Sir Horace Plunkett
KCVO, FRS

IRELAND IN THE
NEW CENTURY

COOPERATIVE STUDIES

BOOKS IN THIS SERIES

Sir Horace Plunkett

KCVO, FRS

IRELAND IN THE NEW CENTURY

With a foreword by
TREVOR WEST

IRISH ACADEMIC PRESS
1982

This book was first published in 1904 and was reprinted twice in that year. In 1905 a Popular Edition was published containing an Epilogue (which edition has been reprinted, to form the present volume, in 1982, the fiftieth anniversary of the author's death).

Printed in the Republic of Ireland

ISBN 0 7165 0294 1

ACKNOWLEDGEMENT
The Society for Cooperative Studies in Ireland gratefully acknowledges the generous support of Allied Irish Banks which has made possible the publication of this new edition of Horace Plunkett's *Ireland in the New Century*.

FOREWORD

Ireland in the New Century was first published in March 1904,
when Horace Plunkett was at the zenith of his career. Much of
the book was written between 5 a.m. (he was a poor sleeper
and rose early) and the start of a full day in the Georgian offices
of the Department of Agriculture and Technical Instruction in
Upper Merrion Street, Dublin. Plunkett, from a landowning
family, was a Protestant and an (at least nominal) unionist; he
was Vice-President of the first Irish government department to
be created independent of the inefficient, and dated, administration centred in Dublin Castle. He would now have been
called the minister of agriculture; but vocational education,
scientific education (except in the universities), the School of
Art, the museums, all came under his department besides the
veterinary service, agricultural education, fisheries and forestry.
Even more was true, for Plunkett had, in a very real sense,
built the department with his own bare hands; a stirring
account of his endeavours and of his plans for the future is
contained in Part II, the practical part of this fascinating book.

However, it was upon the theoretical section in Part I (or
more accurately upon a single chapter in Part I) that Irish
attention was focussed as soon as the book appeared. The pub-
licity which ensued led to a gradual decline in Plunkett's influence, to difficulties for the movement with which his name
was associated, and to ammunition for his opponents, which
they used to such good effect that, three years later, he was
forced to resign his office.

Plunkett's career as a social reformer began after an English
education and ten years of cattle ranching in the foothills of
the Rocky Mountains. Returning to Ireland in 1888, he set
about establishing a rural self-help movement centred around
co-operative creameries. By 1894 this was sufficiently large to

warrant the formation of a coordinating body, the Irish Agricultural Organisation Society. Deftly exploiting the splits in the two Irish political parties, he persuaded the Parnellite nationalists to join with the liberal unionists in a demand for a department to develop agriculture (for the south) and technical education (sorely needed by the industries of Ulster). The Recess Committee (so called as it met in the parliamentary recesses of 1895-6) produced a report which forced the government's hand and the act establishing the new department was passed at Westminster in 1899.

But, en route to the vice-presidency, Plunkett had made enemies; the co-operative movement was opposed by traders, gombeen men and the anti-Parnellite nationalists led by John Dillon. Plunkett had entered parliament in 1892 as a unionist M.P. for South Dublin — a somewhat unusual decision for the leader of an avowedly non-sectarian and non-political movement; his aim in this was not political aggrandisement but to further his economic plan. Never cut out to be a politician (he compared himself to a dog on a tennis court — of equal nuisance to both sides), his progressive policies (which involved alliance with the nationalists) alienated traditional unionism. In the election of 1900 he was opposed by a 'loyal' unionist who split the vote and handed the seat over to the nationalists.

Thus, by 1904, Plunkett was not only an English-educated Protestant from a landed family holding a senior Irish post, but he was a minister without a seat in parliament. It was a delicate position from which to launch one's theories of the defects in Irish character, or the anti-industrial nature of catholicism. But, Plunkett, displaying a characteristic, if naive, honesty, expressed his opinion on these sensitive matters, against the best advice of all his friends. As one of his severest critics put it:

> Sir Horace Plunkett's *Ireland in the New Century*
> is an instructive book.... That he is sincere and
> means well, the work he is doing for some years is
> the best evidence. Moreover, strange as it may
> seem, those things in his book, from which I most

differ, give me strong testimony of his honesty, if
not his prudence.

His unflattering views on Irish character, which he inherited
from the historian Lecky (to whom the book is dedicated)
seemed patronizing to the majority of his Irish readers; the section on religion exhibits some widely held prejudices against
catholicism which now appear dated and irrelevant. The 'non-
economic tendencies' which he observed in Irish Roman Catholics derived more from the backward state of Ireland's development than from an attachment to any particular set of
religious beliefs, while the thrift and industry of Ulster Protestants, strongly emphasised by Plunkett, has not been sufficient
to ward off serious economic decline. But there was an extra
reason for caution, of which Plunkett was well aware, for the
sectarian flames had recently been fanned by the hysterically
anti-clerical writings of the catholic unionist M.J.F. McCarthy,
author of *Priests and People in Ireland* (1902).

Unionist failings and protestant bigotry had come under the
author's critical gaze, but this did not prevent the *Belfast Tele-
graph* from commenting that, although somewhat controversial,
the book was free from bitterness and from traces of the party
spirit. English reviews were generally favourable, and the author
was pleasantly surprised at the comments on his literary accomplishment. The attack, when it came, was on religious
grounds. The *Freeman's Journal* suggested that the author had
demonstrated his unfitness for his position as the book was
'one prolonged libel on the Irish people'. Provincial papers
piled on more virulent condemnation, his name was linked
with M.J.F. McCarthy, and a succession of county councils
and public bodies discussed resolutions calling for the banning
of this filthy book. Cardinal Logue issued a pastoral letter
carrying a thinly veiled reference to enemies of the Church,
and Monsignor O'Riordan, Rector of the Irish College in Rome,
published a rebuttal which was twice the length of the original
(evoking a comment from the author that this was a book
about a chapter, whereas a review was normally a chapter about
a book). Criticisms were repeated upon the floor of the House

of Commons as the nationalists made yet another attempt to have Plunkett removed from office, three years later they succeeded; the legacy of strain between the co-operative movement and the state was to prove a stumbling block to the remainder of his work.

The controversy over *Ireland in the New Century*, which the author attempted to deal with in an Epilogue, added in 1905, had a second, and in the long run perhaps, a more unfortunate consequence, for the concentration upon a single chapter meant that the remainder of the book, constructive in tone and content, went largely ignored. Plunkett aimed to change the current of Irish opinion from its obsession with politics to a consideration of the ways in which his countrymen could work together in a new, revitalised Ireland. His great achievement had been to persuade Protestant and Catholic, unionist and nationalist to combine for their country's good; thus his view of Irish history, his discussions on the state of Ireland in his own day and his optimistic view of the possibilities for Ireland's future have an enduring interest and importance.

His book was written at a time when, in political terms, everything was yet possible. Unionists and nationalists were joined together in a movement for their country's economic regeneration; the battle lines were not yet drawn up for Ulster's resistance to the next instalment of home rule. For pragmatic, unemotional reasons (he had established home rule in agriculture and was convinced that some form of self-government was, by now, inevitable) Plunkett was veering away from a tepid unionism towards acceptance of dominion home rule. He held a unique view of the tangled relationships between the two islands: 'Anglo-Irish history is for Englishmen to remember, for Irishmen to forget', and he believed in the unity of Ireland within an imperial framework. This is a remarkable book, its author the most stimulating thinker on Irish affairs since the days of Thomas Davis and the *Nation*.

Trinity College, Dublin
2 August 1982

TREVOR WEST
Society for
Co-operative Studies

TO THE MEMORY OF

W. E. H. LECKY,

I DEDICATE ALL IN THIS BOOK
THAT IS WORTHY OF THE FRIENDSHIP
WITH WHICH HE HONOURED ME,
AND OF THE COUNSEL WHICH HE GAVE ME
FOR MY GUIDANCE IN IRISH PUBLIC LIFE.

b

Preface to Popular Edition

Some months ago a Roman Catholic priest, who had occasion to write to me on an official matter, thought it would interest me to know the opinions of his brethren upon *Ireland in the New Century*, which he had gathered at a recent clerical meeting. The minority, who had read the book, were, he told me, agreeably surprised; the majority, who had not read it, were very emphatic in their disapproval. On the evidence before them they were both right. Ninety-nine out of every hundred Irishmen who have heard of the book have been given a wrong impression of its contents. In the circumstances, the best defence I can offer is the book itself. Hence this edition issued at a popular price.

I have added an epilogue in reply to some of my critics. It will, I think, serve also to elucidate and further develop the central idea of the book—the application to Ireland of the principle that all true national progress must rest upon a moral foundation.

March, 1905.

Preface to First Edition

Those who have known Ireland for the last dozen years cannot have failed to notice the advent of a wholly new spirit, clearly based upon constructive thought, and expressing itself in a wide range of fresh practical activities. The movement for the organisation of agriculture and rural credit on co-operative lines, efforts of various kinds to revive old or initiate new industries, and, lastly, the creation of a department of Government to foster all that was healthy in the voluntary effort of the people to build up the economic side of their life, are each interesting in themselves. When taken together, and in conjunction with the literary and artistic movements, and viewed in their relation to history, politics, religion, education, and the other past and present influences operating upon the Irish mind and character, these movements appear to me to be worthy of the most thoughtful consideration by all who are responsible for, or desire the well-being of, the Irish people.

I should not, however, in days when my whole time and energies belong to the public service, have undertaken the task of writing a book on a subject so complex and apparently so inseparable from heated controversy, were I not convinced that the expression of certain thoughts which have come to me from practical contact with Irish problems, was the best contribution I could make to the work on which I was engaged. I wished, if I could, to bring into clearer light the essential unity of the various progressive movements in Ireland, and to do something towards promoting a greater definiteness of aim and method, and a better understanding of each other's work, among those who are in various ways striving for the upbuilding of a worthy national life in Ireland.

So far the task, if difficult, was congenial and free from embarrassment. Unhappily, it had been borne in upon me, in the course of a long study of Irish life, that our failure to rise to our opportunities and to give practical evidence of the intellectual qualities with which the race is admittedly gifted, was due to certain defects of character, not ethically grave, but economically paralysing. I need hardly say I refer to the lack of moral courage, initiative, independence and self-reliance— defects which, however they may be accounted for, it is the first duty of modern Ireland to recognise and overcome. I believe in the new movements in Ireland, principally because they seem to me to exert a stimulating influence upon our moral fibre.

Holding such an opinion, I had to decide between preserving a discreet silence and speaking my full mind. The former course would, it appeared to me, be a poor example of the moral courage which I hold to be Ireland's sorest need. Moreover, while I am full of hope for the future of my country, its present condition does not, in my view, admit of any delay in arriving at the truth as to the essential principles which should guide all who wish to take a part, however humble, in the work of national regeneration.

I desire to state definitely that I have not written in any representative capacity except where I say so explicitly. I write on my own responsibility, with the full knowledge that there is much in the book with which many of those with whom I work do not agree.

December, 1903.

CONTENTS

PART I.

THEORETICAL.

CHAPTER I.

THE ENGLISH MISUNDERSTANDING.

CHAPTER II.

The Irish Question in Ireland.

CHAPTER III.

The Influence of Politics upon the Irish Mind.

CHAPTER IV.

The Influence of Religion upon Secular Life in Ireland.

CHAPTER V.

A PRACTICAL VIEW OF IRISH EDUCATION.

CHAPTER VI.

THROUGH THOUGHT TO ACTION.

PART II.

PRACTICAL.

CHAPTER VII.

THE NEW MOVEMENT; ITS FOUNDATION ON SELF-HELP.

CHAPTER VIII.

THE RECESS COMMITTEE.

CHAPTER IX.

A NEW DEPARTURE IN IRISH ADMINISTRATION.

CHAPTER X.

Government with the Consent of the Governed.

EPILOGUE.

PART I.

THEORETICAL.

———

" It is hard to say where history ends, and where religion and politics begin ; for history, religion and politics grow on one stem in Ireland, an eternal trefoil."—*Lady Gregory.*

CHAPTER I.

The English Misunderstanding.

Whatever may be the ultimate verdict of history upon the long struggle of the majority of the Irish people for self-government, the picture of a small country with large aspirations giving of its best unstintingly to the world, while gaining for itself little beyond sympathy, will appeal to the imagination of future ages long after the Irish Question, as we know it, has been buried. It may then, perhaps, be seen that the aspirations came to nought because they were opposed to the manifest destiny of the race, and that it should never have been expected or desired that the Dark Rosaleen should ' reign and reign alone.' Nevertheless, the fidelity and fortitude with which the national ideal had been pursued would command admiration, even if the ideal itself were to be altogether abandoned, or if it were to be ultimately realised in a manner which showed that the methods by which its attainment had been sought were the cause of its long postponement. Whatever the future may have in store for the remnant of the Irish people at home, the continued pursuit of a separate national existence by a nation which is rapidly dis-

B

appearing from the land of all its hopes, and the cherish-
ing of these hopes, not only by those who stay but also
by those who go, will stand as a monument to human
constancy.

The picture will be all the more remarkable when
emphasised by a contrast which the historian will not
fail to draw. Across a narrow streak of sea another
people, during the same period, increased and multiplied
and prospered mightily, spread their laws and institutions, and achieved in every portion of the globe material
success which they can call their own. Yet, although
Irishmen have done much to win that success for the
English people to enjoy, and are to-day foremost in
maintaining the great empire which their brain and
muscle were ever ready to augment, Ireland makes no
claim for herself in respect of the achievement. It is to
her but a proof of what her sons will do for her in the
coming time ; it does not bring her nearer to her heart's
desire.

Although the nineteenth century, with all its mar-
vellous contributions to human progress, left Ireland
with her hopes unfulfilled ; although its sun went down
upon the British people with their greatest failure still
staring them in the face, its last decade witnessed at
first a change in the attitude of England towards Ireland,
and afterwards a profound revolution in the thoughts of
Ireland about herself. The strangest and most interesting feature of these developments was that in practical
England the Irish Question became the great political

issue, while in sentimental Ireland there set in a reaction from politics and an inclination to the practical. The twentieth century has already brought to birth the new Ireland upon whose problems I shall write. If the human interest of these problems is to be realized, if their significance is not to be as wholly misunderstood as that of every other Irish movement which has perplexed the statesmen who have managed our affairs, they must be studied in their relation to the English and Irish events of the period in which the new Ireland was conceived.

In 1885 Gladstone, appealing to an electorate with a large accession of newly enfranchised voters, transferred the struggle over the Irish Question from Ireland to Great Britain. The position taken up by the average English Home Ruler was, it will be remembered, simple and intelligible. The Irish had stated in the proper constitutional way what they wanted, and that, in the first flush of a victorious democracy, when counting heads irrespective of contents was the popular method of arriving at political truth, was assumed to be precisely what they ought to have. A long but inconclusive contest ensued. At times it looked as if the Liberal-Irish alliance might snatch a victory for their policy. But when Gladstone was forced to break with the Irish Leader, and Parnellism without Parnell became obviously impossible, the English realised that the working of representative institutions in Ireland had produced not a democracy but a dictatorship, and they

began to attach a lesser significance to the verdict of the
Irish polls. Their faith in democracy was unimpaired,
but, in their opinion, the Irish had not yet risen to its
dignity. So most English Radicals came round to a
view which they had always reprobated when advanced by the English Conservatives, and political
inferiority was added to the other moral and
intellectual defects which made the Irish an inferior
race!

The anti-climax to the Gladstone crusade was reached
when Lord Rosebery in 1894 took over the premiership
from the greatest English advocate of the Irish cause.
The position of the new leader was very simple. In effect,
he told the Irish Nationalists that the English party he
was about to lead had done its best for them. They must
now regard themselves as partners in the United Kingdom, with the British as the predominant partner. Until
the predominant partner could be brought to take the
Irish view of the partnership, the relations between them
must remain substantially as they were. And not only
must the concession of Home Rule await the conversion
of the British electorate, but before the demand could be
effectively preferred, another leader must rise up among
the Irish; and he, for all Lord Rosebery knew, was at the
moment being wheeled in a perambulator. This apparently cynical avowal of the new premier's own attitude
towards Home Rule accurately stated the facts of the
situation, and fairly reflected the mind of the British
electorate, after Irish obstruction had given them an

opportunity of studying the bearing of the Irish Question on English politics.

If the logic of events was thus making for the removal of Home Rule from the region of practical politics in England, an even more momentous change was taking place in Ireland. Whilst the Home Rule controversy was at its height in the 'eighties and early 'nineties, some Irish grievances were incidentally dealt with—not always under the best impulses or in the best way. The concentration of all the available thought and energy of Irish public men upon an appeal to the passions and prejudices of English parties had led to the further postponement of all Irish endeavour to deal rationally and practically with her own problems at home. But during the welter of contention which prevailed after the fall of Parnell, there grew up in Ireland a wholly new spirit, born of the bitter lesson which was at last being learned. The Irish still clung undaunted to their political ideal, but its pursuit to the exclusion of all other national aims had received a wholesome check. Thought upon the problems of national progress broadened and deepened, in a manner little understood by those who knew Ireland from without, and, indeed, by many of those accounted wise among the observers from within. Was the realisation of a distinctive national existence, many began to ask themselves, to be for ever dependent upon the fortunes of a political campaign? In any scheme of a reconstructed national life to which the

Irish would give of their best, there must be distinctiveness—that much every man who is in touch with Irish
life is fully aware of—but the question of existence must
not be altogether ignored.   At the rate the people were
leaving the sinking ship, the Irish Question would be
settled in the not distant future by the disappearance of
the Irish.   Had we not better look around and see how
other countries with more or less analogous conditions
fared?   Could we not—Unionists and Nationalists alike
—do something towards material progress without
abandoning our ideals?   Could we not learn something
from a study of what our people were doing abroad?
One seemed to hear the voice of Bishop Berkeley,
the biting pertinence of whose *Queries* is ever fresh,
asking from the grave in which he had been laid to rest
nearly a century and a half ago ' whether it would not be
more reasonable to mend our state than complain of it ;
and how far this may be in our own power? '

These questionings, though not generally heard on
the platform or even in the street, were none the less
working in the depths of the Irish mind, and found
expression not so much in words as in deeds.   Yet
though the downfall of Parnell released many minds from
the obsession of politics, the influence of that event was
of a negative character, and it took time to produce a
beneficial effect.   That fruitful last decade of the
nineteenth century saw the foundation of what will
some day be recognised as a new philosophy of Irish
progress.   Certain new principles were then promul-

gated in Ireland, and gradually found acceptance ; and upon those principles a new movement was built. It is partly, indeed, to expound and justify some, at any rate, of the principles and to give an intelligible account of the practical achievement and future possibilities of this movement that I write these pages.

For English readers, to whom this introductory chapter is chiefly addressed, I may here reiterate the opinion, which I have always held and often expressed, that there is no real conflict of interest between the two peoples and the two countries, and that the mutual mis-understanding which we may now hope to see removed is due to a wide difference of temperament and mental outlook. The English mind has never understood the Irish mind—least of all during the period of the ' Union of Hearts.' It is equally true that the Irish have largely misunderstood both the English character and their own responsibility. The result has been that their leaders, despite the brilliant capacity they have shown in presenting the unhappy case of their country to the rest of the world, have rarely presented it in the right way to the English people. There have been many occasions during the last quarter of a century when a calm, well-reasoned statement of the economic dis-advantages under which Ireland labours would, I am convinced, have successfully appealed to British public opinion. It could have been shown that the development of Ireland—the development not only of the resources of her soil but of the far greater wealth which lies in the latent capacities of her people—was demanded quite as much in the interest of one country as in that of the other.

Here, indeed, is an untilled field for those to whom the Irish Question is yet a living one. If I could think that each country fully realised its own responsibility in the matter, if I could think that the long-continued misunderstanding was at an end, nothing would induce me to trouble the waters at this auspicious hour, when a better feeling towards Ireland prevails in Great Britain, and when the Irish people are fully appreciative of the obviously sincere desire of England to be generous to Ireland. But an examination of the events upon which the prevailing optimism is based will show that, unhappily, misunderstanding, though of another sort, still exists, and that Ireland is as much as ever a riddle to the English mind.

Now this new optimism in the English view of Ireland seems to be based, not upon a recognition of the development of what I have ventured to dignify with the title of a new philosophy of Irish progress, but upon a belief that the spirit of moderation and conciliation displayed by so many Irishmen in connection with the Land Act is due to the fact that my incomprehensible countrymen have, under a sudden emotion, put away childish things and learned to behave like grown-up Englishmen. Throughout the press comments upon the Dunraven Conference and in public speeches both inside and outside Parliament there has run a sense that a sort of portent, a transformation scene, a sudden and magical alteration in the whole spirit and outlook of the Irish people, has come to pass.

I feel some hesitation in asking the reader to believe that a great and lasting revolution in Irish thought has been brought about in such a moment in the life of a people as twelve short years. But a lesser number of months seemed to the English mind adequate for the accomplishment of the change. And what a change it was that they conceived! To them, less than a year ago, the Irish Question was not merely unsolved, but in its essential features appeared un-altered. After seven centuries of experimental state-craft—so varied that the English could not believe any expedient had yet to be tried—the vast majority of the Irish people regarded the Government as alien, disputed the validity of its laws, and felt no responsibility for administration, no respect for the legislature, or for those who executed its decrees. And this in a country forming an integral part of the United Kingdom, where the funda-mental basis of government is assumed to be the consent of the governed! Nor were any hopes entertained that the cloud would quickly pass. During the Boer war the prophets of evil, in predicting the calamity which was to fall upon the British Empire, took as their text the failure of English government in Ireland. When they wanted to paint in the darkest colours the coming heritage of woe, they wrote upon the wall, 'Another Ireland in South Africa'; and if any exception was taken to the appropriateness of the phrase, it was certainly not on tne ground that Ireland had ceased to be a warning to British statesmen.

I believe, quite as strongly as the most optimistic Englishman, that there has been a great change from this state of things in Irish sentiment, and my explanation of that change, if less dramatic than the transformation theory, affords more solid ground for optimism. This change in the sentiment of Irishmen towards England is due, not to a sudden emotion of the incomprehensible Celt, but really to the opinion—rapidly growing for the last dozen years—that great as is the responsibility of England for the state of Ireland, still greater is the responsibility of Irishmen. The conviction has been more and more borne in upon the Irish mind that the most important part of the work of regenerating Ireland must necessarily be done by Irishmen in Ireland. The result has been that many Irishmen, both Unionists and Nationalists, without in any way abandoning their opposition to, or support of, the attempt to solve the political problem from without, have been trying—not without success—to solve some part of the Irish Question from within. The Report of the Recess Committee, on which I shall dwell later, was the first great fruit of this movement, and the Dunraven Treaty, which paved the way for Mr. Wyndham's Land Act, was a further fruit, and not the result of an inexplicable transformation scene.

The reason why I dwell on the true nature of the

undoubted change in the Irish situation is not in order to exaggerate the importance of the part played by the new movement in bringing it about, nor to detract from the importance of Parliamentary action, but because a mistaken view of the change would inevitably postpone the firm establishment of an improved mutual understanding between the two countries, which I regard as an essential of Irish progress. I confess that my apprehension of a new misunderstanding was aroused by the debates on the Land Bill in the House of Commons. As regards the spirit of conciliation and moderation displayed by the Irish, and the sincere desire exhibited by the British to heal the chief Irish economic sore, the speeches were, if not epoch-making, at any rate epoch-marking ; but they showed little sense of perspective or proportion in viewing the Irish Question, and little grasp or appreciation of the large social and economic problems which the Land Act will bring to the front. Temporary phenomena and legislative machinery have been endowed with an importance they do not possess, and miracles, it is supposed, are about to be worked in Ireland by processes which, whatever rich good may be in them, have never worked miracles, though they have not seldom excited very similar enthusiasms in the economic history of other European lands.

I agree, then, with most Englishmen in thinking, though for a different reason, that the passing of the Land Act marked a new era in Ireland. They regard it

as productive of, or co-incident in time with, the dawn of
the practical in Ireland. I antedate that event by some
dozen years, and regard the Land Act rather as marking
a new era, because it removes the great obstacle which
obscured the dawn of the practical for so many, and
hindered it for all.

Whatever may have been the expectations upon which
this great measure was based, I, in common with most Irish
observers, watched its progress with unfeigned delight.
The vast majority regarded the hundred millions of
credit and the twelve millions of ' bonus ' as a generous
concession to Ireland ; and I sympathised with those who
deprecated the mischievous suggestion, not infrequently
heard in English political circles, that this m nificence
was the ' price of peace.'   On one point all were agreed :
the Bill could never have become law had not Mr.
Wyndham handled the Parliamentary situation with
masterly tact, temper, and ability.   To him is chiefly due
the credit for the fact that the Land Question, in
its old form at any rate, no longer blocks the way,
and that the large problems which remain to be
solved, and, above all, the spirit in which they will have
to be approached by those who wish the existing peace
to be the forerunner of material and social progress, can
be freely and frankly discussed.

It is true, as I have said, that Ireland is becoming more
and more practical, and that England is becoming more
anxious than ever to do her substantial justice.   But still
the manner of the doing will continue to be as important

as the thing which is done. Of the Irish qualities none is stronger than the craving to be understood. If the English had only known this secret we should have been the most easily governed people in the world. For it is characteristic of the conduct of our most important affairs that we care too little about the substance and too much about the shadow. It is for this reason that I have discussed the real nature of one phase of Irish sentiment which has been largely misunderstood, and it is for the same reason that I propose to preface my examination of the Irish Question with some reference to the cause and nature of the anti-English sentiment, for the long continuance of which I can find no other explanation than the failure of the English to see into the Irish mind.

I am well acquainted with this sentiment because, in my practical work in Ireland, it has ever been the main current of the stream against which I have had to swim. Years spent in the United States had made me familiar with its full and true significance, for there it can be studied in an atmosphere not dominated by any present Irish controversies or struggles. I have found this sentiment of hatred deeply rooted in the minds of Irishmen who had themselves never known Ireland, who had no connection, other than a sentimental one, with that country, who were living quiet business lives in the United States, but who were ever ready to testify with their dollars, and genuinely believed that they only lacked opportunity to demonstrate in a more enterprising way, their "undying hatred of the English name."*

With such men I have reasoned, and sometimes not in vain, upon the injustice and unreason of their attitude. I have not attempted to controvert the main facts of Ireland's grievances, which they frequently told me they had gleaned from Froude and Lecky. I used to deprecate the unqualified application of modern standards to the policies of other days, and to protest against the injustice of punishing one set of persons for the misdoings of another set of persons, who have long since passed beyond the reach of any earthly tribunal. I have given them my reasons for believing that, even if such a course were morally admissible, the wit of man could not devise any means of inflicting a blow upon England which would not react injuriously with tenfold force upon Ireland. I have gone on to show that the sentiment itself, largely the accident of untoward circumstances, is alien to the character and temperament of the Irish people. In short, I have urged that the policy of revenge is un-Christian and unintelligent, and, that, as the Irish people are neither irreligious nor stupid, it is un-Irish. I well remember taking up this position in conversation with some very advanced Irish-Americans

---

* My own experience confirms Mr. Lecky's view of the chief cause of this extraordinary feeling. "It is probable," he writes, " that the true source of the savage hatred of England that animates great bodies of Irishmen on either side of the Atlantic has very little real connection with the penal laws, or the rebellion, or the Union. It is far more due to the great clearances and the vast unaided emigrations that followed the famine."—*Leaders of Public Opinion in Ireland*, Vol. II., p. 177.

in the Far West and the reply which one of them made. "Wal," said my half-persuaded friend, "mebbe you're right. I have two sons, whom I have raised in the expectation that they will one day strike a blow for old Ireland. Mebbe they won't. I'm too old to change."

I have chosen this incident from a long series of similar reminiscences of my study of Irish life, to illustrate an attitude of mind, the historical explanation of which would seem to the practical Englishman as academic as a psychological exposition of the effect of a red rag upon a bull. The English are not much to be blamed for resenting the survival of the feeling, but it appears to me to argue a singular lack of political imagination that they should still fail to appreciate the reality, the significance, and the abiding force of a sentiment which has so far successfully resisted the influence of those governing qualities which have played a foremost part in the civilisation of the modern world. The *Spectator* some time ago came out bluntly with a truth which an Irishman may, I presume, quote without offence from so high an English authority :—" The one blunder of average Englishmen in considering foreign questions is that with white men they make too little allowance for sentiment, and with coloured men they make none at all."* I am afraid it must be added that 'average Englishmen' make exactly the same blunder in under-estimating the force of sentiment when considering Irish questions, with the not unnatural consequence

* *Spectator*, 6th September, 1902.

that the Irish regard them as foreigners, and that, as those foreigners happen to govern them, the sentiment of nationality becomes political and anti-English.

There is one reason why this sentiment is not allowed to die which should always be remembered by those who wish to grasp the inner workings of the Irish mind. Briefly stated, the view prevails in Ireland that in dealing with questions affecting our material well-being, the government of our country by the English was, in the past, characterised by an unenlightened self-interest. Thoughtful Englishmen admit this charge, but they say that the past referred to is beyond living memory and should now be buried. The Irish mind replies that the life of a nation is not to be measured by the life of individuals, and that a wrong inflicted by a Government upon a community entitles those who inherit the consequences of the injury to claim reparation at the hands of those who inherit the government. With this attitude on the part of the Irish mind I am not only most heartily in sympathy, but I find every Englishman who understands the situation equally so. In the later portions of this book it will be shown that practical recognition, in no small measure, has been given by England to the righteousness of this part of the Irish case, and that if the effect thus produced has not found as full an outward expression as might have been expected, the Irish people have at any rate responded to the new treatment in a manner which must, in no distant future, bring about a better understanding.

The only historical causes of our present discontents to which I need now particularly refer, are the commercial restrictions and the land system of the past, which stand out from the long list of Irish grievances as those for which their victims were the least responsible. No one can be more anxious than I am that we should cease to be for ever seeking in the past excuses for our present failures. But it is essential to a correct estimation of Irish agricultural and industrial possibilities that we should notice the true bearings of these historical grievances upon existing conditions.

In this connection there arises a question which is very pertinent to the present inquiry and which must therefore be considered. I have seen it argued by English economists that the industrial revolution which took place at the end of the eighteenth and commencement of the nineteenth century would in any case have destroyed, by force of open competition, industries which, it is admitted, were previously legislated away. They point out that the change from the order of small scattered home industries to the factory system would have suited neither the temperament nor the industrial habits of the Irish. They tell us that with the industrial revolution the juxtaposition of coal and iron became an all-important factor in the problem, and they recall how the north and west of England captured the industrial supremacy from the south and east. Incidentally they point out that the people of the English counties which suffered by these economic causes braced themselves to meet the changes, and it is suggested that if the people of Ireland had shown the same resourcefulness, they, too, might have weathered the storm. And, finally, we are reminded that England, by her stupid Irish policy, punished her own supporters, and even herself, quite as much as the ' mere Irish.'

Much of this may be true, but this line of argument only shows that these English economists do not thoroughly understand the real grievance which the Irish people still harbour against the English for past misgovernment. The commercial restraints sapped the industrial instinct of the people—an evil which was intensified in the case of the Catholics by the working of the penal laws. When these legislative restrictions upon industry had been removed, the Irish, not being trained in industrial habits, were unable to adapt themselves to the altered conditions produced by the Industrial Revolution, as did the people in England. And as for commerce, the restrictions, which had as little moral sanction as the penal laws, and which invested smuggling with a halo of patriotism, had prevented the development of commercial morality, without which there can be no commercial success. It is not, therefore, the destruction of specific industries, or even the sweeping of our commerce from the seas, about which most complaint is now made. The real grievance lies in the fact that something had been taken from our industrial character which could not be remedied by the mere removal of the restrictions. Not only had the tree been stripped, but the roots had been destroyed. If ever there was a case where President Kruger's 'moral and intellectual damages' might fairly be claimed by an injured nation, it is to be found in the industrial and commercial history of Ireland during the period of the building up of England's commercial supremacy.

The English mind quite failed, until the very end of the nineteenth century, to grasp the real needs of the situation which had thus been created in Ireland. The industrial revolution, as I have indicated, found the Irish people fettered by an industrial past for which they themselves were not chiefly responsible. They needed exceptional treatment of a kind which was not conceded. They were, instead, still further handicapped, towards the middle of the century, by the adoption of Free Trade, which was imposed upon them when they were not only unable to take advantage of its benefits, but were so situated as to suffer to the utmost from its inconveniences.

I am convinced that the long-continued misunderstanding of the conditions and needs of this country, the withholding, for so long, of necessary concessions, was due not to heartlessness or contempt so much as to a lack of imagination, a defect for which the English cannot be blamed. They had, to use a modern term, 'standardised' their qualities, and it was impossible to get out of their minds the belief that a divergence, in another race, from their standard of character was synonymous with inferiority. This attitude is not yet a thing of the past, but it is fast disappearing; and thoughtful Englishmen now recognise the righteousness of the claim for reparation, and are willing liberally to apply any stimulus to our industrial life which may place us, so far as this is possible, on the level we might have occupied had we been left to work out our own economic salvation.   Unfortunately, all Englishmen are not thoughtful, and hence I emphasise the fact that England is largely responsible for our industrial defects, and must not hesitate to face the financial results of that responsibility.

When we pass from the domain of commerce, where we have seen that circumstances reduced to the minimum Ireland's participation in the industrial supremacy of England, and come to examine the historical development of Irish agrarian life, we find a situation closely related to, and indeed, largely created by, that which we have been discussing. 'Debarred from every other trade and industry,' wrote the late Lord Dufferin, 'the entire nation flung itself back upon the land, with as fatal an impulse as when a river, whose current is suddenly impeded, rolls back and drowns the valley which it once fertilised.' The energies, the hopes, nay, the very existence of the race, became thus intimately bound up with agriculture. This industry, their last resort and sole dependence, had to be conducted by a people who in every other avocation had been unfitted for material success.   And this industry, too, was crippled from without, for a system of land tenure had been imposed upon Ireland that was probably the most effective that could have been devised for the purpose of perpetuating and accentuating every disability to which other causes had given rise.

The Irish land system suffered from the same ills as we all know the political institutions to have suffered from—a partial and intermittent conquest. Land holding in Ireland remained largely based on the tribal system of open fields and common tillage for nearly eight hundred years after collective ownership had begun to pass away in England. The sudden imposition upon the Irish, early in the seventeenth century, of a land system which was no part of the natural development of the country, ignored, though it could not destroy, the old feeling of communistic ownership, and, when this vanished, it did not vanish as it did in countries where more normal conditions prevailed. It did not perish like a piece of outworn tissue pushed off by a new growth from within: on the contrary, it was arbitrarily cut away while yet fresh and vital, with the result that where a bud should have been there was a scar.

This sudden change in the system of land-holding was followed by a century of reprisals and confiscations, and what war began the law continued. The Celtic race, for the most part impoverished in mind and estate by the penal laws, became rooted to the soil, for, as we have seen, they had, on account of the repression of industries, no alternative occupation, and so became, in fact, if not in law, *adscripti glebae.* Upon the pro-

ductiveness of their labour the landlord depended for
his revenues, but he did little to develop that productiveness, and the system which was introduced did everything to lessen it.*   The wound produced by the original
confiscation of the land was kept from healing by the
way in which the tenants' improvements were somewhat
similarly treated.   I do not mean that they were system-
atically confiscated—the Devon and Bessborough Commissions, as well as Gladstone, bore witness to the
contrary—but the right and the occasional exercise of the
right to confiscate operated in the same way.   In the Irish
tenant's mind dispossession was nine-tenths of the law.

An enlightened system of land tenure might have
made prosperity and contentment the lot of the
native race, and, perhaps, have rendered possible such a
solution of the Irish problem as was effected between
England and Scotland two centuries ago.   What was
chiefly required for agrarian peace was a recognition of
that sense of partnership in the land—a relic of the
tribal days—to which the Irish mind tenaciously
adhered.   But, like most English concessions, it was not
granted until too late, and then granted in the wrong
way.   The natural result was that, when at last the recognition of partnership was enacted, it became a
lever for a demand for complete ownership.   But this
was the aftermath, for in the meantime, from the seed

* The title to the greater part of Irish land is based on confiscation.   This is true of many other countries, but what was exceptional
in the Irish confiscations was that the grantees for the most part did
not settle on the lands themselves, drive away the dispossessed, or
come to any rational working agreement with them.

sown by English blundering, Ireland—native population
and English garrison alike—had reaped the awful harvest of the Irish famine, which was followed by a long
dark winter of discontent. Upon the England that
sowed the wind there was visited a whirlwind of hostility from the Irish race scattered throughout the globe.

It would be altogether outside the scope or purpose of
this chapter to present a complete history of the
remedial legislation applied to Irish land tenure. That
history, however, illustrates so vividly the English
misunderstanding, that a short survey of one phase
of it may help to point the moral. The English intellect at long last began to grasp the
agrarian, though not the industrial side of the
wrong that had been done to Ireland, and the English
conscience was moved; there came the era of concessions to which I have alluded, and for over a quarter of
a century attempts, often generous, if not very dis-
criminating, were made to deal with the situation.
In 1870, dispossession was made very costly to the
landlord. In 1881, it became impossible, except on
the tenant's default, and the partnership was fully
recognised, the tenant's share being made his own to sell,
and being preserved for his profitable use by a right to
have the rent payable to his sleeping partner, the landlord, fixed by a judicial tribunal. These rights were the
famous three F's—fixity of tenure, free sale, and fair
rent—of the Magna Charta of the Irish peasant. If
these concessions had only been made in time,

they would probably have led to a strengthening
of the economic position and character of the Irish
tenantry, which would have enabled them to take full
advantage of their new status, and meet any condition
which might arise ; and it is just possible that the system
might have worked well, even at the eleventh hour,
had it been launched on a rising market.   Unhappily, it
fell upon evil days.   The prosperous times of Irish agriculture, which culminated a few years before the passing
of the ' Tenants' Charter,' were followed by a serious
reaction, the result of causes which, though long
operative, were only then beginning to make themselves felt, and some of which, though the fact was not
then generally recognised, were destined to be of no
temporary character.   The agricultural depression which
has continued ever since was due, as is now well known,
to foreign competition, or, in other words, to the opening up of vast areas in the Far West to the plough and
herd, and the bringing of the products of distant
countries into the home markets in ever-increasing
quantity, in ever fresher condition, and at an ever-
decreasing cost of transportation.   Great changes were
taking place in the market which the Irish farmer supplied, and no two men could agree as to the relative influence of the new factors of the problem, or as to their
probable duration.

Whatever may be said in disparagement of the great
experiment commenced in 1881, there can be no doubt
that it enormously improved the legal position of the

Irish tenantry, and I, for one, regard it as a necessary contribution to the events whose logic was finally to bring about the abolition of dual ownership. But what a curious instance of the irony of fate is afforded by this genuine attempt to heal an Irish sore, what a commentary it is upon the English misunderstanding of the Irish mind! Mr. Gladstone found the land system intolerable to one party; he made it intolerable to the other also. For half a century *laissez-faire* was pedantically applied to Irish agriculture, then suddenly the other extreme was adopted; nothing was left alone, and political economy was sent on its famous planetary excursion.

When Mr. Gladstone was attempting to settle the land question on the basis of dual ownership, the seed of a new kind of single ownership—peasant proprietorship—was sown through the influence of John Bright. The operations of the land purchase clauses in the Church Disestablishment Act of 1869, and the Land Acts of 1870 and 1881, were enormously extended by the Land Purchase Acts introduced by the Conservative Party in 1885 and in 1891, and the success which attended these Acts accentuated the defects and sealed the fate of dual ownership, which all parties recently united to destroy. In other words, Parliament has been undoing a generation's legislative work upon the Irish land question.

This is all I need say about that stage of the Irish agrarian situation at which we have now arrived. What I wish my readers to bear in mind is that the effect of a bad system of land tenure upon the other aspects of the

Irish Question reaches much further back than the struggles, agitations, and reforms in connection with Irish land which this generation has witnessed. The same may be said with regard to the other economic grievances. No one can be more anxious than I am to fasten the mind of my countrymen upon the practical things of to-day, and to wean their sad souls from idle regrets over the sorrows of the past. If I revive these dead issues, it is because I have learned that no man can move the Irish mind to action unless he can see its point of view, which is largely retrospective. I cannot ignore the fact that the attitude of mind which causes the Irish people to put too much faith in legislative cures for economic ills is mainly due to the belief that their ancestors were the victims of a long series of laws by which every industry that might have made the country prosperous was jealously repressed or ruthlessly destroyed. Those who are not too much appalled by the quantity to examine into the quality of popular oratory in Ireland are familiar with the subordination of present economic issues to the dreary reiteration of this old tale of woe. Personally I have always held that to foster resentment in respect of these old wrongs is as stupid as was the policy which gave them birth ; and, even if it were possible to distribute the blame among our ancestors, I am sure we should do ourselves much harm, and no living soul any good, in the reckoning. In my view, Anglo-Irish history is for Englishmen to remember, for Irishmen to forget.

I may now conclude my appeal to outside observers for a broader and more philosophic view of my country and my countrymen with a suggestion born of my own early mistakes, and with a word of warning which is called for by my later observation of the mistakes of others. The difficulty of the outside observer in understanding the Irish Question is, no doubt, largely due to the fact that those in intimate touch with the actual conditions are so dominated by vehement and passionate conviction that reason is not only at a discount but is fatal to the acquisition of popular influence. Of course the power of knowledge and thought, though kept in the background, is not really eliminated. But it is in the circumstances not unnatural that most of us should fall into the error of attributing to the influence of prominent individuals or organisations the events and conditions which the superficial observer regards as the creation of the hour, but which are in reality the outcome of a slow and continuous process of evolution. I remember as a boy being captivated by that charming corrective to this view of historical development, Buckle's *History of Civilization*, which in recent years has often recurred to my mind, despite the fact that many of his theories are now somewhat discredited. Buckle, if I remember right, almost eliminates the personal factor in the life of nations. According to his theory, it would not have made much difference to modern civilisation if Napoleon had happened, as was so near being the case, to be born

a British instead of a French subject. It would also
have followed that if O'Connell had limited his activities
to his professional work, or if Parnell had chanced to
hate Ireland as bitterly as he hated England, we should
have been, politically, very much where we are to-day.
The student of Irish affairs should, of course, avoid the
extreme views of historical causation; but in the search
for the truth he will, I think, be well advised to attach
less significance to the influence of prominent personality
than is the practice of the ordinary observer in Ireland.

The warning I have to offer, I think, will be justified by
a reflection upon the history of the panaceas which we
have been offered, and upon our present state. To those
of my British readers who honestly desire to understand
the Irish Question, I would say, let them eschew the
sweeping generalisations by which Irish intelligence is
commonly outraged.   I may pass by the explanation
which rests upon the cheap attribution of racial inferiority
with the simple reply that our inferior race has much
of the superior blood in its veins; yet the Irish problem
is just as acute in districts where the English blood
predominates as where the people are 'mere Irish.'
If this view be disputed, the matter is not worth arguing
about, because we cannot be born again.   But there
are three other common explanations of the Irish difficulty, any one of which taken by itself only leads away
from the truth.   I refer, I need hardly say, to the
familiar assertions that the origin of the evil is political,
that it is religious, or that it is neither one nor the

other, but economic. In Irish history, no doubt, we may find, under any of these heads, cause enough for much of our present wrong-goings. But I am profoundly convinced that each of the simple explanations to which I have just alluded—the racial, the political, the religious, the economic—is based upon reasoning from imperfect knowledge of the facts of Irish life. The cause and cure of Irish ills are not chiefly political, broaden or narrow our conception of politics as we will; they are not chiefly religious, whatever be the effect of Roman Catholic influence upon the practical side of the people's life; they are not chiefly economic, be the actual poverty of the people and the potential wealth of the country what they may. The Irish Question is a broad and deeply interesting human problem which has baffled generation after generation of a great and virile race, who complacently attribute their incapacity to master it to Irish perversity, and pass on, leaving it unsolved by Anglo-Saxons, and therefore insoluble!

CHAPTER II.

The Irish Question in Ireland.

Whilst attributing the long continued failure of English rule in Ireland largely to a misunderstanding of the Irish mind, I have given England—at least modern England—credit for good intentions towards us. I now come to the case of the misunderstood, and shall from henceforth be concerned with the immeasurably greater responsibility of the Irish people themselves for their own welfare. The most characteristic, and by far the most hopeful feature of the change in the Anglo-Irish situation which took place in the last decade of the nineteenth century, and upon the meaning of which I dwelt in the preceding chapter, is the growing sense amongst us that the English misunderstanding of Ireland is of far less importance, and perhaps less inexcusable, than our own misunderstanding of ourselves.

When I first came into practical touch with the extraordinarily complex problems of Irish life, nothing impressed me so much as the universal belief among my countrymen that Providence had endowed them with capacities of a high order, and their country with resources of unbounded richness, but that both the capacities and the resources remained undeveloped owing to the stupidity—or worse—of British rule. It was asserted, and generally taken for granted, that the exiles of Erin sprang to the front in every walk of life throughout the world, in every country but their own—though I notice that in quite recent times endeavours have been made to cool the emigration fever by painting the fortunes of the Irish in America in the darkest colours. To suggest that there was any use in trying at home to make the best of things as they were was indicative of a leaning towards British rule; and to attempt to give practical effect to such a heresy was to draw a red herring across the path of true Nationalism.

It is not easy to account for the long continuance of this attitude of the Irish mind towards Irish problems, which seems unworthy of the native intelligence of the people. The truth probably is that while we have not allowed our intellectual gifts to decay, they have been of little use to us because we have neglected the second part of the old Scholastic rule of life, and have failed to develop the moral qualities in which we are deficient. Hence we have developed our critical faculties, not, unhappily, along constructive lines. We have been throughout alive to the muddling of our affairs by the English, and have accurately gauged the incapacity of our governors to appreciate our needs and possibilities. But we recognised their incapacity more readily than our own deficiencies, and we estimated the failure of the English far more justly than we apportioned the responsibility between our rulers and ourselves. The sense of the duty and dignity of labour has been lost in the contemplation of circumstances over which it was assumed that we have no control.

It is a peculiarity of destructive criticism that, unlike charity, it generally begins and ends abroad; and those who cultivate the gentle art are seldom given to morbid introspection. Our prodigious ignorance about ourselves has not been blissful. Mistaking self-assertion for self-knowledge, we have presented the pathetic spectacle of a people casting the blame for their shortcomings on another people, yet bearing the consequences themselves. The national habit of living in the past seems to give us a present without achievement, a future without hope. The conclusion was long ago forced upon me that whatever may have been true of the past, the chief responsibility for the remoulding of our national life rests now with ourselves, and that in the last analysis the problem of Irish ineffectiveness at home is in the main a problem of character—and of Irish character.

I am quite aware that such a diagnosis of our mind disease—from which Ireland is, in my belief, slowly but surely recovering—will not pass unchallenged, but I would ask any reader who dissents from this view to take a glance at the picture of our national life as it might unfold itself to an unprejudiced but sympathetic outsider who came to Ireland not on a political tour but with a sincere desire to get at the truth of the Irish Question, and to inquire into the conditions about which all the controversy continues to rage.

This hypothetical traveller would discover that our resources are but half developed, and yet hundreds of thousands of our workers have gone, and are still going, to produce wealth where it is less urgently needed. The remnant of the race who still cling to the old country are not only numerically weak, but in many other ways they show the physical and moral effects of the drain which emigration has made on the youth, strength, and energy of the community. Our four and a quarter millions of people, mainly agricultural, have, speaking generally, a very low standard of comfort which they like to attribute to some five or six millions sterling paid as agricultural rent, and three millions of alleged over-taxation. They face the situation bravely—and, incidentally, swell the over-taxation—with the help of the thirteen or fourteen millions worth of alcoholic stimulants which they annually consume. The still larger consumption in Great Britain may seem to lend at least a respectability to this apparent over-indulgence, but it looks odd. The people are endowed with intellectual capacities of a high order. They have literary gifts and an artistic sense. Yet, with a few brilliant exceptions, they contribute nothing to invention and creat' nothing in literature or in art. One would say that there must be something wrong with the education of the country; and most people declare that it is too literary, though the Census returns show that there are still large numbers who escape the tyranny of books. The people have an extraordinary belief in political remedies for economic ills;

D

and their political leaders, who are not as a rule themselves actively engaged in business life, tell the people, pointing to ruined mills and unused water power, that the country once had diversified industries, and that if they were allowed to apply their panacea, Ireland would quickly rebuild her industrial life. If our hypothetical traveller were to ask whether there are no other leaders in the country besides the eloquent gentlemen who proclaim her helplessness, he would be told that among the professional classes, the landlords, and the captains of industry, are to be found as competent popular advisers as are possessed by any other country of similar economic standing. But these men take only a dilettante part in politics, and no value is set on industrial, commercial or professional success in the choice of public men. Can it be that to the Irish mind politics are, what Bulwer Lytton declared love to be, " the business of the idle, and the idleness of the busy " ?

These, though only a few of the strange ironies of Irish life, are so paradoxical and so anomalous that they are not unnaturally attributed to the intrusion of an alien and unfriendly power ; and this furnishes the reason why everything which goes wrong is used to nourish the anti-English sentiment. At the same time they give emphasis to the growing doubt as to the wisdom of those to whom the Irish Question presents itself only as a single and simple issue—namely, whether the laws which are to put all these things right shall be made at St. Stephen's by the collective wisdom of the United Kingdom, aided

by the voice of Ireland—which is adequately represented
—or whether these laws shall be made by Irishmen alone
in a Parliament in College Green.

It is obviously necessary that, in presenting a comprehensive scheme for dealing with the conditions I have
roughly indicated, I should make some reference to the
attitude towards Home Rule of both the Nationalists and
the Unionists who have joined in work which, whatever
be its irregularity from the standpoint of party discipline as enforced in Ireland, has succeeded in some
degree in directing the energies of our countrymen to the
development of the resources of our country. Many of
my fellow-workers were Nationalists who, while stoutly
adhering to the prime necessity for constitutional changes,
took the broad view, which was unpopular among the
Irish Party, that much could be done, even under present
conditions, to build up our national life on its social, intellectual, and economic sides. The well-known constitutional changes which were advocated in the political
party to which they belonged would then, they believed,
be more effectively demanded by Ireland, and more
readily conceded by England. Unionists who worked
with me were similarly affected by the changing mental
outlook of the country. They, too, had to break loose
from the traditions of an Irish party, for they felt that
the exclusively political opposition to Home Rule was not
less demoralising than the exclusively political pursuit of
Home Rule. Just as the Nationalists who joined the
movement believed that all progress must make for self·

government, so my Unionist fellow-workers believed it would ultimately strengthen the Union. Each view was thoroughly sound from the standpoint of those who held it, and could be regarded with respect by those who did not. We were all convinced that the way to achieve what is best for Ireland was to develop what is best in Irishmen. And it was the conviction that this can be done by Irishmen in Ireland that brought together those whose thought and work supplies whatever there may be of interest in this book.

If I have fairly stated the attitude towards each other of the workers to whose coming together must be attributed as much of the change in the Irish situation as is due to Irish initiation, it will be seen that what had so long kept them apart in public affairs, outside politics, was a difference of opinion, not so much as to the conditions to be dealt with, nor, indeed, as to the end to be sought, but rather as to the means most effective for the attainment of that end. I naturally regard the view which I am putting forward as being broader than that which has hitherto prevailed. Some Nationalists may, however, contend that it is essential to progress that the thoughts and energies of the nation should be focussed upon a single movement, and not dissipated in the pursuit of a multiplicity of ideals. I quite admit the importance of concentration. But I strongly hold that any movement which is closely related to the main currents of the people's life and subservient to their urgent economic necessities, and which gives free play to

the intellectual qualities, while strengthening the moral
or industrial character, cannot be held to conflict with
any national programme of work, without raising a
strong presumption that there is something wrong with
the programme. The exclusively political remedy I
shall discuss in the next chapter, but here I propose to
consider some of the problems which the new movement
seeks to solve without waiting for the political millenium.

It is a commonplace that there are two Irelands, differing in race, in creed, in political aspiration, and in
what I regard as a more potent factor than all the others
put together—economic interest and industrial pursuit.
In the mutual misunderstanding of these two Irelands,
still more than in the misunderstanding of Ireland by
England, is to be found the chief cause of the still
unsettled state of the Irish Question. I shall not seek
to apportion the blame between the two sections of the
population; but as the mists clear away and we can
begin to construct a united and contented Ireland, it is
not only legitimate, but helpful in the extreme, to assign
to the two sections of our wealth-producers their
respective parts in repairing the fortunes of their country.
In such a discussion of future developments chief prominence must necessarily be given to the problems
affecting the life of the majority of the people, who
depend directly on the land, and conduct the industry
which produces by far the greater portion of the wealth
of the country. It is, of course, essential to the prosperity
of the whole community that the North should pursue

and further develop its own industrial and commercial
life.   That section of the community has also, no doubt,
economic and educational problems to face, but these·
are much the same problems as those of industrial communities in other parts of the United Kingdom*; and if
they do not receive, vitally important as is their solution
to the welfare of Ireland, any large share of attention in
this book, it is because they are no part of what is
ordinarily understood by the Irish Question.

Nevertheless, the interest of the manufacturing population of Ulster in the welfare of the Roman Catholic
agricultural majority is not merely that of an onlooker,
nor even that of the other parts of the United Kingdom,
but something more.   It is obvious that the internal
trade of the country depends mainly upon the demand
of the rural population for the output of the manufacturing towns, and that this demand must depend
on the volume of agricultural production.   I think
the importance of developing the home market has not
been sufficiently appreciated, even by Belfast.   The
best contribution the Ulster Protestant population can
make to the solution of this question is to do what they
can to bring about cordial co-operation between the two

----

* I speak from personal knowledge when I say that the leaders of Irish
industry and commerce are fully alive to the practical consideration
which they have now to devote to the new conditions by which they
are surrounded.   They recognise that the intensified foreign competition which harasses them is due chiefly to German education and
American enterprise.   They are deep in the consideration of the form
which technical education should take to meet their peculiar needs;
and I am confident that Ulster will make a sound and useful contribution to the solution of the commercial and industrial problems which
confront the manufacturers of the United Kingdom.

great sections of the wealth-producers of Ireland. They should, I would suggest, learn to take a broader and more patriotic view of the problems of the Roman Catholic and agricultural majority, upon the true nature of which I hope to be able to throw some new light. My purpose will be doubly served if I have, to some extent, brought home to the minds of my Northern friends that there is in Ireland an unsettled question in which they are largely concerned, a rightly unsatisfied people by helping whom they can best help themselves.

The Irish Question is, then, in that aspect which must be to Irishmen of paramount importance, the problem of a national existence, chiefly an agricultural existence, in Ireland. To outside observers it is the question of rural life, a question which is assuming a social and economic importance and interest of the most intense character, not only for Ireland North and South, but for almost the whole civilised world. It is becoming increasingly difficult in many parts of the world to keep the people on the land, owing to the enormously improved industrial opportunities and enhanced social and intellectual advantages of urban life. The problem can be better examined in Ireland than elsewhere, for with us it can, to a large extent, be isolated, since we have little highly developed town life. Our rural exodus takes our people, for the most part, not into Irish or even into British towns, but into those of the United States. What is migration in other countries is emigration with us, and the mind of the country, brooding over the dreary statistics of this perennial drain, naturally and longingly turns to schemes for the rehabilitation of rural life—the only life it knows.

We cannot exercise much direct influence upon the desire to emigrate beyond spreading knowledge as to the real conditions of life in America, for which home life in Ireland is often ignorantly bartered.* We cannot isolate the phenomenon of emigration and find a cure for it apart from the rest of the Irish Question. We must recognise that emigration is but the chief symptom of a low national vitality, and that the first result of our efforts to stay the tide may increase the outflow. We cannot fit the people to stay without fitting them to go. Before we can keep the people at home we have got to construct a national life with, in the first place, a secure basis of physical comfort and decency. This life must have a character, a dignity, an outlook of its own. A comfortable Boeotia will never develop into a real Hibernia Pacata. The standard of living may in some ways be lower than the English standard : in some ways it may be higher. But even if statesmanship and all the forces of philanthropy and patriotism combined can construct a contented rural Ireland for the people, it can only be

* That such a knowledge is still required, though the need is becoming less urgent, is shown by an incident which illustrates the pathos of the Irish exodus. A poor woman once asked me to help her son to emigrate to America, and I agreed to pay his passage. Early in the negotiations, finding that she was somewhat vague as to her boy's prospects, I asked her whether he wanted to go to North or South America. This detail she seemed to consider immaterial. "Ach, glory be to God, I lave that to yer honner. Why wouldn't I ?" Had I shipped him to Peru she would have been quite satisfied. Why wouldn't she ?

maintained by the people. It will have to accord with the national sentiment and be distinctively Irish. It is this national aspiration, and the remarkable promise of the movements making for its fruition, which give to the work of Irish social and economic reform the fascination which those who do not know the Ireland of to-day cannot understand. This work of reform must, of course, be primarily economic, but economic remedies cannot be applied to Irish ills without the spiritual aids which are required to move to action the latent forces of Irish reason and emotion.

The task which we have to face is, then, a two-sided one, but its economic and its purely practical aspects first demand consideration. Many even of the agrarian aspects of the question have, so far, been somewhat neglected in Ireland owing to a cause which is not far to seek. It has often been asserted that the Irish Question is, at bottom, the Land Question. There is a great deal of truth in this view, but almost all those who hold it have fallen into the grave error of tacitly identifying the land question with the tenure question—an error which vitiates a great deal of current theorising about Ireland. It was, indeed, inevitable that Irish agriculturists, with such an economic history behind them as I have outlined in the previous chapter, should have concentrated their attention during the latter half of the nineteenth century upon obtaining a legislative cure for the ills produced by legislation, to the comparative neglect of those equally difficult, if less obvious economic questions, which have been brought into special prominence by the agricultural depression of the last quarter of a century. Now, however, that the Land Act of 1903 has been passed and the solution of the tenure question is in sight, we in Ireland are more free to direct our attention to what is at present the most important aspect of the agrarian situation—the necessity for determining the social and economic conditions essential to the well-being of the peasant proprietary, which, though it is to be started with as bright an outlook as the law can give, must stand or fall by its own inherent merits or defects. Not only are we now free to give adequate consideration to this question, but it is also imperative that we should do so, for whilst I am hopeful that the Land Act will settle the question of tenure, it will obviously not merely leave the other problems of agricultural existence—problems some of which are not unknown in other parts of the United Kingdom—still unsolved, but will also increase the necessity for their solution, and will, moreover, bring in its train complex difficulties of its own.

The main features of the depressing outlook of rural life in the United Kingdom are well known. The land steadily passes from under the plough and is given over to stock raising. As the kine increase the men decay. In Ireland the rural exodus takes, as I have already said, the shape, mainly, not of migration to Irish urban centres, but rather the uglier form of an emigration which not only depletes our population but drains it of the very elements which can least be spared.

The reason generally given for the widespread resort to the lotus-eating occupation of opening and shutting gates, in preference to tilling the soil, is that in the existing state of agricultural organisation, and while urban life is ever drawing away labour from the fields, the substitution of pasturage for tillage is the readiest way to meet the ruinous competition of Eastern Europe, the Western Hemisphere, and Australasia. Yet upon the economic merits of this process I have heard the most diverse opinions stated with equal conviction by men thoroughly well informed as to the conditions. One of the largest graziers in Ireland recently gave me a picture of what he considered to be an ideal economic state for the country. If two more Belfasts could be established on the east coast, and the rest of the country divided into five hundred acre farms, grazing being adopted wherever permanent grass would grow, the limits of Irish productivity would be reached. On the other hand, Dr. O'Donnell, the Roman Catholic Bishop of Raphoe, who may be taken as an authoritative exponent of the trend of popular thought in the country, not long ago advocated ploughing the grazing lands of Leinster right up to the slopes of Tara.* Moreover, many theories have been

* Yet another view which seems to uproot most agrarian ideas in Ireland has been put forward by Dr. O'Gara in *The Green Republic* (Fisher Unwin, 1902). His main conclusion is that the present disastrous state of our rural economy is due to our treating land as an object of property and not of industry. He advocates the cultivation of the land by syndicates holding farms of 20,000 acres and tilling them

advanced to show that the decline of tillage, whatever be its cause, involves an enormous waste of national resources. But of practical suggestion, making for a remedy, there is very little forthcoming.

The solution of all such problems largely depends upon certain developments which, for many reasons, I regard as absolutely essential to the success of the new agrarian order. One of these developments is the spread of agricultural co-operation through voluntary associations. Without this agency of social and economic progress, small landholders in Ireland will be but a body of isolated units, having all the drawbacks of individualism, and none of its virtues, unorganised and singularly ill-equipped for that great international struggle of our time, which we know as agricultural competition. Moreover, there is another equally important, if less obvious, consideration which renders urgent the organisation of our rural communities. From Russia, with its half-communistic Mir to France with its modern village commune, there is no country in Europe except the United Kingdom where the peasant land-holders have not some form of corporate existence. In Ireland the transition from landlordism to a peasant proprietary not only does not create any corporate existence among the

by the lavish application of modern machinery as the only way to meet American competition. His book is able and suggestive, but it is perhaps, a work of supererogation to discuss a theory the whole moral of which is the expediency of absolutely divorcing the functions of the proprietor and the manager of land at a time when the consensus of opinion in Ireland is in favour of uniting them, and in view of the fact that under the new Land Act the future of the country seems inevitably to lie for a long time in the hands of a peasant proprietary.

occupying peasantry but rather deprives them of the slight social coherence which they formerly possessed as tenants of the same landlord. The estate office has its uses as well as its disadvantages, and the landlord or agent is by no means without his value as a business adviser to those from whom he collects the rent.

The organisation of the peasantry by an extension of voluntary associations, which is a condition precedent of social and economic progress, will not, however, suffice to enable them to face and solve the problems with which they are confronted, and whose solution has now become a matter of very serious concern to the British taxpayer. The condition of our agrarian life clearly indicates the necessity for supplementing voluntary effort with a sound system of State aid to agriculture and industry—a necessity fully recognised by the governments of every progressive continental country and of our own colonies. An altogether hopeful beginning of combined self-help and State assistance has been already made. Those who have been studying these problems, and practically preparing the way for the proper care of a peasant proprietary, have overcome the chief obstacles which lay in their path. They have gained popular acceptance for the principle that State aid should not be resorted to until organised voluntary effort has first been set in motion, and that any departure from this principle would be an unwarrantable interference with the business of the people, a fatal blow to private enterprise.*

* The reader may wonder why I touch so lightly upon a fact of

The task before the people, and before the State, of placing the new agrarian order upon a permanent basis of decency and comfort is no light one. Indeed, I doubt whether Parliament realises one-tenth of the problems which the latest land legislation—by far the best we have yet had—leaves unsolved. This becomes only too clear the moment we consider seriously the fundamental question of the relation of population to area in rural Ireland, or, in other words, when we inquire how many people the agricultural land will support under existing circumstances, or under any attainable improvement of the conditions in our rural life. Roughly speaking, the surface area of the island is 20,000,000 acres, of which 5,000,000 are described in the official returns as 'barren mountain, bog and waste.' This leaves us with some 15,000,000 acres available for agriculture and grazing, which area is now divided into some 500,000 holdings. Thus we have an average of thirty acres in extent for the Irish agricultural holding. But, unhappily, the returns show that some 200,000 of these holdings are from one to fifteen acres in extent. Nor do the mere figures show the case at its worst. For it happens that the small holdings in Ireland, unlike those on the Continent, are generally on the poorest land, and the majority of them

such profound significance as the Irishman's acceptance of self-help as a condition precedent of State aid in the development of agriculture and industry. But such a cursory treatment, in the early chapters, of this and of other equally important aspects of the Irish situation is necessitated by the plan I have adopted. I am attempting to give in the first part of the book a philosophic insight into the chief Irish problems, and then, in the second part of the book, to present the facts which appear to me to illustrate these problems in process of solution.

cannot come within any of the definitions of an ' economic holding.'

These 200,000 holdings, the homes of nearly a million persons, threaten to prove the greatest danger to the future of agricultural Ireland. As the majority of them, as at present constituted, do not provide the physical basis of a decent standard of living, the question arises, how are they to be improved? Putting aside emigration, which at one period was necessary and ought to have been aided and controlled by the State, but which is now no longer a statesman's remedy, there is obviously no solution except by the migration of a portion of the occupiers, and the utilisation of the vacated holdings in order to enable the peasants who remain to prosper— much as a forest is thinned to promote the growth of trees. In typical congested districts this operation will have to be carried out on a much larger scale than is generally realised, for a considerable majority of families will have to be removed, in order to allow a sufficient margin for the provision of adequate holdings for those who remain. In some cases, there are large grazing tracts in close proximity to the congested area which might be utilised for the re-settlement, but where this is not so and the occupiers of the vacated holdings have to migrate a considerable distance, the problem becomes far more difficult. I need not dwell upon the administrative difficulties of the operation, which are not light. I may assume, also, that there will be no difficulty in obtaining suitable land somewhere. I do

not myself attach much weight to the unwillingness of
the people to leave their old holdings for better ones, or
to the alleged objection of the clergy to allow their
parishioners to go to another parish. More serious is
the possible opposition of those who live in the vicinity
of the unoccupied land about to be distributed, and who
feel that they have the first claim upon the State in any
scheme for its redistribution with the help of public
credit.   Mr. Parnell promoted a company with the sole
object of practically demonstrating how this problem
could be solved.   A large capital was raised, and a large
estate purchased ; but the company did not effect the
migration of a single family. Still these are minor
considerations compared with the larger one, to which I
must briefly refer.

Under the Land Act of 1903 much has been done to
facilitate the transfer of peasants to new farms, but
it is obvious that land cannot be handed over as a gift
from the State to the families which migrate. They
will become debtors for the value of the land itself, less
perhaps a small sum which may be credited to them in
respect of the tenant's interest in the holdings they have
abandoned. This deduction will, however, be lost in the
expenditure required upon houses, buildings, fences, and
other improvements which would have to be effected
before the land could be profitably occupied. Speaking
generally they will have no money or agricultural implements, and their live stock will in many cases be
moitgaged to the local shopkeeper who has always

financed them. It will be necessary for the future welfare of the country to give them land which admits of cultivation upon the ordinary principles of modern agriculture; but without working capital, and bringing with them neither the skill nor the habits necessary for the successful conduct of their industry under the new conditions, it will be no easy task to place them in a position to discharge their obligations to the State. It is all very easy to talk about the obvious necessity of giving more land to cultivators who have not enough to live upon; and there is, no doubt, a poetic justice in the Utopian agrarianism which dangles before the eyes of the Connaught peasantry the alternative of Heaven or Leinster. But when we come down to practical economics, and face the task of giving to a certain number of human beings, in an extremely backward industrial condition, the opportunity of placing themselves and their families on a basis of permanent well-being, it will be evident that, so far, at any rate, as this particular community is concerned, the mere provision of an economic holding is after all but a part of an economic existence.

I have touched upon this question of migration from uneconomic to economic holdings because it signally illustrates the importance of the human, in contradistinction to the merely material considerations involved in the solution of the many-sided Irish Question. I must now return to the wider question of the relation of population to area in rural Ireland, as it affects the general scheme of agricultural and industrial development.

E

It is obvious that there must be a limit to the number of individuals that the land can support. Allowing an average of five members for each family, and allowing for a considerable number of landless labourers, it seems that the land at present directly supports about 2,500,000 persons—a view which, I may add, is fully borne out by the figures of the recent census; and it is hard to see how a population living by agriculture can be much increased beyond this number. Even if all the land in Ireland were available for re-distribution in equal shares, the higher standard of comfort to which it is essential that the condition of our people should be raised would forbid the existence of much more than half a million peasant proprietors.* Hence the evergreen query, ' What shall we do with our boys? ' remains to be answered; for while the abolition of dual ownership will enable the present generation to bring up their children according to a higher standard of living, the change will not of itself provide a career for the children when they have been brought up. The next generation will have to face this problem :—the average farm can support only one of the children and his family, what is to become of the others? The law forbids sub-division for two generations, and after that, *ex hypothesi*, the then prevailing conditions of life will also prevent such partition. A few of the next generation may become

* The best expert agricultural opinion tells me that under present conditions a family cannot live in any decent standard of comfort—such as I hope to see prevail in Ireland—on less than 30 acres of Irish land, taking the bad land with the good.

agricultural labourers, but this involves descending to the lowest standard of living of to-day, and in any case the demand for agricultural labourers is not capable of much extension in a country of small peasant proprietors.

Against this view I know it is pointed out that in the earlier part of the nineteenth century the agricultural population of Ireland was as large as is the total population of to-day; but we know the sequel. Instances are also cited of peasant proprietaries in foreign countries which maintain a high standard of living upon small, sometimes diminutive, and highly-rented holdings. We must remember, however, that in these foreign countries State intervention has undoubtedly done much to render possible a prosperous peasant proprietary by, for example, the dissemination of useful information, admirable systems of technical education in agriculture, cheap and expeditious transport, and even State attention to the distribution of agricultural produce in distant markets. Again, in many of these countries rural life is balanced by a highly industrial town life, as, for instance, in the case of Belgium; or is itself highly industrialised by the existence of rural industries, as in the case of Switzerland; while in one notable instance —that of Württemberg—both these conditions prevail.

The true lesson to be drawn from these foreign analogies is that not by agriculture alone is Ireland to be saved. The solution of the rural problem embraces many spheres of national activity. It involves, as I have already said, the further development of manufactures

in Irish towns.   One of the best ways to stimulate our
industries is to develop the home market by means of an
increased agricultural production, and a higher standard
of comfort among the peasant producers.   We shall thus
be, so to speak, operating on consumption as well as on
production, and so increasing the home demand for Irish
manufactures.   Perhaps more urgent than the creation
or extension of manufactures on a larger scale is the
development of industries subsidiary to agriculture in
the country.   This is generally admitted, and most
people have a fair knowledge of the wide and varied
range of peasant industries in all European countries
where a prosperous peasantry exists.   Nor is there
much difficulty in agreeing upon the main conditions
to be satisfied in the selection of the industries
to meet the requirements of our case.   The men and
boys require employment in the winter months, or they
will not stay, and the rural industries promoted should,
as far as possible, be those which allow of intermittent
attention.   The female members of the family must have
profitable and congenial employment.   The handicrafts
to be promoted must be those which will give scope to
the native genius and æsthetic sense.   But unless we
can thus supply the demand of the peasant-industry
market with products of merit or distinctiveness, we
shall fail in competition with the hereditary skill and old
established trade of peasant proprietors which have
solved this part of the problem generations ago.   This
involves the vigorous application of a class of in-

struction of which something will be said in the proper place.

So far the rural industry problem, and the direction in which its solution is to be found, are fairly clear. But there is one disadvantage with which we have to reckon, and which for many other reasons besides the one I am now immediately concerned with, we must seek to remove. A community does not naturally or easily produce for export that for which it has itself no use, taste, or desire. Whatever latent capacity for artistic handicrafts the Irish peasant may possess, it is very rarely that one finds any spontaneous attempt to give outward expression to the inward æsthetic sense. And this brings me to a strange aspect of Irish life to which I have often wished, on the proper occasion, to draw public attention. The matter arises now in the form of a peculiar difficulty which lies in the path of those who endeavour to solve the problem of rural life in Ireland, and which, in my belief, has profoundly affected the fortunes of the race both at home and abroad.

To a sympathetic insight there is a singular and significant void in the Irish conception of a home—I mean the lack of appreciation for the comforts of a home, which might never have been apparent to me had it not obtruded itself in the form of a hindrance to social and economic progress.* In the Irish love of home, as in

---

* It is, of course, unnecessary for me to dwell upon the part played by the home in the standard of living, especially amongst a rural community. But it may not be irrelevant to note that M. Desmolins, who, in his remarkable book, *A quoi tient la superiorité des Anglo-*

the larger national aspirations, the ideal has but a meagre material basis, its appeal being essentially to the social and intellectual instincts. It is not the physical environment and comfort of an orderly home that enchain and attract minds still dominated, more or less unconsciously, by the associations and common interests of the primitive clan, but rather the sense of human neighbourhood and kinship which the individual finds in the community. Indeed the Irish peasant scarcely seems to have a home in the sense in which an Englishman understands the word. If he love the place of his habitation he does not endeavour to improve or to adorn it, or indeed to make it in any sense a reflection of his own mind and taste. He treats life as if he were a mere sojourner upon earth whose true home is somewhere else, a fact often attributed to his intense faith in the unseen, but which I regard as not merely due to this cause, but also, and in a large measure, as the natural outcome of historical conditions, to which I shall presently refer.

What the Irishman is really attached to in Ireland is not a home but a social order. The pleasant amenities, the courtesies, the leisureliness, the associations of religion, and the familiar faces of the neighbours, whose ways and minds are like his and very unlike those of any other people; these are the things to which he clings in Ireland and which he

saxons ? hands over the future of civilisation to the Anglo-Saxons, ascribes to the English rural home much of the success of the race.

remembers in exile. And the rawness and eagerness of America, the lust of the eye and the pride of life that meet him, though with no welcoming aspect, at every turn, the sense of being harshly appraised by new standards of the nature of which he has but the dimmest conception, his helplessness in the fierce current of industrial life in which he is plunged, the climatic extremes of heat and cold, the early hours and few holidays: all these experiences act as a rude shock upon the ill-balanced refinement of the Irish immigrant. Not seldom, he or she loses heart and hope and returns to Ireland mentally and physically a wreck, a sad disillusionment to those who had been comforted in the agony of the leave-taking by the assurance that to emigrate was to succeed.

The peculiar Irish conception of a home has probably a good deal to do with the history of the Irish in the United States. It is well known that whatever measure of success the Irish emigrant has there achieved is pre-eminently in the American city, and not where, according to all the usual commonplaces about the Irish race, they ought to have succeeded, in American rural life. There they were afforded, and there they missed, the greatest opportunity which ever fell to the lot of a people agriculturally inclined. During the days of the great emigrations from Ireland, a veritable Promised Land, rich beyond the dreams of agricultural avarice, was gradually opened up between the Alleghanies and the Rocky Mountains, which the Irish had only to occupy in order to possess. Making all allowances for

the depressing influences which had been brought to
bear upon the spirit of enterprise, and for their impoverished condition, I am convinced that a prime cause
of the failure of almost every effort to settle them upon
the land was the fact that the tenement house, with all its
domestic abominations, provided the social order which
they brought with them from Ireland, and the lack of
which on the western prairie no immediate or prospective
physical comfort could make good.

Recently a daughter of a small farmer in County
Galway with a family too 'long' for the means of
subsistence available, was offered a comfortable home
on a farm owned by some better-off relatives, only
thirty miles away, though probably twenty miles
beyond the limits of her utmost peregrinations. She
elected in preference to go to New York, and being
asked her reason by a friend of mine, replied in
so many words, 'because it is nearer.' She felt
she would be less of a stranger in a New York
tenement house, among her relatives and friends who
had already emigrated, than in another part of County
Galway. Educational science in Ireland has always
ignored the life history of the subject with which it
dealt. In no respect has this neglect been so unconsciously cruel as in its failure to implant in the Irish
mind that appreciation of the material aspects of the
home which the people so badly need both in Ireland
and in America. If the Irishman abroad became 'a
rootless colonist of alien earth,' the lot of the Irishman

in Ireland has been not less melancholy. Sadness there is, indeed, in the story of ' the sea-divided Gael,' but, to me, it is incomparably less pathetic than their homelessness at home.

There are, as I have said, historic reasons for the Celtic view of home to which my personal observation and experience has induced me to devote so much space. The Irish people have never had the opportunity of developing that strong and salutary individualism which, amongst other things, imperiously demands, as a condition of its growth, a home that shall be a man's castle as well as his abiding place. In this, as in so much else, a healthy evolution was constantly thwarted by the clash of two peoples and two civilisations. The Irish had hardly emerged from the nomad pastoral stage, when the first of that series of invasions, which had all the ferocity, without the finality of conquest, made settled life impossible over the greater part of the island. An old chronicle throws some vivid light upon the way in which the idea of home life presented itself to the mind of the clan chiefs as late as the days of the Tudors. "Con O'Neal," we are told, "was so right Irish that he cursed all his posterity in case they either learnt English, sowed wheat or built them houses ; lest the first should breed conversation, the second commerce, and with the last they should speed as the crow that buildeth her nest to be beaten out by the hawk."* The penal laws, again, acted as a disin-

* Speed's Chronicle, quoted in *Calendar of State Papers, Ireland*, 1611-14, p. xix.

tegrant of the home and the **family**; and, finally, the
paralysing effect of the abuses of a system of land tenure,
under which evidences of thrift and comfort might at any
time become determining factors in the calculation of
rent, completed a series of causes which, in unison or
isolation, were calculated to destroy at its source the
growth of a wholesome domesticity. These causes
happily, no longer exist, and powerful forces are arising
to overcome the defects and disadvantages which they
have bequeathed to us; and I have little doubt that it
will be possible to deal successfully with this obstacle
which adds so peculiar a feature to the problem of rural
life in Ireland.

If I have dwelt at what may appear to be a dispropor-
tionate length upon the Irishman's peculiar conception of
a home, it is because this difficulty, which Irish social and
economic reformers still encounter, and with which they
must deal sympathetically if they are to succeed in the
work of national regeneration, strikingly illustrates the
two-sided character of the Irish Question and the never-
to-be-forgotten inter-dependence of the sentimental and
the practical in Ireland. I admit that this condition which
adds to the interest of the problem, and perhaps makes
it more amenable to rapid solution, is an indication
of a weakness of moral fibre to which must be largely
attributed our failure to be master of our circumstances.
Indeed, as I come into closer touch with the efforts
which are now being made to raise the material condition of the people, the more convinced I become, much

as my practical training has made me resist the conviction, that the Irish Question is, in its most difficult
and most important aspects, the problem of the Irish
mind, and that the solution of this problem is to be
found in the strengthening of Irish character.

With this enunciation of the main proposition of my
book, I may now indicate the order in which I shall
endeavour to establish its truth. I have said enough to
show that I do not ignore the historical causes of our
present state; but with so many facts with which we
can deal confronting us, I propose to review the chief
living influences to which the Irish mind and character
are still subjected. These influences fall naturally into
three distinct categories and will be treated in the three
succeeding chapters. The first will show the effect upon
the Irish mind of its obsession by politics. The next will
deal with the influence of religious systems upon the
secular life of the people. I shall then show how education, which should not only have been the most potent of
all the three influences in bringing our national life into
line with the progress of the age, but should also have
modified the operation of the other two causes, has
aggravated rather than cured the malady.

Whatever impression I may succeed in making upon
others, I may here state that, as the result of observation
and reflection, the conclusion has been forced upon me
that the Irish mind is suffering from considerable
functional derangement, but not, so far as I can discern,
from any organic disease. This is the basis of my

optimism. I shall submit in another chapter, which will
conclude the first, the critical part of my book, certain
new principles of treatment which are indicated by the
diagnosis ; and I would ask the reader, before he rejects
the opinions which are there expressed, to persevere
through the narrative contained in the second part of the
book. There he will find in process of solution some of
the problems which I have indicated, and the principles
for which a theoretical approval has been asked, in
practical operation, and already passing out of the
experimental stage. The story of the Self-help Movement will strike the note of Ireland's economic hopes.
The action of the Recess Committee will be explained,
and the concession of their demand by the establishment
of a ' Department of Agriculture and other rural industries and for Technical Instruction for Ireland,' will be
described. This will complete the story of a quiet,
unostentatious movement which will some day be seen to
have made the last decade of the nineteenth century
a fit prelude to a future commensurate with the
potentialities of the Irish people.

CHAPTER III.

THE INFLUENCE OF POLITICS UPON THE IRISH MIND.

Among the humours of the Home Rule struggle, the story was current in England that a peasant in Connemara ceased planting his potatoes when the news of the introduction of the Home Rule Bill in 1886 seemed to bring the millenium into the region of practical politics. Those who used the story were not slow to suggest that, had the Bill become law, the failure of spontaneous generation in the Connemara potato patch might have been typical of much analogous disillusionment elsewhere. Even to those who are familiar with our history, the faith of the Irish people in the potentialities of government, which this little tale illustrates by caricature, will give cause for reflection of another and more serious kind. The moral to be drawn by Irish politicians is that we in Ireland have yet to free ourselves from one of the worst legacies of past misgovernment, the belief that any legislation or any legislature can provide an escape from the physical and mental toil imposed through our first parents upon all nations for all time.

' The more business in politics, and the less politics in business, the better for both,' is a maxim which I brought

home from the Far West and ventured to advocate publicly
some years ago.   Being still of the same mind, I regret
that I am compelled to introduce a whole chapter of
politics into this book, which is a study of Irish affairs
mainly   from   a   social and economic   point   of   view.
But to ignore, either in the diagnosis or in the treatment
of the 'mind diseased,' the political obsession of our
national life would be about as wise as to discuss and
plan a Polar expedition without taking account of the
climatic conditions to be encountered.

In such an examination of Irish politics as thus becomes necessary I shall have to devote the greater part
of my criticism to the influence of the Nationalist party
upon the Irish mind.   But it will be seen that this course
is not taken with a view to making party capital for my
own side.   As I read Irish history, neither party need
expect very much credit for more than good intentions.
Whichever proves to be right in its main contention, each
will have to bear its share of the responsibility for the
long continuance of the barren controversy.   Each has
neglected to concern itself with the settlement of vitally
important questions the consideration of which need not
have been postponed because the constitutional question
still remained in dispute.   Therefore, though I seem
to throw upon the Nationalist party the chief blame for
our present political backwardness, and, so far as politics
affect other spheres of national activity, for our industrial
depression, candour compels me to admit that Irish
Unionism has failed to recognise its obligation—an

obligation recognised by the Unionist party in Great Britain—to supplement opposition to Home Rule with a positive and progressive policy which could have been expected to commend itself to the majority of the Irish people—the Irish of the Irish Question.

To my own party in Ireland then, I would first direct the reader's attention. I have already referred to the deplorable effects produced upon national life by the exclusion of representatives of the landlord and the industrial classes from positions of leadership and trust over four-fifths of the country. I cannot conceive of a prosperous Ireland in which the influence of these leaders is restricted within its present bounds. It has been so restricted because the Irish Unionist party has failed to produce a policy which could attract, at any rate, moderate men from the other side, and we have, therefore, to consider why we have so failed. Until this is done, we shall continue to share the blame for the miserable state of our political life which, at the end of the nineteenth century, appeared to have made but little advance from the time when Bishop Berkeley asked 'Whether our parties are not a burlesque upon politics.'

The Irish Unionist party is supposed to unite all who, like the author, are opposed to the plunge into what is called Home Rule. But its propagandist activities in Ireland are confined to preaching the doctrine of the *status quo*, and preaching it only to its own side. From the beginning the party has been intimately connected with the landlord class ; yet even upon

the land question it has thrown but few gleams of the
constructive thought which that question so urgently
demanded, and which it might have been expected to
apply to it. Now and again an individual tries to
broaden the basis of Irish Unionism and to bring himself into touch with the life of the people. But the
nearer he gets to the people the farther he gets from
the Irish Unionist leaders. The lot of such an individual
is not a happy one: he is regarded as a mere intruder
who does not know the rules of the game, and he is
treated by the leading players on both sides like a dog
in a tennis court.

Two main causes appear to me to account for the
failure of the Irish Unionist party to make itself an
effective force in Irish national life. The great misunderstanding to which I have attributed the unhappy
state of Anglo-Irish relations kept the country in a condition of turmoil which enabled the Unionist party to declare itself the party of law and order. Adopting Lord
Salisbury's famous prescription, 'twenty years of resolute
government,' they made it what its author would have
been the last man to consider it, a sufficient justification for a purely negative and repressive policy.
Such an attitude was open to somewhat obvious
objections. No one will dispute the proposition
that the government of Ireland, or of any other country,
should be resolute, but twenty years of resolute government, in the narrow sense in which it came to be interpreted, needed for its success, what cannot be had under

party government, twenty years of consistency. It may be better to be feared than to be loved, but Machiavelli would have been the first to admit that his principle did not apply where the Government which sought to establish fear had to reckon with an Opposition which was making capital out of love. Moreover, the suggestion that the Irish Question is not a matter of policy but of police, while by no means without influential adherents, is altogether vicious. You cannot physically intimidate Irishmen, and the last thing you want to do is morally to intimidate a people whose greatest need at the moment is moral courage.

The second cause which determined the character of Irish Unionism was the linking of the agrarian with the political question; the one being, in effect, a practical, the other a sentimental issue. The same thing happened in the Nationalist party; but on their side it was intentional and led to an immense accession of strength, while on the Unionist side it made for weakness. If the influence of Irish Unionists was to be even maintained, it was of vital importance that the interest of a class should not be allowed to dominate the policy of the party. But the organisation which ought to have rallied every force that Ireland could contribute to the cause of imperial unity came to be too closely identified with the landlord class. That class is admittedly essential to the construction of any real national life. But there is another element equally essential, to which the political leaders of Irish

F

Unionism have not given the prominence which is
its due. The Irish Question has been so successfully narrowed down to two simple policies, one
positive but vague, the other negative but definite, that
to suggest that there are three distinct forces—three
distinct interests—to be taken into account seems like
confusing the issue.   It is a fact, nevertheless, that
a very important element on the Unionist side, the industrial element, has been practically left out of the calculation by both sides.   Yet the only expression of real
political thought which I have observed in Ireland, since
I have been in touch with Irish life, has emanated from
the Ulster Liberal-Unionist Association, whose weighty
pronouncements, published from time to time, are
worthy of deep consideration by all interested in the
welfare of Ireland.

It will be remembered that when the Home Rule controversy was at its height, the chief strength of the Irish
opposition to Mr. Gladstone's policy, and the consideration
which most weighed with the British electorate, lay in the
business objection of the industrial population of Ulster ;
though on the platform religious and political arguments
were more often heard.   The intensely practical nature
of the objection which came from the commercial and
industrial classes of the North who opposed Home Rule
was never properly recognised in Ireland.   It was, and is
still unanswered.   Briefly stated, the position taken up by
their spokesmen was as follows :—'We have come,' they
said in effect, ' into Ireland, and not the richest portion

of the island, and have gradually built up an industry and commerce with which we are able to hold our own in competition with the most progressive nations in the world. Our success has been achieved under a system and a polity in which we believe. Its non-interference with the business of the people gave play to that self-reliance with which we strove to emulate the industrial qualities of the people of Great Britain. It is now proposed to place the manufactures and commerce of the country at the mercy of a majority which will have no real concern in the interests vitally affected, and who have no knowledge of the science of government. The mere shadow of these changes has so depressed the stocks which represent the accumulations of our past enterprise and labour that we are already commercially poorer than we were.'*

My sole criticism of those leaders of commerce and industry in Belfast, who, whenever they turn their attention from their various pre-occupations, import into Irish politics the valuable qualities which they display in the conduct of their private affairs, is that they do not go further and take the necessary steps to give practical effect to their views outside the ranks of their immediate associates and followers. Had the industrial section made its voice heard in the councils of the Irish Unionist

---

* This view of the case was powerfully stated by the deputation from the Belfast Chamber of Commerce which waited on Mr. Gladstone in the spring of 1893. They pointed out *inter alia* that the members of the deputation were poorer by thousands of pounds owing to the fall in Irish stocks consequent upon the introduction of the Home Rule Bill in that year.

party, the Government which that party supports might have had less advice and assistance in the maintenance of law and order, but it would have had invaluable aid in its constructive policy. For the lack of the wise guidance which our captains of industry should have provided, Irish Unionism has, by too close adherence to the traditions of the landlord section, been the creed of a social caste rather than a policy in Ireland. The result has been injurious alike for the landlords, the leaders of industry, and the people. The policy of the Unionist party in Ireland has been to uphold the Union by force rather than by a reconciliation of the people to it. It has held aloof from the masses, who, bereft of the guidance of their natural leaders, have clung the more closely to the chiefs of the Nationalist party; and these in their turn have not, as I shall show presently, risen to their responsibility, but have retarded rather than advanced the march of democracy in Ireland. If there is to be any future for Unionism in Ireland, there must be a combination of the best thought of the country aristocracy and that of the captains of industry. Then, and not till then, shall we Unionists as a party exercise a healthful and stimulating influence on the thought and action of the people.

I cannot, therefore, escape from the conclusion that whilst the Irish section of the party to which I belong is, in my opinion, right on the main political question, its influence is now for the most part negative. Hence I direct attention mainly to the Home Rule party, as the more forceful element in Irish political life ; and if it receives the more criticism it is because it is more closely in touch with the people, and because any reform in its principles or methods would more generally and more rapidly prove beneficial to the country than would any change in Unionist policy.

In examining the policy of the Nationalist party my chief concern will be to arrive at a correct estimate of the effect which is produced upon the thought and action of the Irish people by the methods employed for the attainment of Home Rule. I propose to show that these methods have been in the past, and must, so long as they are employed, continue to be injurious to the political and industrial character of the people, and consequently a barrier to progress. I know that most of the Nationalist leaders justify the employment of these methods on the ground that, in their opinion, the constitutional reforms they advocate are a condition precedent to industrial progress. I believe, on the contrary, and I shall give my reasons for believing, that their tactics have been not only a hindrance to industrial progress, but destructive even to the ulterior purpose they were intended to fulfil.

It is commonly believed—a belief very naturally fostered by their leaders—that, if there is one thing the Irish do understand, it is politics. Politics is a term obviously capable of wide interpretation, and I fear that those who say that my countrymen are pre-eminently politicians use the term in a sense more applicable to

the conceptions of Mr. Richard Croker than of Aristotle.
In intellectual capacity for discrimination upon political
issues the average Irish elector is, I believe, far superior
to the average English elector. But there is as yet
something wanting in the character of our people which
seems to prohibit the exercise by them of any independent political thought and, consequently, of any
effective or permanent political influence.

The assumption that Irishmen are singularly good
politicians seems to stand seriously in the way of their
becoming so; and yet it is a matter of the greatest
importance that they should become good politicians in
a real sense, for in no country would sound political
thought exercise a more beneficial influence upon the
life of the people than in Ireland. Indeed I would go
further and give it as my strong conviction that, properly
developed and freed from the narrowing influences of
the party squabbles by which it has been warped and
sterilised, the political thought of the Irish people would
contribute a factor of vital importance to the life of the
British empire. But at the moment I am dealing only
with the influence of politics on Irish social and economic
life.

I am aware that any political deficiencies which the
Irish may display at home, are commonly attributed to
the political system which has been imposed upon
Ireland from without. If you want to see Irish
genius in its highest political manifestation, it must
be studied, we are told, in the United States, the

widest and freest arena which has ever been offered to
the race. This view is not in accordance with the
facts as I have observed them. These facts are
somewhat obscured by the natural, but misleading habit
of reckoning to the account of Ireland at large achievements really due to the Scotch-Irish, who helped to
colonise Pennsylvania, and who undoubtedly played a
dominant part in developing the characteristic features
of the American political system. The Scotch-Irish, however, do not belong to the Ireland of the Irish Question.
Descended, largely, as their names so often testify, from
the early Irish colonists of western Scotland, they came
back as a distinct race, dissociating themselves from
the Irish Celts by refusing to adopt their national traditions, or intermarry with them, and both here and in
America disclaiming the appellation of Irish.*

Leaving, then, out of consideration the political
achievements of the Scotch-Irish, it appears to me that
the part played in politics by the Irish in America does
not testify to any high political genius. They have shown
there an extraordinary aptitude for political organisation, which, if it had been guided by anything approaching to political thought, would have placed them
in a far higher position in American public life than that

---

* The term 'Scotch-Irish' does not mean an amalgam of Scotch
and Irish, but a race of Scottish immigrants who settled in north-
east Ireland. I may point out that in these criticisms of Irish-American
politics I refer, of course, mainly to the Irish-born immigrants and not
to the Irish, Scotch-Irish or other, who are American-born. Nobody
can have a higher appreciation than I of the great part played by the
American-Irish once they have assimilated the full spirit of American
institutions.

which they now occupy. But the fact is that it would be much easier to find evidence of high political capacity and success in the history of the Irish in British colonies ; and the reason for this fact is not only very germane to the purpose of this book, but has a strong practical interest for Americans as well. Irishmen when they go to America find themselves united by a bond which does not and could not exist in the Colonies— though it does exist in Ireland—the bond of anti-English feeling, and by the hope of giving practical effect to this feeling through the policy of their adopted country. Imbued with this common sentiment, and influenced by their inherited clannishness, the Irish in America readily lend themselves to the system of political groups, a system which the 'boss' for his own ends seeks to perpetuate. The result is a sort of political paradox—it has made the Irish in America both stronger and weaker than they ought to be. They suffer politically from the defects of their political qualities: they are strong as a voting machine, but the secret of their collective strength is also the secret of their individual weakness. This organisation into groups is much commoner among the Irish than among other American immigrants, for the anti-English feeling with which so many of the Irish land in America is carefully kept alive by the 'boss,' whose sedulous fostering of the instinctive clannishness and inherited leader-following habits of the Irish saps their independence of thought and prevents them from ceasing to be mere political agents and developing a citizenship which would furnish its due quota of states-men to the service of the Republic. They lack in the United States just what they lack at home, the capacity, or at any rate the inclination, to use their undoubted abilities in a large and foreseeing manner, and so are becoming less and less powerful as a force in American politics.

The fallacious views about the nature and sphere of politics, which the Irish bring with them from Ireland, and which are perpetuated in America, have the effect not only of debarring the Irish from real political progress, but also, as at home, from gaining success in industrial pursuits which their talents would otherwise win for them. They succeed as journalists owing to their quick intelligence and versatility, and as contractors mainly owing to their capacity for organising gangs of workmen —a faculty which seems to be the only good thing result-ing from their political education. They are as brilliant soldiers in the service of the United States as they are in that of Britain—more it would be impossible to say—and they have produced types of daring, endurance, and shrewdness like the 'Silver Kings' of Nevada which testify to the exceptional powers always developed by the Irish in exceptional circumstances. But in the humdrum business of everyday life in the United States they suffer from defects which are the outcome of their devotion to mistaken political ideals and of their subordination of industry to politics, which are not always purely

American, but are often influenced by considerations of
the country of their birth.   On the whole, a quarter of a
century of not unsympathetic observation of the Irish in
the United States has convinced me that the position
they occupy there is not one which either they or the
American people can look on with entire satisfaction.
The Irish immigrants are felt to belong to a kind of
imperium in imperio, and to carry into American politics
ideas which are not American, and which might easily
become an embarrassment if not a danger to America.
Hence the powerful interest which America shares with
England, though of course in a less degree, in understanding and helping to settle the complex difficulty
called the Irish Question.   The Irish remember Ireland
long after they have left it.   They are not in the same
position as the German or English immigrants who have
no cause at home which they wish to forward.   Every
echo in the States of political or social disturbance in
Ireland rouses the immigrant and he becomes an Irishman
once more, and not a citizen of the country of his adoption.   His views and votes on international questions, in
so far as they affect these Islands, are thus often dictated
more by a passionate sympathy for and remembrance of
the land he no longer lives in, than by any right understanding of the interests of the new country in which
he and his children must live.

The only reason why I have examined the assumption
that Irishmen display marked political capacity in the
United States is to make it clear that the political defi-

ciencies they manifest at home are to be attributed mainly to defects of character, and to a conception of politics for which modern English government is very slightly responsible. I admit that English government in the past had no small share in producing the results we deplore to-day, but the motives and manner of its action have, it seems to me, been very imperfectly understood.

The fact is that the difficulties of English government in Ireland, until a complete military conquest had been effected, were of a peculiarly complex character. Before the English could impose upon Ireland their own political organisation—and the idea that any other system could work better among the Irish never entered the English mind—it was obviously necessary that the very antithesis of that organisation, the clan system, should be abolished. But there were military and financial objections to carrying out this policy. Irish campaigns were very costly, and England was in those days by no means wealthy. English armies in Ireland, after a short period spent in desultory warfare with light armed kernes in the fever stricken Munster forests, began to melt away. For many generations, therefore, England, adopting a policy of *divide et impera*, set clan against clan. Later on, statecraft may be said to have supervened upon military tactics. It consisted of attempts made by alternate threats and bribes to induce the chiefs to transform the clan organisation by the acceptance of English institutions. But any systematic endeavours to complete the transformation were soon

rendered abortive by being coupled with huge confiscations of land.   The policy of converting the members
of the clans into freeholders was subordinated to the
policy of planting British colonists. After this there was
no question of fusion of races or institutions. Plantations
on a large scale, self-supporting, self-protecting, became
the policy alike of the soldier and the statesman.

The inevitable result of these methods was that it was
not until a comparatively late date that a political conception of an Irish nation first began to emerge out of
the congeries of clans.   In the State Papers of the
sixteenth century the clans are frequently spoken of as
' nations.'   Even as late as the eighteenth century a
Gaelic poet, in a typical lament, thus identifies his
country with the fortunes of her great families :—

> The O'Doherty is not holding sway, nor his noble race ;
> The O'Moores are not strong, that once were brave—
> O'Flaherty is not in power, nor his kinsfolk ;
> And sooth to say, the O'Briens have long since become English.
>
> Of O'Rourke there is no mention—my sharp wounding !
> Nor yet of O'Donnell in Erin ;
> The Geraldines they are without vigour—without a nod,
> And the Burkes, the Barrys, the Walshes of the slender ships.*

The modern political idea of Irish nationality at
length asserted itself as the result of three main causes.
The bond of a common grievance against the English
foe was created by the gradual abandonment of the
policy of setting clan against clan in favour of impartial

* *Poems of Egan O'Rahilly*.   Edited, with translation, by the
Rev. P. S. Dinneen, M.A., for the Irish Texts Society, p. 11.
O'Rahilly's charge against Cromwell is that he " gave plenty to the
man with the flail," but beggared the great lords, p. 167.

confiscation of land from friendly as well as from hostile chiefs. Secondly, when the English had destroyed the natural leaders, the clan chiefs, and attempted to proselytise their adherents, the political leadership largely passed to the Roman Catholic Church, which very naturally defended the religion common to the members of all the clans, by trying to unite them against the English enemy. Nationality, in this sense, of course applied only to Celtic Roman Catholic Ireland. The first real idea of a United Ireland arose out of the third cause, the religious grievances of the Protestant dissenters and the commercial grievances of the Protestant manufacturers and artisans in the eighteenth century, who suffered under a common disability with the Roman Catholics, and many of whom came in the end to make common cause with them. But even long after this conception had become firmly established, the local representative institutions corresponding to those which formed the political training of the English in law and administration either did not exist in Ireland or were altogether in the hands of a small aristocracy, mostly of non-Irish origin, and wholly non-Catholic. O'Connell's great work in freeing Roman Catholic Ireland from the domination of the Protestant oligarchy showed the people the power of combination, but his methods can hardly be said to have fostered political thought. The efforts in this direction of men like Gavan Duffy, Davis, and Lucas were neutralised by the Famine, the after effects of which also did much to thwart Butt's attempts to develop serious public opinion amongst a people whose political education had been so long delayed. The prospect of any early fruition of such efforts vanished with the revolutionary agrarian propaganda, and independent thinking—so necessary in the modern democratic state—never replaced the old leader-following habit which continued until the climax was reached under Parnell.

The political backwardness of the Irish people revealed itself characteristically when, in 1884, the English and Irish democracies were simultaneously endowed with a greatly extended franchise. In theory this concession should have developed political thought in the people and should have enhanced their sense of political responsibility. In England no doubt this theory was proved by the event to be based on fact; but in Ireland it was otherwise. Parnell was at the zenith of his power. The Irish had the man, what mattered the principles? The new suffrages simply became the figures upon the cheques handed over to the Chief by each constituency, with the request that he would fill in the name of the payee. On one or two occasions a constituency did protest against the payee, but all that was required to settle the matter was a personal visit from the Chief. Generally speaking, the electorate were quite docile, and instances were not wanting of men discovering that they had found favour with electors to whom their faces and even their names were previously unknown.

No doubt, the one-man system had a tactical

value, of which the English themselves were ever ready to make use. " If all Ireland cannot rule this man, then let this man rule all Ireland," said Henry VII. of the Earl of Kildare ; and the echo of these words was heard when the Kilmainham Treaty was negotiated with the last man who wore the mantle of the chief.   But whatever may be said for the one-man system as a means of political organisation, it lacked every element of political education.   It left the people weaker, if possible, and less capable than it found them ; and assuredly it was no fit training for Home Rule.   While Parnell's genius was in the ascendant, all was well— outwardly.   When a tragic and painful disclosure brought about a crisis in his fate, it will hardly be contended by the most devoted admirer of the Irish people that the situation was met with even moderate ability and foresight.   But the logic of events began to take effect. The decade of dissension which followed the fall of Parnell will, perhaps, some day be recognised as a most fruitful epoch in modern Irish history. The re-action from the one-man system set in as soon as the one man had passed away.   The independence which Parnell's former lieutenants began to assert when the laurels faded upon the brow of the uncrowned King communicated itself to some extent to the rank and file.   The mere weighing of the merits of several possible successors led to some wholesome questioning as to the merits of the policies, such as they were, which they respectively represented. The critical spirit which was now called forth, did not,

at first, go very far; but it was at least constructive and
marked a distinct advance towards real political thought.
I believe the day will come, and come soon, when
Nationalist leaders themselves will recognise that while
bemoaning faction and dissension and preaching the
cause of 'unity' they often mistook the wheat for the
tares.   They will, I feel sure, come to realise that the
passing of the dictatorship, which to outward appearances left the people as "sheep without a shepherd, when
the snow shuts out the sky," in fact turned the thoughts
of Ireland in some measure away from England into her
own bosom, and gave birth there to the idea of a national
life to which the Irish people of all classes, creeds, and
politics could contribute of their best.

I sometimes wonder whether the leaders of the Nationalist party really understand the full effect of their
tactics upon the political character of the Irish people,
and whether their vision is not as much obscured by a too
near, as is the vision of the Unionist leaders by a too
distant, view of the people's life.   Everyone who
seeks to provide practical opportunities for Irish intellect
to express itself worthily in active life—and this, I take
it, is part of what the Nationalist leaders wish to achieve
—meets with the same difficulty.   The lack of initiative
and shrinking from responsibility, the moral timidity
in glaring contrast with the physical courage—which has
its worst manifestation in the intense dread of public
opinion, especially when the unknown terrors of edito-
rial power lurk behind an unfavourable mention 'on the

paper,' are, no doubt, qualities inherited from a primitive social state in which the individual was nothing and the community everything. These defects were intensified in past generations by British statecraft, which seemed unable to appreciate or use the higher instincts of the race; they remain to-day a prominent factor in the great human problem known as the Irish Question—a factor to which, in my belief, may be attributed the greatest of its difficulties.

It is quite clear that education should have been the remedy for the defects of character upon which I am forced to dwell so much; and I cannot absolve any body of Irishmen, possessed of actual or potential influence, of failure to recognise this truth. But here I am dealing only with the political leaders, and trying to bring home to them the responsibility which their power imposes upon them, not only for the political development but also for the industrial progress of their followers. They ought to have known that the weakness of character which renders the task of political leadership in Ireland comparatively easy is in reality the quicksand of Irish life, and that neither self-government nor any other institution can be enduringly built upon it.

The leaders of the Nationalist party are, of course, entitled to hold that, in existing political conditions, any non-political movement towards national advancement, which in its nature cannot be linked, as the land question was linked, to the Home Rule movement constitutes an unwarrantable sacrifice of ends to means. And

G

so holding, they are further entitled to subject any proposal to elevate popular thought, or to direct popular
activities, to a strict censorship as to its remote as well as
to its immediate effect upon the electorate. I know, too,
that it is held by some thinking Nationalists who take
no active part in politics that the politicians are justified
on tactical grounds in this exclusive pursuit of their
political aims, and in the methods by which they pursue
them. They consider the present system of government too radically wrong to mend, and they can
undoubtedly point to agrarian legislation as evidence of
the effectiveness of the means they employ to gain their
end.

This view of things has sunk very deep into the Irish
mind. The policy of ' giving trouble ' to the Government
is looked upon as the one road to reform and is believed
in so fervently that, except for religion, which sometimes
conflicts with it, there is scarcely any capacity left for
belief in anything else. I am far from denying that the
past offers much justification for the belief that nothing
can be gained by Ireland from England except through
violent agitation. Until recently, I admit, Ireland's
opportunity had to wait for England's difficulty. But, as
practised in the present day, I believe this doctrine
to be mischievous and false. For one thing, there
is a new England to deal with. The England
which, certainly not in deference to violent agitation,
established the Congested Districts Board, gave Local
Government to Ireland, and accepted the recom-

mendations of the Recess Committee for far-reaching
administrative changes, as well as those of the Land
Conference which involved great financial concessions,
is not the England of fifty years ago, still less the
England of the eighteenth century. Moreover, in
riveting the mind of the country on what is to
be obtained from England, this doctrine of 'giving
trouble,' the whole gospel of the agitator, has blinded
the Irish people to the many things which Ireland
can do for herself. Whatever may be said of
what is called 'agitation' in Ireland as an engine for
extorting legislation from the Imperial Parliament, it is
unquestionably bad for the much greater end of building
up Irish character and developing Irish industry and
commerce. 'Agitation,' as Thomas Davis said, 'is one
means of redress, but it leads to much disorganisation,
great unhappiness, wounds upon the soul of a country
which sometimes are worse than the thinning of a people
by war.'* If Irish politicians had at all realised this
truth, it is difficult to believe that the popular movement
of the last quarter of a century would not have been
conducted in a manner far less injurious to the soul of

---

* *Prose Writings of Thomas Davis*, p. 284. 'The writers of
The Nation,' wrote Davis in another place, 'have never concealed the
defects or flattered the good qualities of their countrymen. They have
told them in good faith that they wanted many an attribute of a free
people, *and that the true way to command happiness and liberty was by
learning the arts and practising the culture that fitted men for their
enjoyment*' (p. 176). The thing that especially distinguished Davis
among Nationalist politicians was the essentially constructive
mind which he brought to bear on Irish questions, as illustrated
in the passage I have italicised. It is, I am afraid, the part of his
legacy of thought which has been least regarded by his admirers.

Ireland and equally or more effective for legislative reform as well as all other material interests.

Now, modern Nationalism in Ireland is open to damaging criticism not only from my Unionist point of view, which was also, in many respects, the view of so strong a Nationalist as Thomas Davis; it is also open to grave objection from the point of view of the effectiveness of the tactics employed for the attainment of its end—the winning of Home Rule.

Before examining the effect of these tactics I may point out that this conception of Nationalist policy, even if justifiable from a practical point of view, does not relieve the leaders from the obligation of giving some assurance that they are ready with a consistent scheme of re-construction, and are prepared to build when the ground has been cleared. In this connection I might make a good deal of Unionist capital, and some points in support of my condemnation of the political absorption of the Irish mind, out of the total failure of the Nationalist party to solve certain all-important constitutional and financial problems which months of Parliamentary debate in 1893 tended rather to obscure than to elucidate. I am, however, willing for argument's sake to postpone all such questions, vital as they are, to the time when they can be practically dealt with. I am ready to assume that the wit of man can devise a settlement of many points which seemed insoluble in Mr. Gladstone's day. But even granting all this, I think it can easily be shown that the means which the political thought available on the Nationalist side has evolved for the attainment of their end, and which *ex hypothesi* are only to be justified on tactical grounds, are the least likely to succeed; and that, consequently, they should be abandoned in favour of a constructive policy which, to say the least, would not be less effective towards advancing the Home Rule cause, if that cause be sound, and which would at the same time help the advancement of Ireland in other than political directions.

Tactics form but a part of generalship, and half the success of generalship lies in making a correct estimate of the opposing forces. This is as true of political as it is of military operations. Now, of what do the forces opposed to Home Rule consist? The Unionists, it may be admitted, are numerically but a small minority of the population of Ireland—probably not more than one-fourth. But what do they represent? First, there are the landed gentry. Let us again make a concession for the sake of argument and accept the view that this class so wantonly kept itself aloof from the life of the majority of the people that the Nationalists could not be expected to count them among the elements of a Home Rule Ireland. I note, in passing, with extreme gratification that at the recent Land Conference it was declared by the tenants' representatives that it was desirable, in the interests of Ireland, that the present owners of land should not be expatriated, and that inducements should be afforded to selling owners to continue to reside in the country.

But I may ignore this as I wish here to recall attention to that other element, which was, as I have already said, the real force which turned the British democracy against Home Rule—I mean the commercial and industrial community in Belfast and other hives of industry in the north-east corner of the country, and in scattered localities elsewhere. I have already admitted that the political importance of the industrial element was not appreciated in Irish Unionist circles. No less remarkable is the way in which it has been ignored by the Nationalists. The question which the Nationalists had to answer in 1886 and 1893, and which they have to answer to-day, is this:— In the Ireland of their conception is the Unionist part of Ulster to be coerced or persuaded to come under the new regime? To those who adopt the former alternative my reply is simply that, if England is to do the coercion, the idea is politically absurd. If we were left to fight it out among ourselves, it is physically absurd. The task of the Empire in South Africa was light compared with that which the Nationalists would have on hands. I am aware that, at the time when we were all talking at concert pitch on the Irish Question, a good deal was said about dying in the last ditch by men who at the threat of any real trouble would be found more discreetly perched upon the first fence. But those who know the temper and fighting qualities of the working-men opponents of Home Rule in the North are under no illusion as to the account they would give of

themselves if called upon to defend the cause of Protestantism, liberty, and imperial unity as they understand it.
Let us, however, dismiss this alternative and give
Nationalists credit for the desire to persuade the
industrial North to come in by showing it that it will
be to its advantage to join cordially in the building
up of a united Ireland under a separate legislature.

The difficulties in the way of producing this conviction
are very obvious. The North has prospered under the
Act of Union—why should it be ready to enter upon a
new ' variety of untried being '? What that state of
being will be like, it naturally gauges from the forces
which are working for Home Rule at present. Looking
at these simply from the industrial standpoint and leaving
out of account all the powerful elements of religious and
race prejudice, the man of the North sees two salient facts
which have dominated all the political activity of the
Nationalist campaign. One is a voluble and aggressive
disloyalty, not merely to ' England ' and to the present
system of government, but to the Crown which repre-
sents the unity of the three kingdoms, and the other is
the introduction of politics into business in the very
virulent and destructive form known as boycotting.

Now, hostility to the Crown, if it means anything,
means a struggle for separation as soon as Home Rule
has given to the Irish people the power to organise and
arm. And (still keeping to the sternly practical point
of view) that would, for the time being at least, spell
absolute ruin to the industrial North. The practice of

boycotting, again, is the very antithesis of industry—it creates an atmosphere in which industry and enterprise simply cannot live. The North has seen this practice condoned as a desperate remedy for a desperate ill, but it has seen it continued long after the ill had passed away, used as a weapon by one Nationalist section against another, and revived when anything like a really oppressive or arbitrary eviction had become impossible. There seems to have been in Nationalist circles, since the time of O'Connell, but little appreciation of the deadly character of this social curse ; and the prospect of a Government which would tolerate it naturally fills the mind of the Northern commercial man with alarm and aversion.

Again, the democratisation of local government which gave the Nationalist leaders a unique opportunity of showing the value, has but served to demonstrate the ineffectiveness, of their political tactics. North of Ireland opinion was deeply interested in this reform, and appreciated its far-reaching importance. Elsewhere, I think it will be safe to say, people generally were indifferent to it until it came, and the leaders seemed to see in it only a weapon to be used for political purposes. To the great vista of useful and patriotic work opened out by the Act of 1898, to the impression that a proper use of that Act might make on Northern opinion, they were blind. It is true that the Councils when left to themselves did admirably, and fully justified the trust reposed in them. But at the inauguration of local government it was naturally not the work of the Councils but the attitude of the party leaders which appeared to stamp the reception of the Act by the Irish people.

It is true, of course, that many thoughtful men among the Nationalist party repudiate the idea that the methods of to-day would be continued in a self-governed Ireland. I fail to see any reason why they should not. Under any system of limited Home Rule questions would arise which would afford much the same sort of justification for the employment of such methods, and they could hardly be worse for the welfare of the country then than they are now. There is abundant need and abundant work in the present day for thoughtful and far-seeing men in a party constitutionally so strong as that of the Irish Nationalists. If those among them who possess, or at any rate can make effective use of qualities of con-structive statesmanship are as few as the history of recent years would lead us to suppose, what assurance can Ulster Unionists feel that such men would spring up spontaneously in an Ireland under Home Rule? I admit, indeed, that a considerable measure of such assurance might be derived from the attitude of the leaders of the party at and since the Land Conference. But this adoption of statesmanlike methods which cannot be too widely understood or too warmly commended is a matter of very recent history; and though we may hope that the success attending it will help materially in the political education of the Irish people, that will not, by itself, undo the effect of a quarter of a century of political agitation governed by ideas the very reverse of those which are now happily beginning to find favour.

I have thought it necessary to examine at some length the defence on the ground of tactics which is often made for Nationalist politics, because it is the only defence ever made by those apologists who admit the disturbing influence upon our economic and social life of Nationalist methods. A broader and saner view of political tactics than prevailed ten years ago is now possible, for circumstances are becoming friendly and helpful to the development of political thought. Though the United Irish League apparently restored ' unity ' to the ranks of the Nationalists, the country is, I believe, getting restless under the political bondage, and is seething with a wholesome discontent. In this very matter of political education, the stir of corporate life, the sense of corporate responsibility which in every parish of Ireland are now being fostered by the reformed system of local government, must make their influence felt in wider spheres. Even now I believe that the field is ready for the work of those who would bid the old leader-following habit, the product partly of the dead clan system, partly of dying national animosities, depart as a thing that has had its day, and who would endeavour to train up a race of free, self-reliant, and independent citizens in a free state.

In this work the very men whose mistaken conception of a united Ireland I have criticised will, I doubt not, take a leading part. In many respects,

and these not the least important, no one could
desire a better instrument for the achievement of
great reforms than the Irish party. They are
far beyond any similar group of English members
in rhetorical skill and quickness of intelligence
and decision, qualities which no doubt belong to the
mechanism rather than the soul of politics, but which the
practical worker in public life will not despise. But even
when tried by a higher standard the Irish members need
not fear the judgment of history. They have often, in my
opinion, misconceived the true interests of their country,
but they have been faithful to those interests as they
understood them, and have proved themselves notably
superior to sordid personal aims. These gifts and
virtues are not common, but still rarer is it to see such
gifts and virtues cursed with the doom of futility. The
influence of the Irish political leaders has neither
advanced the nation's march through the wilderness
nor taught the people how they are to dispense with
manna from above when they reach the Promised Land.
With all their brilliancy, they have thrown but little
helpful light on any Irish problem. In this want of political and economic foresight Irish Nationalist politicians,
with some exceptions whom it would be invidious to
name, have fallen lamentably short of what might be expected of Irish intellect. For the eight years during which
I represented an Irish constituency I always felt that an
Irish night in the House of Commons was one of the
strangest and most pathetic of spectacles. There were

the veterans of the Irish party hardened by a hundred fights, ranging from Venezuela to the Soudan in search of battlefields, making allies of every kind of foreign potentate, from President Cleveland to the Mahdi, from Mr. Kruger to the Akhoom of Swat, but looking with suspicion on every symptom of an independent national movement in Ireland; masters of the language of hate and scorn, yet mocked by inevitable and eternal failure; winners of victories that turn to dust and ashes; devoted to their country, yet, from ignorance of the real source of its malady, ever widening the gaping wound through which its life-blood flows. While I recall these scenes, there rises before my mind the picture vividly drawn by Miss Lawless of their prototypes, the 'Wild Geese,' who carried their swords into foreign service after the final defeat of the Stuarts :—

> War-battered dogs are we,
> Fighters in every clime,
> Fillers of trench and of grave,
> Mockers, bemocked by Time;
> War-dogs, hungry and grey,
> Gnawing a naked bone,
> Fighting in every clime
> Every cause but our own.*

Irishmen have been long in realising that the days of the 'Wild Geese' are over, and that there are battles for Ireland to be fought and won in Ireland—battles in which England is not the enemy she was in the days of

---

* *With the Wild Geese.* Poems by the Hon. Emily Lawless. I have never read a better portrayal of the historic Irish sentiment than is set forth in this little volume. By the way, there is a preface by Mr. Stopford Brooke, which is singularly interesting and informing.

Fontenoy, but a friend and helper. But there will be little gain in replacing the traditional conception of England as the inexorable foe by the more modern conception, which threatened to become traditional in its turn, of England as the source of all prosperity and her favour as the condition of all progress in Ireland. In the recent Land Conference I recognise something more valuable even than the financial and legislative results which flowed from it, for it showed that the conception of reliance upon Irishmen in Ireland, not under some future and problematical conditions, but here and now, for the solution of Irish questions, is gaining ground among us. If this conception once takes firm hold, as I think it is beginning to do, of the Nationalist party in Ireland, much of the criticism of this chapter will lose its meaning. The mere substitution of a positive Irish policy for a negative anti-English policy will elevate the whole range of Nationalist political activity in and out of Ireland. And I am certain that if the ultimate goal of Nationalist politics be desirable, and continue to be desired, it will not be rendered more difficult, but on the contrary very much easier of attainment if those who seek it take possession of the great field of work which, without waiting for any concessions from Westminster, is offered by the Ireland of to-day.

CHAPTER IV.

THE INFLUENCE OF RELIGION UPON SECULAR LIFE IN IRELAND.

In the preceding chapter I attempted to estimate the influence of our political leaders as a potential and as an actual force. I come now to the second great influence upon the thought and action of the Irish people, the influence of religion, especially the power exercised by the priests and by the unrivalled organisation of the Roman Catholic Church. I do not share the pessimism which sees in this potent influence nothing but the shackles of mediævalism restraining its adherents from falling into line with the progress of the age. I shall, indeed, have to admit much of what is charged against the clerical leaders of popular thought in Ireland, but I shall be able to show, I hope, that these leaders are largely the product of a situation which they themselves did not create, and that not only are they as susceptible as are the political leaders to the influences of progressive movements, but that they can be more readily induced to take part in their promotion. In no other country in the world, probably, is religion so dominant an element in the daily life of the people as in Ireland, and certainly nowhere else has the minister of religion so wide and undisputed an authority. It is obvious, therefore, that, however foreign such a theme may *prima facie* appear to the scope and aim of the present volume, I have no choice but to analyse frankly and as fully as my personal experience justifies, what I conceive to be the true nature, the salutary limits, and the actual scope of clerical influence in this country.

But before I can discuss what I may call the religious situation, there is one fundamental question—a question which will appear somewhat strange to anyone not in touch with Irish life—which I must, with a view to a general agreement on essentials, submit to some of my co-religionists. In all seriousness I would ask, whether in their opinion the Roman Catholic Church in Ireland is to be tolerated. If the answer be in the negative, I can only reply that any efforts to stamp out the Roman Catholic faith would fail as they did in the past ; and the practical minds among those I am now addressing must admit that in toleration alone is to be found the solution of that part of the Irish difficulty which is due to sectarian animosities.

This brings us face to face with the question, What is religious toleration—I do not mean as a pious sentiment which we are all conscious of ourselves possessing in a truer sense than that in which it is possessed by others, but rather toleration as an essential of the liberty which we Protestants enjoy under the British Constitution, and boast that all other creeds equally enjoy? Perhaps I had better state simply how I answer this question in my own mind. Toleration by the Irish minority, in regard to the religious faith and ecclesiastical system of the Irish majority, implies that we admit the right of Rome to say what Roman Catholics shall believe and what outward forms they shall observe, and that they shall not suffer before the State for these beliefs and observances. I do not think exception can be taken to the statement that toleration in this narrow sense cannot be refused consistently with the fundamental principles of British government.

Now, however, comes a less obvious, but, as I think, no less essential condition of toleration in the sense above indicated. The Roman Catholic Hierarchy claim the right to exercise such supervision and control over the education of their flock as will enable them to safeguard faith and morals as preached and practised by their Church. I concede this second claim as a necessary corollary of the first. Having lived most of my life among Roman Catholics—two branches of my own family belonging to that religion—I am aware that this control is an essential part of the whole fabric of Roman Catholicism. Whether the basis of authority upon which that system is founded be in its origin divine or human is beside the point. If we profess to tolerate the faith and religious system of the majority of our countrymen we must at least concede the conditions essential to the maintenance of both the one and the other, unless our tolerance is to be a sham.

So far all liberal-minded Protestants, who know what Roman Catholicism is, will be with me ; and for the main purposes of the argument contained in this chapter it is not necessary to interpret toleration in any wider sense than that which I have indicated. Many Protestants, among whom I am one, do, it is true, make a further concession to the claim of our Roman Catholic fellow-countrymen. We would give them in Ireland facilities for higher education which we would not give them in England, and we would advocate liberal endowment by the State to this end. To us this is not a concession of privilege, but of simple justice, in view of all the circumstances, historical and other. It is, however, only fair to say that those who think otherwise, may be, and often are, actuated by a perfectly legitimate conception of educational principles, or by other considerations which are neither of a narrow nor sectarian character.

I need hardly say that in criticising religious systems and their ministers I have not the faintest intention of entering on the discussion of doctrinal issues. I am, of course, here concerned with only those aspects of the religious situation which bear directly on secular life. I am endeavouring, it must be remembered, to arrive at a comprehensive and accurate appreciation of the chief influences which mould the character, guide the thought, and, therefore, direct the action of the Irish people as citizens of this world and of their own country. From this standpoint let us try to make a dispassionate survey

H

of Protestantism and Roman Catholicism in Ireland, and see wherein their votaries fulfil, or fail to fulfil, their mission in advancing our common civilisation. Let us examine, in a word, not merely the direct influence which the creed of each of the two sections of Irishmen produces on the industrial character of its adherents, but also its indirect effects upon the mutual relations and regard for each other of Protestants and Roman Catholics.

Protestantism has its stronghold in the great industrial centres of the North and among the Presbyterian far-mers of five or six Ulster counties. These communities, it is significant to note, have developed the essentially strenuous qualities which, no doubt, they brought from England and Scotland. In city life their thrift, industry, and enterprise, unsurpassed in the United Kingdom, have built up a world-wide commerce. In rural life they have drawn the largest yield from relatively infertile soil. Such, in brief, is the achievement of Ulster Protestantism in the realm of industry. It is a story of which, when a united Ireland becomes more than a dream, all Irishmen will be proud.

But there is, unhappily, another side to the picture. This industrial life, otherwise so worthily cultivated, is disturbed by manifestations of religious bigotry which sadly tarnish the glory of the really heroic deeds they are intended to commemorate. It is impos-sible for any close observer of these deplorable exhibi-tions to avoid the conclusion that the embers of the old fires are too often fanned by men who are actuated by motives, which, when not other than religious, are certainly based upon an unworthy conception of religion. I am quite aware that it is only a small and decreasing minority of my co-religionists who are open to the charge of intolerance, and that the former extravagances of the July celebrations are now less frequent. But this bigotry is so notorious, as for instance in the exclusion of Roman Catholics from many responsible positions, that it unquestionably reacts most unfavourably upon the general relations between the two creeds throughout the whole of Ireland. The existence of such a spirit of suspicion and hatred, from whatever motive it emanates, is bound to retard our progress as a people towards the development of a healthy and balanced national life.

Many causes have recently contributed to the unhappy continuance of sectarian animosities in Ireland. The Ritualistic movement and the struggle over the Education Bill in England, the renewed controversy on the University Question in Ireland, instances of bigotry towards Protestants displayed by County, District, and Urban Councils in the three southern provinces of Ireland, the formation of the Catholic Association, the question of the form of the King's oath, and, more remotely, the protest against clericalism in such Roman Catholic countries as France and Austria, have one and all helped to keep alive the flame of anti-Roman feeling among Irish Protestants.*

* The reproach which is brought upon Irish Christianity mainly by

There are, happily, other influences now at work in a contrary direction. Among the industrial leaders a better spirit prevails. A well-known Ulster manufacturer told me recently that only a few years ago, when an applicant for employment appeared at certain Northern factories, which my friend named, the first question always put was, 'Are you a Protestant or Roman Catholic?' Now, he said, it is not what a man believes, but what he can do, which is considered when engaging workers. And outside the cities there are most gratifying signs of better relations between the two creeds. We are on the eve of the creation of a peasant proprietary, involving the rehabilitation of rural life, and one essential condition of the successful inauguration of the new agrarian order is the elimination of anything approaching to sectarian bitterness in communities which will require every advantage derivable from joint deliberation and common effort to enable them to hold their own against foreign competition. I recall a trivial but significant incident in the course of my Irish work which left a deep impression on my mind. After attending a meeting of farmers in a very backward district in the extreme west of Mayo, I arrived one winter's

the extravagances of a section of my co-religionists, to which I have been obliged to refer, came home to me not long ago in a very forcible way. I happened to remark to a friend that it was a disgrace to Christianity that Mussulman soldiery were employed at the Holy Sepulchre to keep the peace between the Latin and Greek Christians. He reminded me that the prosperous and progressive municipality of Belfast, with a population eminently industrious, and predominantly Protestant, has to be policed by an Imperial force in order to restrain two sections of Irish Christians from assaulting each other in the name of religion.

evening at the Roman Catholic priest's house. Before the meeting I had been promised a cup of tea, which, after a long, cold drive, was more than acceptable. When I presented myself at the priest's house, what was my astonishment at finding the Protestant clergyman presiding over a steaming urn and a plate of home-made cakes, having been requested to do the honours by his fellow-minister, who had been called away to a sick bed. A cycle of homilies on the virtue of tolerance could add nothing to the simple lesson which these two clergymen gave to the adherents of both their creeds. I felt as I went on my way that night that I had had a glimpse into the kind of future for Ireland towards which my fellow-workers are striving.

It is, however, with the religion of the majority of the Irish people and with its influence upon the industrial character of its adherents that I am chiefly concerned. Roman Catholicism strikes an outsider as being in some of its tendencies non-economic, if not actually anti-economic. These tendencies have, of course, much fuller play when they act on a people whose education has (through no fault of their own) been retarded or stunted. The fact is not in dispute, but the difficulty arises when we come to apportion the blame between ignorance on the part of the people and a somewhat one-sided religious zeal on the part of large numbers of their clergy. I do not seek to do so with any precision here. I am simply adverting to what has appeared to me, in the course of my experience in Ireland, to be a defect in the industrial character of Roman Catholics which, however caused, seems to me to have been intensified by their religion. The reliance of that religion on authority, its repression of individuality, and its complete shifting of what I may call the moral centre of gravity to a future existence— to mention no other characteristics—appear to me calculated, unless supplemented by other influences, to check the growth of the qualities of initiative and self-reliance, especially amongst a people whose lack of education unfits them for resisting the influence of what may present itself to such minds as a kind of fatalism with resignation as its paramount virtue.

It is true that one cannot expect of any church or religion, as a condition of its acceptance, that it will furnish an economic theory; and it is also true that Roman Catholicism has, at different periods of history, advantageously affected economic conditions, even if it did not act from distinctively economic motives—for example, by its direct influence in the suppression of slavery* and its creation of the mediæval craft guilds. It may, too, be admitted that during the Middle Ages, when Roman Catholicism was freer than now to manifest its influence in many directions, owing to its practically unchallenged supremacy, it favoured, when it did not originate, many forms of sound economic activity, and was, to say the least, abreast of the time in its conception of the working of economic causes. But from the

---

* '*Pro salute animae meae*' was, I am reminded, the consideration usually expressed in the old charters of manumission.

time when the Reformation, by its demand for what
we Protestants conceive to be a simpler Christianity,
drove Roman Catholicism back, if I may use the expression, on its first line of defence, and constrained it to
look to its distinctively spiritual heritage, down to the
present day, it has seemed to stand strangely aloof from
any contact with industrial and economic issues. When
we consider that in this period Adam Smith lived
and died, the industrial revolution was effected, and
the world-market opened, it is not surprising that we
do not find Roman Catholic countries in the van of
economic progress, or even the Roman Catholic element
in Protestant countries, as a rule, abreast of their fellow-
countrymen. It would, however, be an error to ignore
some notable exceptions to this generalisation.   In
Belgium, in France, in parts of Germany and Austria, and
in the north of Italy economic thought is making headway amongst Roman Catholics, and the solution of social
problems is being advanced by Roman Catholic laymen
and clergymen. Even in these countries, however, much
remains to be done. The revolution in the industrial
order, and its consequences, such as the concentration of
immense populations within restricted areas, have brought
with them social and moral evils that must be met with
new weapons. In the interests of religion itself, principles first expounded to a Syrian community with the
most elementary physical needs and the simplest of
avocations, have to be taught in their application to the
conditions of the most complex social organisation and

economic life. Taking people as we find them, it may be said with truth that their lives must be wholesome before they can be holy, and while a voluntary asceticism may have its justification, it behoves a Church to see that its members, while fully acknowledging the claims of another life, should develop the qualities which make for well-being in this life. In fact, I believe that the influence of Christianity upon social progress will be best maintained by co-ordinating these spiritual and economic ideals in a philosophy of life broader and truer than any to which the nations have yet attained.

What I have just been saying with regard to Roman Catholicism generally, in relation to economic doctrines and industrial progress, applies, of course, with a hundred fold pertinence to the case of Ireland. Between the enactment of the first Penal Laws and the date of Roman Catholic Emancipation, Irish Roman Catholics were, to put it mildly, afforded scant opportunity, in their own country, of developing economic virtues or achieving industrial success. Ruthlessly deprived of education, are they to be blamed if they did not use the newly acquired facilities to the best advantage? With their religion looked on as the badge of legal and social inferiority, was it any wonder that priests and people alike, while clinging with unexampled fidelity to their creed, remained altogether cut off from the current of material prosperity? Excluded, as they were, not merely from social and political privileges, but from the most ordinary civil rights, denied altogether the right of ownership of

real property, and restricted in the possession of person-
alty, is it any wonder that they are not to-day in the van of
industrial and commercial progress? Nay, more, was it to
have been expected that the character of a people so per-
secuted and ostracised should have come out of the
ordeal of centuries with its adaptability and elasticity
unimpaired? That would have been impossible. Those
who are intimate with the Roman Catholic people
of Ireland, and at the same time familiar with their
history, will recognise in their character and mental outlook many an inheritance of that epoch of serfdom.
I speak, of course, of the mass, for I am not unmindful of
many exceptions to this generalisation.

But I must now pass on to a more definite consideration of the present action and attitude of the Irish
Roman Catholic clergy towards the economic, educational, and other issues discussed in this book. The
reasons which render such a consideration necessary
are obvious. Even if we include Ulster, three quarters
of the Irish people are Roman Catholics, while, excluding the Northern province, quite nine-tenths of the
population belong to that religion. Again, the three
thousand clergymen of that denomination exercise an
influence over their flocks not merely in regard to
religious matters, but in almost every phase of their
lives and conduct, which is, in its extent and character,
quite unique, even, I should say, amongst Roman
Catholic communities. To a Protestant, this authority
seems to be carried very far beyond what the legitimate

influence of any clergy over the lay members of their congregation should be. We are, however, dealing with a national life explicable only by reference to a very exceptional and gloomy history of religious persecution. What I may call the secular shortcomings of the Roman Catholics in Ireland cannot be fairly judged except as the results of a series of enactments by which they were successively denied almost all means of succeeding as citizens of this world.

From such study as I have been able to give to the history of their Church, I have come to the conclusion that the immense power of the Irish Roman Catholic clergy has been singularly little abused. I think it must be admitted that they have not exhibited in any marked degree bigotry towards Protestants. They have not put obstacles in the way of the Roman Catholic majority choosing Protestants for political leaders, and it is significant that refugees, such as the Palatines, from Catholic persecutions in Europe, found at different times a home amongst the Roman Catholic people of Ireland. My own experience, too, if I may again refer to that, distinctly proves that it is no disadvantage to a man to be a Protestant in Irish political life, and that where opposition is shown to him by Roman Catholics it is almost invariably on political, social, or agrarian, but not on religious grounds.

A charge of another kind has of late been often brought against the Roman Catholic clergy, which has a direct bearing upon the economic aspect of this question.

Although, as I read Irish history, the Roman Catholic priesthood have, in the main, used their authority with personal disinterestedness, if not always with prudence or discretion, their undoubted zeal for religion has, on occasion, assumed forms which enlightened Roman Catholics, including high dignitaries of that Church, think unjustifiable on economic grounds, and discourage even from a religious standpoint. Excessive and extravagant church-building in the heart and at the expense of poor communities has been objected to on the surely not irreligious ground that the best monument of any clergyman's influence and earnestness must always be found in the moral character and the spiritual fibre of his flock, and not in the marbles and mosaics of a gaudy edifice. If, however, in some cases the sense of proportion has been obscured by a misdirected zeal, the excesses complained of cannot be fairly judged without some reference to the past. They may be regarded as an extreme reaction from the penal times, when the hunted *soggarth* had to celebrate the Mass in cabins and caves on the mountain side—a reaction the converse of which was witnessed in Protestant England when Puritanism rose up against Anglicanism in the seventeenth century. This expenditure, however, has been incurred; and, no one, I take it, would advocate the demolition of existing religious edifices on the ground that their erection had been unduly costly! The moral is for the present and the future, and applies not merely to economy in new

buildings, but also in the decoration of existing
churches.*

But it is not alone extravagant church building which
in a country so backward as Ireland, shocks the economic
sense. The multiplication—in inverse ratio to a declining population—of costly and elaborate monastic and
conventual institutions, involving what in the aggregate
must be an enormous annual expenditure for maintenance, is difficult to reconcile with the known conditions of the country. Most of these institutions, it
is true, carry on educational work, often, as in the case
of the Christian Brothers and some colleges and con-
vents, of an excellent kind. Many of them render great
services to the poor, and especially to the sick poor.
But, none the less, it seems to me, their growth in
number and size is anomalous. I cannot believe that so
large an addition to the classes, technically called unproductive, is economically sound, and I have no doubt at
all that the competition with lay teachers of celibates
'living in community' is excessive and educationally injurious. Fully admitting the importance of religion in

* One of the unfortunate effects of this passion for building costly
churches is the importation of quantities of foreign art-work in the
shape of woodcarvings, stained glass, mosaics, and metal work. To
good foreign art, indeed, one could not, within certain limits, object.
It might prove a valuable example and stimulus. But the articles which
have actually been imported, in the impulse to get everything finished
as soon as possible, generally consist of the stock pieces produced in a
spirit of mere commercialism in the workshops of Continental firms
which make it their business to cater for a public who do not know the
difference between good art and bad. Much of the decoration of
ecclesiastical buildings, whether Roman Catholic or Protestant, might
fittingly be postponed until religion in Ireland has got into closer relation with the native artistic sense and industrial spirit now beginning
to seek creative expression.

education, I still hold that teachers who have renounced the world and withdrawn from contact with its stress and strain are at a great disadvantage in moulding the characters of youths who will have to take their part in the hard struggle of modern industrial life. But here again we must accept the situation and work with the instruments ready to hand. The practical and statesmanlike action for all those concerned is to assist these institutions to become as efficient educational agencies as may be possible. They owe their existence largely to the gaps in the educational system of this country which religious and political strife have produced and maintained, and they deserve the utmost credit for endeavouring to supply missing steps in our educational ladder.* If they now fully respond to the spirit of the new movements and supply the demand for technical education by the employment of the most approved methods and equipment, and by the thorough training on sound lines of their staffs, they will meet my criticisms.

* The following extract from a statement of the Most Rev. Dr. O'Dea, the newly elected Bishop of Clonfert, is pertinent.—' There is another cause also—*i.e.* in addition to the absence of university education for Roman Catholic laymen—which has hindered the employment of the laity in the past. Till very recently, the secondary Catholic schools received no assistance whatever from the State, and their endowment from private sources was utterly inadequate to supply suitable remuneration for lay teachers. It is evident that a celibate clergy *can* live on a lower wage than the laity, and they are now charged with having monopolized the schools, because they chose to work for a minimum allowance rather than suffer the country to remain without any secondary education whatever. Two causes, then, operated in the past, and in a large measure still operate, to exclude the laity from the secondary schools,— first, these schools were so poverty-stricken that they could not afford to pay lay teachers at such a rate as would attract them to the teaching profession, and, next, the Catholic laity as a body were uneducated, and, therefore, unfit to teach in the schools.'—*Maynooth and the University Question*, p. 109 (footnote).

But, after all, these criticisms are, for the purposes of my argument, of minor relevance and importance. The real matter in which the direct and personal responsibility of the Roman Catholic clergy seems to me to be involved, is the character and *morale* (still using the terms in the restricted sense which I have, I hope, made sufficiently clear) of the people of this country. No reader of this book will accuse me of attaching too little weight to the influence of historical causes on the present state, social, economic and political, of Ireland, but even when I have given full consideration to all such influences I still think that, with their unquestioned authority in religion, and their almost equally undisputed influence in education, the Roman Catholic clergy cannot be exonerated from some responsibility in regard to Irish character as we find it to-day. Are they, I would ask, satisfied with that character? I cannot think so. The impartial observer will, I fear, find amongst a majority of our people a striking absence of self-reliance and moral courage; an entire lack of serious thought on public questions; a listlessness and apathy in regard to economic improvement which amount to a form of fatalism; and, in backward districts, a survival of superstition, which saps all strength of will and purpose—and all this, too, amongst a people singularly gifted by nature with good qualities of mind and heart.

Nor can the Roman Catholic clergy altogether console themselves with the thought that religious faith, even

when free from superstition, is strong in the breasts of
the people. So long, no doubt, as Irish Roman Catholics remain at home, in a country of sharply defined
religious classes, and with a social environment and a
public opinion so preponderatingly stamped with their
creed, open defections from Roman Catholicism are
rare. But we have only to look at the extent of the
'leakage' from Roman Catholicism amongst the Irish
emigrants in the United States and in Great Britain, to
realise how largely emotional and formal must be the
religion of those who lapse so quickly in a non-Catholic
atmosphere.*

It is not, of course, to the causes of the defections
from a creed to which I do not subscribe that my
criticism is directed. I refer to the matter only in order
to emphasise the large share of responsibility which
belongs to the Roman Catholic clergy for what I strongly
believe to be the chief part in the work of national
regeneration, the part compared with which all legislative, administrative, educational or industrial achievements are of minor importance. Holding, as I do, that
the building of character is the condition precedent to
material, social and intellectual advancement, indeed to

---

* See, *inter alia*, an article "Ireland and America," by Rev. Mr.
Shinnors, O.M., in the *Irish Ecclesiastical Record*, February, 1902. 'Has
the Church,' asks Father Shinnors, 'increased her membership in the
ratio that the population of the United States has increased? No.
There are many converts, but there are many more apostates. Large
numbers lapse into indifferentism and irreligion. There should be
in America about 20,000,000 Catholics; there are scarcely 10,000,000.
There are reasons to fear that the great majority of the apostates are of
Irish extraction, and not a few of them of Irish birth.'

all national progress, I may, perhaps, as a lay citizen, more properly criticise, from this point of view, what I conceive to be the great defect in the methods of clerical influence. For this purpose no better illustration could be afforded than a brief analysis of the results of the efforts made by the Roman Catholic clergy to inculcate temperance.

Among temperance advocates—the most earnest of all reformers—the Roman Catholic clergy have an honourable record. An Irish priest was the greatest, and, for a brief spell, the most successful temperance apostle of the last century, and statistics, it is only fair to say, show that we Irish drink rather less than people in other parts of the United Kingdom. But the real question is whether we more often drink to intoxication, and police statistics as well as common experience seem to disclose that we do. Many a temperate man drinks more in his life than many a village drunkard. Again, the test of the average consumption of man, woman and child is somewhat misleading, especially in Ireland where, owing to the excessive emigration of adults, there is a disproportionately large number of very young and old. Moreover, we Irish drink more in proportion to our means than the English, Scotch, and Welsh, whose consumption is absolutely larger. Anyone who attempts to deal practically with the problems of industrial development in Ireland realises what a terribly depressing influence the drink evil exercises upon the industrial capacity of the people. 'Ireland sober is Ireland free,' is nearer the truth than

much that is thought and most of what is said about
liberty in this country.

Now, the drink habit in Ireland differs from that of
the other parts of the United Kingdom. The Irishman
is, in my belief, physiologically less subject to the craving
for alcohol than the Englishman, a fact which is partially
attributable, I should say, to the less animal dietary to
which he is accustomed. By far the greater proportion of
the drinking which retards our progress is of a festive
character. It takes place at fairs and markets, sometimes,
even yet, at 'wakes,' those ghastly parodies on the
blessed consolation of religion in bereavement.   It is
largely due to the almost universal sale of liquor in the
country shops 'for consumption on the premises,' an evil
the demoralising effects of which are an hundredfold
greater than those of the 'grocer's licences' which temperance reformers so strenuously denounce. It is an
evil for the existence of which nothing can be said, but
it has somehow escaped the effective censure of the
Church. .

The indiscriminate granting of licences in Ireland,
which has resulted in the provision of liquor shops in a
proportion to the population larger than is found in any
other country, is in itself due mainly to the moral
cowardice of magistrates, who do not care to incur local
unpopularity by refusing licences for which there is no
pretence of any need beyond that of the applicant and
his relatives.   Not long ago the magistrates of Ireland
met in Dublin in order to inaugurate common action in

I

dealing with this scandal. Appropriate resolutions were passed, and some good has already resulted from the meeting, but had the unvarnished truth been admissible, the first and indeed the only necessary resolution should have run, "Resolved that in future we be collectively as brave as we have been individually timid, and that we take heart of grace and carry away from this meeting sufficient strength to do, in the exercise of our functions as the licensing authority, what we have always known to be our plain duty to our country and our God." No such resolution was proposed, for though patriotism is becoming real in Ireland, it is not yet very robust.

I do not think it unfair to insist upon the large responsibility of the clergy for the state of public opinion in this matter, to which the few facts I have cited bear testimony. But I attribute their failure to deal with a moral evil of which they are fully cognisant to the fact that they do not recognise the chief defect in the character of the people, and to a misunderstanding of the means by which that character can be strengthened. There are, however, exceptions to this general statement. It is of happy augury for the future of Ireland that many of the clergy are now leading a temperance movement which shows a real knowledge of the *causa causans* of Irish intemperance. The Anti-Treating League, as it is called, administers a novel pledge which must have been conceived in a very understanding mind. Those enlisted undertake neither to treat nor to be treated. They may drink, so far as the pledge is concerned, as much as they like; but they must drink at their own expense; and others must not drink at their expense. The good nature and sociability of Irishmen, too often the mere result of inability to say 'no,' need not be sacrificed. Even if they were, the loss of these social graces would be far more than compensated by a self-respect and seriousness of life out of which something permanent might be built. Still, even this League makes no direct appeal to character, and so acts rather as a cure for than as a preventive of our moral weakness.

The methods by which clerical influence is wielded in the inculcation of chastity may be criticised from exactly the same standpoint as that from which I have found it necessary to deal with the question of temperance. Here the success of the Irish priesthood is, considering the conditions of peasant life, and the fire of the Celtic temperament, absolutely unique. No one can deny that almost the entire credit of this moral achievement belongs to the Roman Catholic clergy. It may be said that the practice of a virtue, even if the motive be of an emotional kind, becomes a habit, and that habit proverbially develops into a second nature. With this view of moral evolution I am in entire accord; but I would ask whether the evolution has not reached a stage where a gradual relaxation of the disciplinary measures by which chastity is insured might be safely allowed without any danger of lowering the high standard of continence which is general in Ireland and which of course it is of supreme importance to maintain.

There are, however, many parishes where in this matter the strictest discipline is rigorously enforced. Amusements, many of them not necessarily, and most of them not often vicious, are objected to as being fraught with dangers which would never occur to any but the rigidly ascetic or the puritanical mind. In many parishes the Sunday cyclist will observe the strange phenomenon of a normally light-hearted peasantry marshalled in male and female groups along the road, eyeing one another in dull wonderment across the forbidden space through the long summer day. This kind of discipline, unless when really necessary, is open to the objection that it eliminates from the education of life, especially during the formative years, an essential of culture—the mutual understanding of the sexes. The evil of grafting upon secular life a quasi-monasticism which, not being voluntary, has no real effect upon the character, may perhaps involve moral consequences little dreamed of by the spiritual guardians of the people. A study of the pathology of the emotions might throw doubt upon the safety of enforced asceticism when unaccompanied by the training which the Church wisely prescribes for those who take the vow of celibacy. But of my own knowledge I can speak only of another aspect of the effect upon our national life of the restrictions to which I refer. No Irishmen are more sincerely desirous of staying the tide of emigration than the Roman Catholic clergy, and while, wisely as I think, they do not dream of a wealthy Ireland, they earnestly work for the

physical and material as well as the spiritual well-being
of their flocks. And yet no man can get into the confidence of the emigrating classes without being told by
them that the exodus is largely due to a feeling that the
clergy are, no doubt from an excellent motive, taking
innocent joy from the social side of the home life.

To go more fully into these subjects might carry me
beyond the proper limits of lay criticism. But, clearly,
large questions of clerical training must suggest themselves to those to whom their discussion properly belongs
—whether, for example, there is not in the instances
which I have cited evidence of a failure to understand
that mere authority in the regions of moral conduct
cannot have any abiding effect, except in the rarest
combination of circumstances, and with a very primitive
people. Do not many of these clergy ignore the vast
difference between the ephemeral nature of moral com-
pulsion and the enduring force of a real moral training?

I have dealt with the exercise of clerical influence in
these matters as being, at any rate in relation to the
subject matter of this book, far more important than
the evil commonly described as "The Priest in Politics."
That evil is, in my opinion, greatly misrepresented. The
cases of priests who take an improper part in politics
are cited without reference to the vastly greater number
who take no part at all, except when genuinely assured
that a definite moral issue is at stake. I also have in
my mind the question of how we should have fared if
the control of the different Irish agitations had been

confined to laymen, and if the clergy had not consistently condemned secret associations. But whatever may be said in defence of the priest in politics in the past, there are the strongest grounds for deprecating a continuance of their political activity in the future. As I gauge the several forces now operating in Ireland, I am convinced that if an anti-clerical movement similar to that which other Roman Catholic countries have witnessed, were to succeed in discrediting the priesthood and lowering them in public estimation, it would be followed by a moral, social, and political degradation which would blight, or at least postpone, our hopes of a national regeneration. From this point of view I hold that those clergymen who are predominantly politicians endanger the moral influence which it is their solemn duty to uphold. I believe however, that the over-active part hitherto taken in politics by the priests is largely the outcome of the way in which Roman Catholics were treated in the past, and that this undesirable feature in Irish life will yield, and is already yielding to the removal of the evils to which it owed its origin and in some measure its justification.*

One has only to turn to the spirit and temper of such representative Roman Catholics as Archbishop Healy and Dr. Kelly, Bishop of Ross—to their words and to their deeds—in order to catch the inspiration of a new movement amongst our Roman Catholic fellow-countrymen at once religious and patriotic. And if my optimism ever

* This view seems to be taken by the most influential spokesmen of the Roman Catholic Hierarchy. See Evidence, *Royal Commission on University Education in Ireland*, vol. iii., p. 238, Questions 8702-6.

wavers, I have but to think of the noble work that many priests are to my own knowledge doing, often in remote and obscure parishes, in the teeth of innumerable obstacles. I call to mind at such times, as pioneers in a great awakening, men like the eminent Jesuit, Father Thomas Finlay, Father Hegarty of Erris, Father O'Donovan of Loughrea, and many others—men with whom I have worked and taken counsel, and who represent, I believe, an ever increasing number of their fellow priests.*

My position, then, towards the influence of the Roman Catholic clergy—and this influence is a matter of vital importance to the understanding of Irish problems—may now be clearly defined. While recognising to the full that large numbers of the Irish Roman Catholic clergy have in the past exercised undue influence in purely political questions, and, in many other matters, social, educational, and economic, have not, as I see things, been on the side of progress, I hold that their influence is now, more than ever before, essential for improving the condition of the most backward section of the population. Therefore I feel it to be both the duty

---

* I may mention that of the co-operative societies organised by the Irish Agricultural Organisation Society there are no fewer than 331 societies of which the local priests are the Chairmen, while to my own knowledge during the summer and autumn of 1902, as many as 50,000 persons from all parts of Ireland were personally conducted over the exhibit of the Department of Agriculture and Technical Instruction at the Cork Exhibition by their local clergy. The educational purpose of these visits is explained in Chap. x. Again, in a great number of cases the village libraries which have been recently started in Ireland with the assistance of the Department (the books consisting largely of industrial, economic, and technical works on agriculture), have been organised and assisted by the Roman Catholic clergy.

and the strong interest of my Protestant fellow-countrymen to think much less of the religious differences which
divide them from Roman Catholics, and much more of
their common citizenship and their common cause. I also
hold with equal strength and sincerity to the belief, which
I have already expressed, that the shortcomings of the
Roman Catholic clergy are largely to be accounted for,
not by any innate tendency on their part towards obscu-
rantism, but by the sad history of Ireland in the past.
I would appeal to those of my co-religionists who think
otherwise to suspend their judgment for a time. That
Roman Catholicism is firmly established in Ireland is a
fact of the situation which they must admit, and as this
involves the continued powerful influence of the priesthood upon the character of the people, it is surely good
policy by liberality and fair dealing, especially in the
matter of education, to turn this influence towards the
upbuilding of our national life.

To sum up the influence of religion and religious controversy in Ireland, as it presents itself from the
only standpoint from which I have approached the
matter in this chapter, namely, that of material, social,
and intellectual progress, I find that while the Protestants
have given, and continue to give, a fine example of thrift
and industry to the rest of the nation, the attitude of a
section of them towards the majority of their fellow-
countrymen has been a bigoted and unintelligent
one. On the other hand, I have learned from practical
experience amongst the Roman Catholic people of Ire-

land that, while more free from bigotry, in the sense
in which that word is usually applied, they are apathetic,
thriftless, and almost non-industrial, and that they especially require the exercise of strengthening influences on
their moral fibre. I have dealt with their shortcomings
at much greater length than with those of Protestants,
because they have much more bearing on the subject
matter of this book. North and South have each virtues
which the other lacks; each has much to learn from the
other; but the home of the strictly civic virtues and effi-
ciencies is in Protestant Ireland. The work of the future
in Ireland will be to break down in social intercourse the
barriers of creed as well as those of race, politics, and
class, and thus to promote the fruitful contact of North
and South, and the concentration of both on the welfare
of their common country. In the case of those of us,
of whatever religious belief, who look to a future for our
country commensurate with the promise of her undeveloped resources both of intellect and soil, it is of
the essence of our hope that the qualities which are in
great measure accountable for the actual economic and
educational backwardness of so many of our fellow-
countrymen, and for the intolerance of too many who
are not backward in either respect, are not purely racial
or sectarian, but are the transitory growth of days and
deeds which we must all try to forget if our work for
Ireland is to endure.

CHAPTER V.

A PRACTICAL VIEW OF IRISH EDUCATION.

A little learning, we are told, is a dangerous thing;
and in their dealings with Irish education the English
should have discovered that this danger is accentuated
when the little learning is combined with much native wit.
In the days when religious persecution was universal—
only, be it remembered, a few generations ago—it was
the policy of England to avert this danger by prohibiting,
as far as possible, the acquisition by Irish Roman
Catholics of any learning at all. After the Union,
Englishmen began to feel their responsibility for the
state of Ireland, a state of poverty and distress which
culminated in the Famine. Knowledge was then no
longer withheld: indeed the English sincerely desired
to dispel our darkness and enable us to share in the
wisdom, and so in the prosperity, of the predominant
partner. In their attempts to educate us they dealt
with what they saw on the surface, and moulded their
educational principles upon what they knew; but they
did not know Ireland. Even if we excuse them for paying scant attention to what they were told by Irishmen,
they should have given more heed to the reports of their
own Royal Commissions.

We have so far seen that the Irish mind has been in

regard to economics, politics, and even some phases of
religious influence, a mind warped and diseased, deprived of good nutrition and fed on fancies or fictions,
out of which no genuine growth, industrial or other, was
possible. The one thing that might have strengthened
and saved a people with such a political, social, and
religious history, and such racial characteristics, was an
educational system which would have had special regard
to that history, and which would have been a just
expression of the better mind of the people whom it
was intended to serve.

Now this is exactly what was denied to Ireland. Not
merely has all educational legislation come from England, in the sense of being based on English models and
thought out by Englishmen largely out of touch and
sympathy with the peculiar needs of Ireland, but whenever there has been genuine native thought on Irish
educational problems, it has been either ignored altogether or distorted till its value and significance were
lost. And in this matter we can claim for Ireland that
there was in the country during the first half of the nineteenth century, when England was trying her best to
provide us with a sound English education, a comparatively advanced stage of home-grown Irish thought upon
the educational needs of the people. Take, for example,
the Society for Promoting Elementary Education among
the Irish Poor, know as the Kildare Street Society,
which was founded as early as the year 1811. The first
resolution passed by this body, which was composed of

prominent Dublin citizens of all religious beliefs, was set out as follows :—

(1.) Resolved—That promoting the education of the poor of Ireland is a grand object which every Irishman anxious for the welfare and prosperity of his country ought to have in view as the basis upon which the morals and true happiness of the country can be best secured.

This Society, it is true, did not see or foresee that any system of mixed religious education was doomed to failure in Ireland, but they took a wide view of the place of education in a nation's development, and the character of the education which their schools actually dispensed was admirable.　This hopeful and enterprising educational movement is described by Mr. Lecky in a passage from which I take a few extracts :—

The " Kildare Street Society " which received an endowment from Government, and directed National education from 1812 to 1831, was not proselytising, and it was for some time largely patronized by Roman Catholics. It is certainly by no means deserving of the contempt which some writers have bestowed on it, and if measured by the spirit of the time in which it was founded it will appear both liberal and useful. . . . The object of the schools was stated to be united education, " taking common Christian ground for the foundation, and excluding all sectarian distinctions from every part of the arrangement ; " " drawing the attention of both denominations to the many leading truths of Christianity in which they agree."　To carry out this principle it was a fundamental rule that the Bible must be read without note or

comment in all the schools.   It might be read either in
the Authorized or in the Douay version. . . . In 1825 there
were 1,490 schools connected with the Society, containing
about 100,000 pupils.   The improvements introduced into
education by Bell, Lancaster, and Pestalozzi were largely
adopted.   Great attention was paid to needlework. . . .
A great number of useful publications were printed by the
Society, and we have the high authority of Dr. Doyle for
stating that he never found anything objectionable [to
Catholics] in them.*

Take, again, as an evidence of the progressive spirit
of the Irish thinkers on education, the remarkable
scheme of national education which, after the passing of the Catholic Emancipation Act, was formulated
by Mr. Thomas Wyse, of Waterford.   In addition to
elementary schools, Mr. Wyse proposed to establish in
every county, 'an academy for the education of the
middle class of society in those departments of knowledge most necessary to those classes, and over those a
College in each of the four provinces, managed by a
Committee representative of the interests of the several
counties of the provinces.'   'It is a matter of importance,' wrote Mr. Wyse, 'for the simple and efficient
working of the whole system of national education, that
each part should as much as possible be brought into
co-operation and accord with the others.'   He foresaw,
too, that one of the needs of the Irish temperament was
a training in science which would cultivate the habits of
'education, observation, and reasoning,' and he pointed

* *Leaders of Public Opinion in Ireland*, II., 122-4.

out that the peculiar manufactures, trades, and occupations of the several localities would determine the course
of studies. Mr. Wyse's memorandum on education led,
as is well known, to the creation of the Board of
National Education, but, to quote Dr. Starkie,* the
present Resident Commissioner of the Board, 'the
more important part of the scheme, dealing with a
university and secondary education, was shelved, in spite
of Mr. Wyse's warnings that it was imprudent, dangerous, and pernicious to the social condition of the
country, and to its future tranquillity, that so much
encouragement should be given to the education of the
lower classes, without at the same time due provision
being made for the education of the middle and upper
classes.'

As still another evidence of the sound thought on
educational problems which came from Irishmen who
knew the actual conditions of their own country and
people, the case of the agricultural instruction administered by the National Board is pertinent. The late Sir
Patrick Keenan has told us that landlords and others who
on political and religious grounds distrusted the National
system, turned to this feature of the operations
of the National Board with the greatest fervour.
A scheme of itinerant instruction in agriculture,
which had a curious resemblance to that which the
Department of Agriculture is now organising, was
developed, and was likely to have worked with the

---

* *Recent Reforms in Irish Education*, p. 7.

greatest advantage to the country at large. Sir Patrick Keenan, who knew Ireland and the Irish people well, speaks of this part of the scheme as 'the most fruitful experiment in the material interests of the country that was ever attempted. It was,' he adds, through the agency of this corps of practical instructors that green cropping as a systematic feature in farming was introduced into the South and West, and even into the central parts of Ireland.' But all the hopes thus raised went down, not before any intrinsic difficulties in the scheme itself, or before any adverse opinion to it in Ireland, but before the opposition of the Liverpool Financial Reform Association, who had their own views as to the limits of State interference with agriculture. These examples, drawn from different stages of Irish educational history, might easily be multiplied, but they will serve as typical instances of that want of recognition by English statesmen of Irish thought on Irish problems, and that ignoring of Irish sentiment—as distinguished from Irish sentimentality—which I insist is the basal element in the misunderstandings of Irish problems.

I now come to a brief consideration of some facts of the present educational situation, and I shall indicate, for those readers who are not familiar with current events in Ireland, the significant evolution, or revolution, through which Irish education is passing. Within the last eight years we have had in Ireland three very remarkable reports—in themselves symptoms of a widespread unrest and dissatisfaction—on the educational systems of the country. I allude to the reports of two Viceregal Commissions, one on Manual and Practical Instruction in our Primary Schools, and the other on our Intermediate Education; and to the recent report by a Royal Commission on University Education. These reports cover the three grades of our educational system, and each of them contains a strong denunciation and a scathing criticism of the existing provision and methods of instruction in elementary, secondary, and university education (outside Dublin University), respectively. One and all showed that the education to be had in our primary and secondary schools, as well as in the examining body known as the Royal University, had little regard to the industrial or economic conditions of the country. We find, for example, agriculture taught out of a text book in the primary schools, with the result that the *gamins* of the Belfast streets secured the highest marks in the subject. In the Intermediate system are to be found anomalies of a similar kind, which could not long have survived if there had been a living opinion on educational matters in Ireland. No careful reader of the evidence given before the Commissions can fail to see that under our educational system the schools were practically bribed to fall in with a stereotyped course of studies which left scant room for elasticity and adaptation to local needs; that the teacher was, to all intents and purposes, deprived of healthy initiative; and that the Irish parents must as a body have been in the dark as to the bearing of their children's studies on their probable careers in life. A deep and wholesome impression was made in Ireland by the exposure of the intrinsic evils of a system calculated in my opinion to turn our youth into a generation of second-rate clerks, with a distinct distaste for any industrial or productive occupation in which such qualities as initiative, self-reliance, or judgment were called for.

I am told by competent authorities that there is not a single educational principle laid down in either the report on Manual Instruction or on Intermediate Education, which was not known and applied at least half a century ago in continental countries. In fact, in the Recess Committee investigations, as any reader of the report of that body can see for himself, the Committee, guided by foreign experience, foreshadowed practically every reform now being put into operation. It is better, of course, that we should reform late than never, but it is well to bear in mind also, so far as the problems of this book are concerned, how far the education of the country has fallen short of any sound standard, and how little could have been expected from the working of our system. The curve of Irish illiteracy has indeed fallen continuously with each succeeding census, but true education as opposed to mere instruction has languished sadly.

Together with my friends and fellow-workers in the self-help movement, I believe that the problem of Irish education, like all other Irish problems, must be recon-

K

sidered from the standpoint of its relation to the practical affairs and everyday life of the people of Ireland. The needs and opportunities of the industrial struggle must, in fact, mould into shape our educational policy and programmes. We are convinced that there is little hope of any real solution of the more general problem of national education, unless and until those in direct contact with the specific industries of the country succeed in bringing to the notice of those engaged in the framing of our educational system the kind and degree of the defects in the industrial character of our people which debar them from successful competition with other countries. Education in Ireland has been too long a thing apart from the economic realities of the country— with what result we know. In the work of the Department of Agriculture and Technical Instruction for Ireland, an attempt is being made to establish a vital relation between industrial education and industrial life. It is desired to try, at this critical stage of our development, the experiment—I call it an experiment only because it does not seem to have been tried before in Ireland—of directing our instruction with a conscious and careful regard to the probable future careers of those we are educating.

This attempt touches, of course, only one department of the whole educational problem, much of which it would be quite outside my present purpose to discuss. But I must guard against the supposition that in our insistence upon the importance of the practical side of

education we are under any doubt as to the great importance of the literary side. My friends and I have been
deeply impressed by the educational experience of
Denmark, where the people, who are as much dependent
on agriculture as are the Irish, have brought it by means
of organisation to a more genuine success than it has
attained anywhere else in Europe. Yet an inquirer will
at once discover that it is to the "High Schools" founded
by Bishop Grundtvig, and not to the agricultural schools,
which are also excellent, that the extraordinary national
progress is mainly due. A friend of mine who was
studying the Danish system of State aid to agriculture,
found this to be the opinion of the Danes of all classes,
and was astounded at the achievements of the associations of farmers, not only in the manufacture of butter,
but in a far more difficult undertaking, the manufacture
of bacon in large factories equipped with all the most
modern machinery and appliances which science had
devised for the production of the finished article. He at
first concluded that this success in a highly technical
industry by bodies of farmers indicated a very perfect
system of technical education. But he soon found another
cause. As one of the leading educators and agriculturists
of the country put it to him : 'It's not technical instruction, it's the humanities.' I would like to add that it is
also, if I may coin a term, the 'nationalities,' for nothing
is more evident to the student of Danish education or, I
might add, of the excellent system of the Christian
Brothers in Ireland, than that one of the secrets of their

success is to be found in their national basis and their foundation upon the history and literature of the country.

To sum up the educational situation in Ireland, it is not too much to say that all our forms of education, technical and general, hang loose. We lack a body of trained teachers ; we have no alert and informed public opinion on education and its function in regard to life ; and there is no proper provision for research work in all branches, a deficiency, which, I am told by those who have given deep thought and long study to these problems, inevitably reacts most disastrously on the general educational system of the country. This state of things appears not unnatural when we remember that the Penal Laws were not repealed till almost the close of the eighteenth century, and that a large majority of the Irish people had not full and free access to even primary and secondary education until the passing of the Emancipation Act in 1829. At the present day, the absence of any provision for higher education of which Roman Catholics will avail themselves is not merely an enormous loss in itself, but it reacts most adversely upon the whole educational machinery, and consequently upon the whole public life and thought of that section of the nation.

One of the very first things I had to learn when I came into direct touch with educational problems, was that the education of a country cannot be divided into water-tight compartments, and each part legislated for or discussed solely on its merits and without reference to the other parts. I see now very clearly that the educational system of a country is an organic whole, the working of any part of which necessarily has an influence on the working of the rest. I had always looked upon the lower, secondary, and higher grades as the first, second, and third storeys of the educational house, and I am not quite sure that I attached sufficient importance to the staircase. My view has now changed, and I find myself regarding the University as a foundation and support of the primary and secondary school.

It was not on purely pedagogic grounds that I added to my other political irregularities the earnest advocacy of such a provision for higher education as Roman Catholics will avail themselves of. This great need was revealed to me in my study of the Irish mind and of the direction in which it could look for its higher development. My belief is based on practical experience ; my point of view is that of the economist. When the new economic mission in Ireland began now fourteen years ago, we had to undertake, in addition to our practical programme, a kind of University extension work with the important omission of the University. We had to bring home to adult farmers whose general education was singularly poor, though their native intelligence was keen and receptive, a large number of general ideas bearing on the productive and distributive side of their industry. Our chief obstacles arose from the lack of trained economic thought among all classes, and especially among those to whom the majority looked for guidance. The air was thick with economic fallacies or

half-truths. We were, it is true, successful beyond our
expectations in planting in apparently uncongenial soil
sound economic principles. But our success was mainly
due, as I shall show later, to our having used the associative instincts of the Irish peasant to help out the
working of our theories; and we became convinced that
if a tithe of our priests, public men, national school
teachers, and members of our local bodies had received
a university education, we should have made much more
rapid progress.

I hardly know how to describe the mental atmosphere in which we were working. It would be no libel
upon the public opinion upon which we sought to make
an impression to say that it really allowed no question
to be discussed on its merits. Public opinion on social
and economic questions is changing now, but I cannot
associate the change with any influence emanating from
institutions of higher education. In other countries, so
far as my investigations have extended, the universities
do guide economic thought and have a distinct though
wholly unofficial function as a court of appeal upon
questions relating to the material progress of the
communities amongst which they are situated. Of
such institutions there are in Ireland only two which
could be expected to direct in any large way the
thought of the country upon economic and other important national questions—Maynooth, and Trinity
College, Dublin. Whether in their widely different
spheres of influence these two institutions could, under

conditions other than those prevailing, have so met
the requirements of the country as to have obviated
what is at present an urgent necessity for a complete
reorganisation of higher education need not be discussed ;
but it is essential to my argument that I should set forth
clearly the results of my own observation upon their
influence, or rather lack of influence, upon the people
among whom I have worked.

The influence of Maynooth, actual and potential, can
hardly be exaggerated, but it is exercised indirectly
upon the secular thought of the country. It is not its
function to make a direct impression. It is in fact only
a professional—I had almost said a technical—school.
It trains its students, most admirably I am told, in
theology, philosophy, and the studies subsidiary to these
sciences, but always, for the vast majority of its students,
with a distinctly practical and definite missionary end in
view. There is, I believe, an arts course of modest
scope, designed rather to meet the deficiencies of students
whose general education has been neglected than to
serve as anything in the nature of a university arts
course. I am quite aware of the value of a sound training
in mental science if given in connection with a full
university course, but I am equally convinced that the
Maynooth education, on the whole, is no substitute for
a university course, and that while its chief end of turning
out a large number of trained priests has been fulfilled,
it has not given, and could not be expected to have
given, that broader and more humane culture which only

a university, as distinguished from a professional school, can adequately provide.

Moreover, under the Maynooth system young clerics are constantly called upon to take a part in the life of a lay community, towards which, when they entered college, they were in no position of responsibility, and upon which, so far as secular matters are concerned, when they emerge from their theological training, they are no better adapted to exercise a helpful influence. In my experience of priests I have met with many in whom I recognised a sincere desire to attend to the material and social well-being of their flocks, but who certainly had not that breadth of view and understanding of human nature which perhaps contact with the laity during the years in which they were passing from discipline to authority might have given to them. However this may be, it is clear and it is admitted that education as opposed to professional training of a high order is still, generally speaking, a want among the priests of Ireland, and I look forward to no greater boon from a University or University College for Roman Catholics than its influence, direct and indirect, on a body of men whose prestige and authority are necessarily so unique.

It is, therefore, to Trinity College, or the University of Dublin, that one would naturally turn as to a great centre of thought in Ireland for help in the theoretic aspects, at least, of the practical problems upon whose successful solution our national well-being depends. Judged

by the not unimportant test of the men it has supplied
to the service of the State and country during its three
centuries of educational activity, by the part it took in
one of the brightest epochs of these three centuries—the
days when it gave Grattan to Grattan's Parliament, by
the work and reputation of the *alumni* it could muster
to-day within and without its walls, our venerable seat
of learning need not fear comparison with any similar
institutions in Great Britain. It may also, of course, be said
that many men who have passed through Trinity College
have impressed the thought of Ireland, and, indeed, of
the world, in one way or another—such men as, to take
two very different examples, Burke and Thomas Davis
—but on some of the very best spirits amongst these
men Trinity College and its atmosphere have exerted influence rather by repulsion than by attraction; and certainly their characteristics of temper or thought have not
been of a kind which those best acquainted with the
atmosphere of Trinity College associate with that institution. Still nothing can detract from the credit of
having educated such men. But these tests and standards are, for my present purpose, irrelevant. I am not
writing a book on Irish educational history, or even a
record of present-day Irish educational achievement. I
am rather trying, from the standpoint of a practical
worker for national progress, to measure the reality and
strength of the educational and other influences which
are actually and actively operating on the character and
intellect of the majority of the Irish people, moulding

their thought and directing their action towards the upbuilding of our national life.

From this point of view I am bound to say that Trinity College, so far as I have seen, has had but little influence upon the minds or the lives of the people. Nor can I find that at any period of the extraordinarily interesting economic and social revolution, which has been in progress in Ireland since the great catastrophe of the Famine period, Dublin University has departed from its academic isolation and its aloofness from the great national problems that were being worked out. The more one thinks of it, indeed, and the more one realises the opportunities of an institution like Trinity College in a country like Ireland, the more one must recognise how small, in recent times, has been its positive influence on the mind of the country, and how little it has contributed towards the solution of any of those problems, educational, economic, or social, that were clamant for solution, and which in any other country would have naturally secured the attention of men who ought to have been leaders of thought.

Whatever the causes, and many may be assigned, this unfortunate lack of influence on the part of Trinity College, has always seemed to me a strong supplementary argument for the creation of another University or University College on a more popular basis, to which the Roman Catholic people of Ireland would have recourse. From the fact that Maynooth by its constitution could never have developed into a great national

University,* and that Trinity College has never, as a matter of fact, done so, and has thus, in my opinion, missed a unique opportunity, it has come about that Ireland has been without any great centre of thought whose influence would have tended to leaven the mass of mental inactivity or random-thinking so prevalent in Ireland, and would have created a body of educated public opinion sufficiently informed and potent to secure the study and discussion on their merits of questions of vital interest to the country. The demoralising atmosphere of partisanship which hangs over Ireland would, I am convinced, gradually give way before an organised system of education with a thoroughly democratic University at its head, which would diffuse amongst the people at large a sense of the value of a balanced judgment on, and a true appreciation of, the real forces with which Ireland has to deal in building up her fortunes.

To discuss the merits of the different solutions which have been proposed for the vexed problem of higher education in Ireland would be beyond the scope of this book. The question will have to be faced, and all I need do here is to state the conditions which the solution will have to fulfil if it is to deal with the aspects of the Irish Question with which the new movement is practically concerned. What is most needed is a University that will

---

* It was not authorised to give degrees to lay students; and even the admission of lay students to an Arts course was prohibited by Government, lest Catholic students should be drawn away from Trinity College. See Cornwallis Correspondence, III., 366-8.

reach down to the rural population, much in the same way as the Scottish Universities do, and a lower scale of fees will be required than Trinity College, with its diminished revenues, could establish.   Already I can see that the work of the new Department, acting in conjunction with local bodies, urban and rural, throughout the country, will provide a considerable number of scholarships, bursaries, and exhibitions for young men who are being prepared to take part in the very real, but rather hazily understood, industrial revival which is imminent.   Leaving sectarian controversies out of the question, the type of institution which is required in order to provide adequately for the classes now left outside the influence of higher education is an institution pre-eminently national in its aims, and one intimately associated with the new movements making for the development of our national resources.

Unfortunately, however, in Ireland, and indeed in England too, there is a tendency to regard educational institutions almost solely as they will affect religion. At least it is difficult to arouse any serious interest in them except from this point of view. I welcome, therefore, the striking answers given to the queries of Lord Robertson, Chairman of the University Commission, by Dr. O'Dwyer, the Roman Catholic Bishop of Limerick, who boldly and wisely placed the question before the country in the light in which cleric and layman should alike regard it :—

The Chairman.—(413) : " I suppose you believe a

Catholic University, such as you propose, will strengthen
Roman Catholicism in Ireland?"—" It is not easy to
answer that ; not so easy as it looks." (414) : —" But it
won't weaken it, or you would not be here?"—" It would
educate Catholics in Ireland very largely, and, of course,
a religious denomination composed of a body of educated
men is stronger than a religious denomination composed of
ignorant men. In that sense it would strengthen Roman
Catholicism." (415) : —" Is there any sense in which it
won't?"—" As far as religion is concerned, I do not know
how a University would work out. If you ask me now
whether I think that that University in a certain number
of years would become a centre of thought, strengthening
the Catholic faith in Ireland, I cannot tell you. It is a
leap in the dark." (416) : —" But it is in the hope that
it will strengthen your own Church that you propose it?"
—" No, it is not, by any means. We are Bishops, but we
are Irishmen, also, and we want to serve our country."*

Equally significant were the statements of Dr. O'Dea,
the official spokesman of Maynooth, when he said,

I regard the interest of the laity in the settlement of
the University Question as supreme. The clergy are but
a small, however important, part of the nation, and the
laity have never had an institution of higher education
comparable to Maynooth in magnitude or resources. I
recognise, therefore, that the educational grievances of the
laity are much more pressing than those of the clergy . .
It is generally admitted that Irish priests hold a position of exceptional influence, due to historical causes, the
intensely religious character of the people, and the want
of Catholic laymen qualified by education and position for
social and political leadership. What Bishop Berkeley
said of them in 1749, in his letter, *A Word to the Wise*,
still holds true, ' That no set of men on earth have it in

* Appendix to First Report, p. 37.

their power to do good on easier terms, with more advantage to others, and less pains or loss to themselves.'
It would be folly to expect that in a mixed community the
State should do anything to strengthen or perpetuate this
power ; but this result will certainly not follow from the
more liberal education of the clergy, provided equal advantages are extended to the laity.   On the contrary, I
am convinced that if the void in the lay leadership of the
country be filled up by higher education of the better
classes among the Catholic laity, the power of the priests,
so far as it is abnormal or unnecessary will pass away ;
and, further, if I believed, with many who are opposed to
the better education of the priesthood, that their power
is based on falsehood or superstition, I would unhesitat-
ingly advocate the spread of higher education among the
laity and clergy alike, as the best means of effectually
sapping and disintegrating it.*

I had for long indulged a hope that a university of
the type which Ireland requires would have been the
outcome of a great national educational movement
emanating from Trinity College, which might, at this
auspicious hour, have surpassed all the proud achievements of its three hundred years.   That hope was dispelled when the cry of ' Hands off Trinity ' was applied
to the profane hands of the Royal Commission.   Perhaps
that attitude may be reconsidered yet.   There is one
hopeful sentiment which is often heard coming from that
institution.   An opinion has been strongly expressed that
nothing ought to be done to separate in secular life two
sections of Irishmen who happen to belong to different
creeds.   Whatever may be the logical outcome of the
position taken up towards the University problem by

* Appendix to Third Report, pp. 283, 296.

those who give expression to this pious opinion, I do not
for a moment doubt their sincerity. But I often think
that too much importance is attached to the danger of building new walls, and that there is too
little appreciation of the wide and deep foundation
of the already existing walls between the two
sections of Irishmen who are so unhappily kept
apart. In dealing with this, as with all large Irish problems, it had better be frankly recognised that there are
in the country two races, two creeds, and, what is too
little considered, two separate spheres of economic interest and pursuit. Socially two separate classes have
naturally, nay inevitably, arisen out of these distinctions.
One class has superior advantages in many ways of
great importance. The other class is far more numerous,
produces far the greater proportion of the nation's
wealth, and is, therefore, from the national point of
view, of greater importance. But both are necessary.
Both must be adequately provided for in the supreme
matter of higher education. Above all, the two classes
must be educated to regard themselves as united by the
bond of a common country—a sentiment which, if
genuine, would treat differences arising from whatever
cause, not as a difficulty in the way of national progress,
but rather as affording a variety of opportunities for
national expansion.

I do not concern myself as to the exact form which the
new institution or institutions which are to give us the
absolutely essential advantage of higher education should

take. If in view of the difference in the requirements to which I have alluded, and the complicated pedagogic and administrative considerations which have to be taken into account, schemes of co-education of Protestants and Roman Catholics are difficult of immediate accomplishment, let that ideal be postponed. The two creeds can meet in the playground now: they can meet everywhere in after life. Ireland will bring them together soon enough if Ireland is given a chance, and when the time is ripe for their coming together in higher education they will come together. If the time is not now ripe for this ideal there is no justification for postponing educational reform until the relations between the two creeds have been elevated to a plane which, in my opinion, they will never reach except through the aid of that culture which a widely diffused higher education alone can afford.

When I was beginning to write this chapter I chanced to pick up the *Chesterfield Letters*. I opened the book at the two hundredth epistle, and, curiously enough, almost the first sentence which caught my eye ran: 'Education more than nature is the cause of that difference you see in the character of men.' I felt myself at first in strong disagreement with this aphorism. But when I came to reflect how much the nature of one generation must be the outcome of the education of those which went before it, I gradually came to see the truth in Lord Chesterfield's words. I must leave it to experts to define the exact steps which ought to be taken to make the general education of this country capable of cultivating the judgment, strengthening the will, and so of building up the character. But every day, every thought, I give to the problems of Irish progress convinces me more firmly that this is the real task of educational reform, a task that must be accomplished before we can prove to those who brand us with racial inferiority that, in Ireland, it was not nature that has been unkind in causing the difference we find in the character of men.

L

CHAPTER VI.

THROUGH THOUGHT TO ACTION.

I have now completed my survey of the main conditions which, in my opinion, must be taken into account by anyone who would understand the Irish mind, and still more by those who seek to work with it in rebuilding the fortunes of the country. The task has been one of great difficulty, as it was necessary to tell, not only the truth—for that even an official person may be excused—but also the whole truth, which, unless made compulsory by the kissing of the book, is regarded as a gratuitous kissing of the rod. From the frying pan of political dispute, I have passed into the fire of sectarian controversy. I have not hesitated to poach on the preserves of historians and economists, and have even bearded the pedagogues in their dens. Before my stock of metaphors is exhausted, let me say that I have one hope of escape from the cross-fire of denunciation which independent speaking about Ireland is apt to provoke. I once witnessed a football match between two villages, one of which favoured a political party called by the name of a leader, with an 'ism' added to indicate a policy, the other adopting the same name, still further elongated by the prefix 'anti.' When I arrived on the scene the game had begun in deadly earnest, but I noticed the ball lying unmolested in another quarter of the field. In Irish public life I have often had reason to envy that ball, and perhaps now its lot may be mine, while the game goes on and the critics pay attention to each other.

To my friendly critics a word of explanation is due. The opinions to which I have given expression are based upon personal observation and experience extending over a quarter of a century during which I have been in close touch with Irish life at home, and not unfamiliar with it abroad. I have referred to history only when I could not otherwise account for social and economic conditions with which I came into contact, or with which I desired practically to deal. Whether looking back over the dreary wastes of Anglo-Irish history, or studying the men and things of to-day, I came to conclusions which differed widely from what I had been taught to believe by those whose theories of Irish development had not been subjected to any practical test. Deeply as I have felt for the past sufferings of the Irish people and their heritage of disability and distress, I could not bring myself to believe that, where misgovernment had continued so long, and in such an immense variety of circumstances and conditions, the governors could have been alone to blame. I envied those leaders of popular thought whose confidence in themselves and in their followers was shaken by no such reflections. But the more I listened to them the more the conviction was borne in upon me that they were seeking to build an impossible future upon an imaginary past.

Those who know Ireland from within are aware that
Irish thought upon Irish problems has been undergoing
a silent, and therefore too lightly regarded revolution.
The surface of Irish life, often so inexplicably ruffled,
and sometimes so inexplicably calm, has just now become
smooth to a degree which has led to hasty conclusions
as to the real cause and the inward significance of the
change. To chime in with the thoughtless optimism of
the hour will do no good ; but a real understanding of the
forces which have created the existing situation will
reveal an unprecedented opportunity for those who
would give to the Irish mind that full and free development which has been so long and, as I have tried to
show, so unnaturally delayed.

Among these new forces in Irish life there is one
which has been greatly misunderstood ; and yet to its
influence during the last few years much of the 'transformation scene' in the drama of the Irish Question is
really due. It deserves more than a passing notice here,
because, while its aims as formulated appear somewhat
restricted, it unquestionably tends in practice towards
that national object of paramount importance, the
strengthening of character. I refer to the movement
known as the Gaelic Revival. Of this movement I am
myself but an outside observer, having been forced to
devote nearly all my time and energies to a variety of
attempts which aim at the doing in the industrial sphere
of very much the same work as that which the Gaelic
movement attempts in the intellectual sphere—the re-

habilitation of Ireland from within. But in the course of my work of agricultural and industrial development I naturally came across this new intellectual force and found that when it began to take effect, so far from diverting the minds of the peasantry from the practical affairs of life, it made them distinctly more amenable to the teaching of the dry economic doctrine of which I was an apostle. The reason for this is plain enough to me now, though, like all my theories about Ireland, the truth came to me from observation and practical experience rather than as the result of philosophic speculation. For the co-operative movement depended for its success upon a two-fold achievement. In order to get it started at all, its principles and working details had to be grasped by the Irish peasant mind and commended to his intelligence. Its further development and its hopes of permanence depend upon the strengthening of character, which, I must repeat, is the foundation of all Irish progress.

The Irish Agricultural Organisation Society* exerts its influence—a now established and rapidly-growing influence—mainly through the medium of associations. The Gaelic movement, on the other hand, acts more directly upon the individual, and the two forces are therefore in a sense complementary to each other. Both will be seen to be playing an important part—I should say a necessary part—in the reconstruction of our national life. At any rate, I feel that it is necessary to my argument that I should explain to those who are as ill-informed

* This body is fully described in the next chapter.

about the Gaelic revival as I was myself until its
practical usefulness was demonstrated to me, what
exactly seems to be the most important outcome of the
work of that movement.

The Gaelic League, which defines its objects as ' The
preservation of Irish as the national language of Ireland
and the extension of its use as a spoken tongue ; the
study and publication of existing Irish literature and the
cultivation of a modern literature in Irish,' was formed
in 1893. Like the Agricultural Organisation Society,
the Gaelic League is declared by its constitution to be
' strictly non-political and non-sectarian,' and, like it, has
been the object of much suspicion, because severance
from politics in Ireland has always seemed to the politician the most active form of enmity. Its constitution,
too, is somewhat similar, being democratically guided in
its policy by the elected representatives of its affiliated
branches. It is interesting to note that the funds with
which it carries on an extensive propaganda are mainly
supplied from the small contributions of the poor. It
publishes two periodicals, one weekly and another
monthly. It administers an income of some £6,000 a
year, not reckoning what is spent by local branches, and
has a paid staff of eleven officers, a secretary, treasurer,
and nine organisers, together with a large number of
voluntary workers. It resembled the agricultural movement also in the fact that it made very little headway
during the first few years of its existence. But it had a
nucleus of workers with new ideas for the intellectual

regeneration of Ireland. In face of much apathy they persisted with their propaganda, and they have at last succeeded in making their ideas understood. So much is evident from the rapidly-increasing number of affiliated branches of the League, which in March, 1903, amounted to 600, almost treble the number registered two years before. But even this does not convey any idea of the influence which the movement exerts. Within the past year the teaching of the Irish language has been introduced into no less than 1,300 National Schools. In 1900 the number of schools in which Irish was taught was only about 140. The statement that our people do not read books is generally accepted as true, yet the sale of the League publications during one year reached nearly a quarter of a million copies. These results cannot be left unconsidered by anybody who wishes to understand the psychology of the Irish mind. The movement can truly claim to have effected the conversion of a large amount of intellectual apathy into genuine intellectual activity.

The declared objects of the League—the popularising of the national language and literature—do not convey, perhaps, an adequate conception of its actual work, or of the causes of its popularity. It seeks to develop the intellectual, moral, and social life of the Irish people from within, and it is doing excellent work in the cause of temperance. Its president, Dr. Douglas Hyde, in his evidence given before the University Commission,*

* See Appendix to Third Report, p. 311.

pointed out that the success of the League was due to
its meeting the people half way ; that it educated them
by giving them something which they could appreciate
and assimilate; and that it afforded a proof that
people who would not respond to alien educational
systems, will respond with eagerness to something they
can call their own.   The national factor in Ireland has
been studiously eliminated from national education, and
Ireland is perhaps the only country in Europe where it
was part of the settled policy of those who had the guidance of education to ignore the literature, history, arts,
and traditions of the people.   It was a fatal policy, for it
obviously tended to stamp their native country in the
eyes of Irishmen with the badge of inferiority and to
extinguish the sense of healthy self-respect which comes
from the consciousness of high national ancestry and
traditions.   This policy, rigidly adhered to for many
years, almost extinguished native culture among Irishmen, but it did not succeed in making another form of
culture acceptable to them.   It dulled the intelligence of
the people, impaired their interest in their own surroundings, stimulated emigration by teaching them to look on
other countries as more agreeable places to live in, and
made Ireland almost a social desert.   Men and
women without culture or knowledge of literature or of
music have succeeded a former generation who were
passionately interested in these things, an interest which
extended down even to the wayside cabin.   The loss of
these elevating influences in Irish society probably

accounts for much of the arid nature of Irish controversies, while the reaction against their suppression has
given rise to those displays of rhetorical patriotism for
which the Irish language has found the expressive term
raimeis, and which (thanks largely to the Gaelic movement) most people now listen to with a painful and
half-ashamed sense of their unreality.

The Gaelic movement has brought to the surface senti-
ments and thoughts which had been developed in Gaelic
Ireland through hundreds of years, and which no repression had been able to obliterate altogether, but which
still remained as a latent spiritual inheritance in the mind.
And now this stream, which has long run underground,
has again emerged even stronger than before, because an
element of national self-consciousness has been added at
its re-emergence.   A passionate conviction is gaining
ground that if Irish traditions, literature, language, art,
music, and culture are allowed to disappear, it will
mean the disappearance of the race ; and that the education of the country must be nationalised if our social,
intellectual, or even our economic position is to be
permanently improved.

With this view of the Gaelic movement my own
thoughts are in complete accord.   It is undeniable that
the pride in country justly felt by Englishmen, a pride
developed by education and a knowledge of their history.
has had much to do with the industrial pre-eminence of
England ; for the pioneers of its commerce have been
often actuated as much by patriotic motives as by the

desire for gain. The education of the Irish people has ignored the need for any such historical basis for pride or love of country, and, for my part, I feel sure that the Gaelic League is acting wisely in seeking to arouse such a sentiment, and to found it mainly upon the ages of Ireland's story when Ireland was most Irish.

It is this expansion of the sentiment of nationality outside the domain of party politics—the distinction, so to speak, between nationality and nationalism—which is the chief characteristic of the Gaelic movement. Nationality had come to have no meaning other than a political one, any broader national sentiment having had little or nothing to feed upon. During the last century the spirit of nationality has found no unworthy expression in literature, in the writings of Ferguson, Standish O'Grady and Yeats, which, however, have not been even remotely comparable in popularity with the political journalism in prose and rhyme in which the age has been so fruitful. It has never expressed itself in the arts, and not only has Ireland no representative names in the higher regions of art, but the national deficiency has been felt in every department of industry into which design enters, and where national art-characteristics have a commercial value. The national customs, culture, and recreations which made the country a pleasant place to live in, have almost disappeared, and with them one of the strongest ties which bind people to the country of their birth. The Gaelic revival, as I understand it, is an attempt to supply these deficiencies, to give to Irish people a culture of their own; and I believe that by awakening the feelings of pride, self-respect, and love of country, based on knowledge, every department of Irish life will be invigorated.

Thus it is that the elevating influence upon the individual is exerted. Politics have never awakened initiative among the mass of the people, because there was no programme of action for the individual. Perhaps it is as well for Ireland that such should have been the case, for, as it has been shown, we have had little of the political thought which should be at the back of political action. Political action under present conditions must necessarily be deputed to a few representatives, and after the vote is given, or the cheering at a meeting has ceased, the individual can do nothing but wait, and his lethargy tends to become still deeper. In the Gaelic revival there is a programme of work for the individual; his mind is engaged, thought begets energy, and this energy vitalises every part of his nature. This makes for the strengthening of character, and so far from any harm being done to the practical movement, to which I have so often referred, the testimony of my fellow-workers, as well as my own observation, is unanimous in affirming that the influence of the branches of the Gaelic League is distinctly useful whenever it is sought to move the people to industrial or commercial activity.

Many of my political friends cannot believe—and I am afraid that nothing that I can say will make them

believe—that the movement is not necessarily, in the
political sense, separatist in its sentiment.   This impression is, in my opinion, founded on a complete misunderstanding of Anglo-Irish history.   Those who look
askance at the rise of the Gaelic movement ignore the
important fact that there has never been any essential
opposition between the English connection and Irish
nationality.   The Elizabethan chiefs of the sixteenth
and the Gaelic poets of the seventeenth and eighteenth
centuries, when the relations between the two countries
were far worse than they are to-day, knew nothing of
this opposition.   The true sentiment of nationality is
a priceless heritage of every small nation which has done
great things, and had it not largely perished in Ireland,
separatist sentiment, the offspring, not of Irish nationality, but of Irish political nationalism, could hardly have
survived until to-day.

But undoubtedly we strike here on a danger to the
Gaelic movement, so far at least as that movement is
bound up with the future of the Gaelic League ; a danger
which cannot be left out of account in any estimate of
this new force in Irish life.   The continuance of the
League as a beneficent force, or indeed a force at all,
seems to me, as in the case of the co-operative organisation to which I have compared it, to be vitally dependent
on a scrupulous observance of that part of its constitution
which keeps the door open to Irishmen of every creed or
political party.   Only thus can the League remain a
truly national body, and attract from all classes Irishmen

who are capable of forwarding its true policy. I do not
think there is much danger of a spirit of sectarian
exclusiveness developing itself in a body mainly composed of Roman Catholics whose President is a Protestant. But it cannot be denied that there has been
an occasional tendency to interpret the 'no politics'
clause of the constitution in a manner which seems
hardly fair to Unionists or even to constitutional Home
Rulers who may have joined the organisation on the
strength of its declaration of political neutrality. If this
is not a mere transitory phenomenon its effect will be
serious. As a political body the League would immediately sink into insignificance and probably disappear
amid a crowd of contending factions. It would certainly
cease to fulfil its great function of creating a nationality
of the thought and spirit, in which all Irishmen who wish
to be anything else than English colonists might aspire
to share. Its early successes in bringing together men of
different political views were remarkable. At the very
outset of its career it enlisted the support of so militant
a politician as the late Rev. R. R. Kane, who declared
that though a Unionist and an Orangeman he had no
desire to forget that he was an O'Cahan. On this basis
it is difficult to set a limit to the fruitfulness of the work
which this organisation might do for Ireland, and I
cannot regard any who would depart from the letter and
spirit of its constitution as sincere, or if sincere as wise,
friends of the movement with which they are associated.

Of minor importance are certain extravagances in the

conduct of the movement which time and practical experience can hardly fail to correct. I have borne witness to the value of the cultivation of the language even from my own practical standpoint, but I cannot think that to sign cheques in Irish, and get angry when those who cannot understand will not honour them, is a good way of demonstrating that value. I should, speaking generally, regard it as a mistake, supposing it were practicable, to substitute Irish for English in the conduct of business. If any large development of the trade in pampooties, turf and potheen between the Aran Islands and the mainland were in contemplation, this attempt might be justified. But on behalf of those Philistines who attach paramount importance to the development of Irish industry, trade and commerce on a large and comprehensive scale, I should regret a course which, from a business point of view, would be about as wise as the advocacy of distinctive Irish currency, weights and measures. And I protest more strongly against the reasons which have been given to me for this policy. I have been told that, in order to generate sufficient enthusiasm, a young movement of the kind must adopt a rigorous discipline and an aggressive policy. Not only are we thus confronted with a false issue, but by giving countenance to the outward acceptance of what the better sense rejects, these over-zealous leaguers are administering to the Irish character the very poison which all Irish movements should combine to eliminate from the national life.

The position which I have given to the Gaelic Revival among the new influences at work and making for progress in Ireland will hardly be understood by those who have never embraced the idea of combining all such forces in a constructive and comprehensive scheme of national advancement. One instance of the potential utility of the Gaelic League will appeal to those of my readers who attach as much importance as I do to the improvement of the peasant home. Concerted action to this end is being planned while I write. It is proposed to take a few districts where the peasants are members of one of the new co-operative societies, and where the clergy have taken a keen interest in the economic and social advancement of the members of the Society, but where the cottages are in the normal condition. The new Department will lend the services of its domestic economy teachers. The Organisation Society, the clergy, and the Department thus working together will, I hope, be able to get the people of the selected districts to effect an improvement in their domestic surroundings which will act as an invaluable example for other districts to follow. But in order that this much needed contribution to the well-being of the peasant proprietary, upon which all our thoughts are just now concentrated, may be assisted with the enthusiasm which belongs in Ireland to a consciously national effort, it is hoped that common action with the Gaelic League may be possible, so that this force also may be enlisted in the solution of this part of our central problem, the rehabilitation of rural life in Ireland.

It is, however, on more general grounds that I have, albeit as an outside observer, watched with some anxiety and much gratification the progress of the Gaelic Revival. In the historical evolution of the Irish mind we find certain qualities atrophied, so to speak, by disuse; and to this cause I attribute the past failures of the race in practical life at home. I have shown how politics, religion, and our systems of education have all, in their respective influences upon the people, missed to a large extent, the effect upon character which they should have made it their paramount duty to produce. Nevertheless, whenever the intellect of the people is appealed to by those who know its past, a recuperative power is manifested which shows that its vitality has not been irredeemably impaired. It is because I believe that, on the whole, a right appeal has been made by the Gaelic League that I have borne testimony to its patriotic endeavours.

The question of the Gaelic Revival seems to be really a form of the eternal question of the interdependence of the practical and the ideal in Ireland. Their true relation to each other is one of the hardest lessons the student of our problems has to learn. I recall an incident in the course of my own studies which I will here recount, as it appears to me to furnish an admirable illustration of this difficulty as it presented itself to a very interesting mind. During the years covering the rise and fall of Parnell, when interest in the Irish Question was at its zenith, the newspapers of the United States kept in

London a corps of very able correspondents, who
watched and reported to their transatlantic readers every
move in the Home Rule campaign. An American
public, by no means limited to the American-Irish,
devoured every morsel of this intelligence with an
avidity which could not have been surpassed if the United
States had been engaged in a war with Great Britain.
Among these correspondents perhaps the most brilliant
was the late Harold Frederic. Not many months before
he died I received a letter from him, in which he said
that, although we were unknown to each other, he
thought, from some public utterances of mine, that we
must have many views in common. He had often intended to get an introduction to me, and now suggested
that we should 'waive things and meet.' We met and
spent an evening together, which left some deep impressions on my mind. He told me that the Irish Question
possessed for him a fascination for which he could give
no rational explanation. He had absolutely no tie of
blood or material interest with Ireland, and his friendship
for it had brought him the only quarrels in which he had
ever been engaged.

What chiefly interested me in Harold Frederic's
philosophy of the Irish Question was that he had arrived
at a diagnosis of the Irish mind not substantially different
from my own. Since that evening I have come across a
passage in one of his novels, which clothes in delightful
language his view of the chaotic psychology of the Irish
Celt:

There, in Ireland, you get a strange mixture of

M

elementary early peoples, walled off from the outer world
by the four seas, and free to work out their own racial
amalgam on their own lines. They brought with them at
the outset a great inheritance of Eastern mysticism.
Others lost it, but the Irish, all alone on their island, kept
it alive and brooded on it, and rooted their whole spiritual
side in it. Their religion is full of it ; their blood is full
of it. . . . The Ireland of two thousand years ago is
incarnated in her. They are the merriest people and the
saddest, the most turbulent and the most docile, the most
talented and the most unproductive, the most practical
and the most visionary, the most devout and the most
pagan. These impossible contradictions war ceaselessly
in their blood.*

In our conversation what struck me most was the
influence which politics had exercised even on his
philosophic mind, notwithstanding a low estimate of our
political leaders.   In one of a series of three notable
articles upon the Irish Question, which appeared anony-
mously in the *Fortnightly Review* † in the winter of
1893-4, and of which he told me he was the writer, he
had given a character sketch of what he called ' The
Rhetoricians.' Their performances since the Union were
summarised in the phrase 'a century of unremitting
gabble,' and he regarded it as a sad commentary on Irish
life that such brilliant talents so largely ran to waste in
destructive criticism.

I naturally turned the conversation on to my own line

* *The Damnation of Theron Ware.* This was the title of the
book I read in the United States. I am told he published it in England
under the title of *Illumination*—a nice discrimination !

† They appeared under the signature of ' X.' in Nov. and Dec.,
1893, and Jan., 1894.

of thought, and discussed the practical conclusions to which his studies had led him. I tried to elicit from him exactly what he had in his mind when, in one of the articles to which I have referred, he advocated ' a reconstruction of Ireland on distinctive national lines.' I hoped to find that his psychological study of my countrymen would enable him to throw some light upon the means by which play could be given at home to the latent capacities of the race. I found that he was in entire accord with my view, that the chief difficulty in the way of constructive statesmanship was the defect in the Irish character about which I have said so much. I was prepared for that conclusion, for I had already seen the lack of initiative admirably appreciated in the following illuminating sentence of his :—' The Celt will help someone else to do the thing that other has in mind, and will help him with great zeal and devotion ; but he will not start to do the thing he himself has thought of.'* But I was disappointed when he bade me his first and la st good-bye that I had not convinced him that there was any way out of the Irish difficulty other than political changes, for which, at the same time, he appeared to think the people singularly unfitted.

The fact is we had arrived at the point where the student of Irish life usually finds himself in a *cul de sac*. If he has accurately observed the conditions, he is face to face with a problem which appears to be in its nature insoluble. For at every turn he finds things being done wrong which might so easily be done right, only that

* *Fortnightly Review*, Jan. 1894, pp. 11, 12.

nobody is concerned that they should be done right.
And what is worse, when he has learned, in the course of
his investigations, to discount the picturesque explanation of our unsuccess in practical life which in Ireland
veils the unpleasant truth, he will find that the people
are quite aware of their defects, although they attribute
them to causes beyond their power to remove. Then,
too, the sympathetic inquirer is shocked by the lack of
seriousness in it all. With all their past griefs and their
high aspirations, the Irish people seem to be play-acting
before the world. The inquirer does not, perhaps, reflect
that, if play-acting be inconsistent with the deepest emotions, and with the pursuit of high ideals, then he con-
demns a little over one half of the human race.* He
probably comes to the main conclusion adopted in these
pages, and realises that the Irish Question is a problem
of character. And as Irish character is the product of
Irish history, which cannot be re-enacted, he leaves the
problem there. Harold Frederic left it there, and there
it has been taken up by those whose endeavour forms
the story which I have to tell.

I now come to the principles which, it appears to me,
must underlie the solution of this problem. The narra-

---

* The difficulties of the writer who is not a writer are great. I sent
this chapter to two literary friends, one of whom, with the help of a
globe, disputed my accuracy in a learned ethnological disquisition with
which he favoured me. The other warned me to be even more obscure
and sent me the following verses, addressed by 'Cynicus' (J. K.
Stephen) to Shakespeare,
> " You wrote a line too much, my sage,
>   Of seers the first, the first of sayers;
> For only half the world's a stage,
>   And only all the women players."

tive contained in the second part of this book is a record of the efforts made during the last decade of the nineteenth and the first two years of the twentieth century by a small, but now rapidly augmenting group of Irishmen, to pluck the brand of Irish intellect from the burning of the Irish Question. The problem before us was, my readers will now understand, how to make headway in view of the weakness of character to which I have had to attribute the paralysis of our activities in the past. We were quite aware that our progress would at first be slow. But as we were satisfied that the defects of character which stood in the way of economic advancement were due to causes which need no longer be operative, and that the intellect of the people was unimpaired, we faced the problem with confidence.

The practical form which our work took was the launching upon Irish life of a movement of organised self-help, and the subsequent grafting upon this movement of a system of State-aid to the agriculture and industries of the country I need not here further elaborate this programme, for the steps by which it has been and is being adopted will be presently described in detail. But there is one aspect of the new movement in Ireland which must be understood by those who would grasp the true significance and the human interest of an evolution in our national life, the only recent parallel for which, as far as I am aware, is to be found in Japan: though to my mind the conscious attempt of the Irish people to develop a civilisation of their own is far more interesting than the recent efforts of the Japanese to westernise their institutions.

The problem of mind and character with which we had to deal in Ireland presented this central and somewhat discouraging fact. In practical life the Irish had failed where the English had succeeded, and this was attributed to the lack of certain English qualities which have been undoubtedly essential to success in commerce and in industry from the days of the industrial revolution until a comparatively recent date. It was the individualism of the English economic system during this period which made these qualities indispensable. The lack of these qualities in Irishmen to-day may be admitted, and the cause of the deficiency has been adequately explained. But those who regard the Irish situation as industrially hopeless probably ignore the fact that there are other qualities, of great and growing importance under modern economic conditions, which can be developed in Irishmen and may form the basis of an industrial system. I refer to the range of qualities which come into play rather in association than in the individual, and to which the term 'associative' is applied.*

---

* These qualities, as will be explained later, happen to have a special economic value in the farming industry, and so are available for the elevation of rural life, with whose problems we are now so deeply concerned in Ireland. Their applicability to urban life need not be discussed here. But my study of the co-operative movement in England has convinced me that, if the English had the associative instincts of the Irish, that movement would play a part in English life more commensurate with its numerical strength and the volume of its commercial transactions, than can be claimed for it so far.

So that although much disparaging criticism of Irish character is based upon the survival in the Celt of the tribal instincts, it is gratifying to be able to show that even from the practical English point of view, our preference for thinking and working in groups may not be altogether a *damnosa hereditas*. If, owing to our deficiency in the individualistic qualities of the English, we cannot at this stage hope to produce many types of the ' economic man ' of the economists, we think we see our way to provide, as a substitute, the economic association. If the association succeeds, and by virtue of its financial success becomes permanent, a great change will, in our opinion, be produced on the character of its members. The reflex action upon the individual mind of the habit of doing, in association with others, things which were formerly left undone, or badly done, may be relied upon to have a tonic effect upon the character of the individual. This is, I suppose, the secret of discipline, which, though apparently eliminating volition, seems in weak characters to strengthen the will.

There is, too, as we have learned, in the association a strange influence which develops qualities and capacities that one would not expect on a mere consideration of the character of its members. This psychological phenomenon has been admirably and most entertainingly discussed by the French psychologist, Le Bon,* who, in the attractive pursuit of paradox, almost goes to the length of the proposition that the association inherently

* *La Psychologie de la Foule.*

possesses qualities the opposite of those possessed by its members. My own experience—and I have had opportunities of observing hundreds of associations formed by my friends upon the principles above laid down—does not carry me quite so far. But, unquestionably, the association in Ireland does often become an entity as distinct from the individualities of which it is composed, as is a new chemical compound from its constituent elements.

Associations of the kind we had in our minds, which were to be primarily for purely business purposes, were bound to have many collateral effects. They would open up outside of politics and religion, but not in conflict with either, a sphere of action where an independence new to the country would have to be exercised. In Ireland public opinion is under an obsession which, whether political, religious, historical, or all three combined, is probably unique among civilised peoples. Until the last few years, for example, it was our habit—one which immensely weakened the influence of Ireland in the Imperial Parliament—to form extravagant estimates of men, exalting and abasing them with irrational caprice, not according to their qualities so much as by their attitude towards the passion of the hour. The ups and downs of the reputations of Lord Spencer and Mr. Arthur Balfour in Ireland are a sufficient illustration of our disregard of the old Latin proverb which tells us that no man ever became suddenly altogether bad. Even now public opinion is too prone to attach excessive value to projects of vague and visionary development, and to underrate

the importance of serious thought and quiet work, which
can be the only solid foundation of our national progress.
In these new associations—humble indeed in their origin,
but destined to play a large part in the people's lives—
projects, professing to be fraught with economic benefit,
have to be judged by the cruel precision of audited
balance sheets, and the worth of men is measured by the
solid contribution they have made to the welfare of the
community.

I have now accomplished one long stage of my journey
towards the conclusion of this discussion of the needs of
modern Ireland. Were I to stop here, probably most of
those who had been induced to open yet another book
upon the Irish Question would accuse me, and not without justice, of being responsible for a barren graft upon
a barren controversy. I fear no such criticism, whatever
other shortcomings may be detected, from those who
have the patience to read on. For when I pass from my
own reflections to record the work to which many
thousands of my countrymen have addressed themselves
in building up the Ireland of the twentieth century, I
shall have a story to tell which must inspire hope in all
who can be persuaded that Ireland in the past has not
often been treated fairly and has never been understood.
I have shown—and it was necessary to show, if a repeti-
tion of misunderstanding was to be avoided—that the
Irish people themselves are gravely responsible for the
ills of their country, and that the forces which have

mainly governed their action hitherto are rapidly bringing about their disappearance as a distinct nationality.
But I shall now have to tell of the widespread and growing adoption of certain new principles of action which I
believe to be consonant with the genius and traditions of
the race, and the acceptance of which seems to me
vitally necessary if the Irish people are to play a worthy
part in the future history of the world.   That part is a
far greater one than they could ever hope to play as an
independent and separate State, yet their success in playing it must closely depend upon their remaining a distinct
nationality, in the sense so clearly and wisely indicated
by his Majesty when, in his reply to the address of the
Belfast Corporation, he spoke of the 'national characteristics and ideals' which he desired his kingdoms to
cherish in the midst of their imperial unity.*   The great
experiment which I am about to relate is, in its own province, one of the many applications which we see around
us of the conception here put forward.   And I believe
that a few more years of quiet work by those who are
taking part in this movement, with its appeal to Irish

* July   27th, 1903,—His Majesty thus confirmed the striking
utterance of imperial policy contained in Lord Dudley's speech to the
Incorporated Law Society, on the 20th of November, 1902.   His
Excellency, after protesting against the conception of empire as a ' huge
regiment' in which each nation was to lose its individuality, said—
" Lasting strength, lasting loyalty, are not to be secured by any attempt
to force into one system or to remould into one type those special
characteristics which are the outcome of a nation's history and of her
religious and social conditions, but rather by a full recognition of the
fact that these very characteristics form an essential part of a nation's
life ; and that under wise guidance and under sympathetic treatment
they will enable her to provide her own contribution and to play her
own special part in the life of the empire to which she belongs."

intellect, and its reliance upon Irish patriotism, is all that is needed to prove that by developing the industrial qualities of the Celt on associative lines we can .in politics as well as in economics, add strength to the Irish character without making it less Irish or less attractive than of old.

PART II.

PRACTICAL.

" For a country so attractive and a people so gifted we cherish the
warmest regard, and it is, therefore with supreme satisfaction that I
have during our stay so often heard the hope expressed that a brighter
day is dawning upon Ireland. I shall eagerly await the fulfilment of
this hope. Its realisation will, under Divine Providence, depend
largely upon the steady development of self-reliance and co-operation,
upon better and more practical education, upon the growth of industrial and commercial enterprise, and upon that incre.se of mutual toleration and respect which the responsibility my Irish people now enjoy
in the public administration of their local affairs is well-fitted to
teach."—*Message of the King to the Irish People*, 1st August, 1903.

CHAPTER VII.

THE NEW MOVEMENT: ITS FOUNDATION ON SELF-HELP.

The movement for the reorganisation of Irish agricultural and industrial life, to which I have already frequently referred, must now be described in practical operation. Before I do this, however, there are two lines of criticism which the very mention of a new movement may suggest, and which I must anticipate. Every year has its tale of new movements, launched by estimable persons whose philanthropic zeal is not balanced by the judgment required to discriminate between schemes which possess the elements of permanence, and those which depend upon the enthusiasm or financial support of their promoters, and are in their nature ephemeral. There is, consequently, a widespread and well justified mistrust of novel schemes for the industrial regeneration of Ireland. I confess to having had my ingenuity severely taxed on some occasions to find a sympathetic circumlocution wherewith to show cause for declining to join a new movement, my real reason being an inward conviction that nothing except resolutions would be moved. In the complex problem of building up the economic and social life of a people with such a history as ours, we must resist the temptation to multiply schemes which, however well intended, are but devices for enabling individuals to devolve their responsibilities upon the community or upon the Government, and which owe their bubble reputation and brief popularity to this unconscious humouring of our chief national defect. On the contrary, we must seek to instil into the mind of each individual the too little recognised importance of his own contribution to the sum of national achievement. The building of character must be our paramount object, as it is the condition precedent of all social and economic reform in Ireland. To explain the principles by the observance of which the agency of the association may be utilised as an economic force, while at the same time the industrial character of the individual may be developed, was one of the chief aims I had in view in the foregoing analysis of the Irish mind and character, as they have emerged from history and are stunted in their growth by present influences. The facts about to be recited will, I hope, suffice to prove that the reformer in Ireland, if he has a true insight into the great human problem with which he is dealing, may find in the association not only a healthy stimulus to national activities, but also a means whereby the assistance of the State may be so invoked and applied that it will concentrate, and not dissipate, the energies of the people.

The other criticism which I think it necessary to anticipate would, if ignored, leave room for a wrong impres-

sion as to much of the work which is being done both
on the self-help and on the State-aid sides of the new
movement. Education, it will be said, is the only real
solvent to the range of problems discussed in this book,
most other agencies of social and economic reform being
of doubtful efficacy and, if they tend to postpone
educational effort, positively harmful. There is much
truth in this view. But it must be remembered
that the backward condition of our economic life is due
mainly to the fact that our educational systems have had
little regard to our history or economic circumstances.
We must, therefore, at this stage in our national development give to education a much wider interpretation than
that which is usually applied to the term. We cannot
wait for a generation to grow up which has been given an
education calculated to fit it for the modern economic
struggle, even if there were any probability that the
necessary reforms would soon be carried against the prejudices which are aroused by any proposal to train the
minds, or even the hands and eyes, of the rising generation. In the meantime much of the work, both voluntary
and State-aided, now initiated in Ireland, must consist of
educating adults to introduce into their business concerns the more advanced economic and scientific methods
which the superior education of our rivals in agriculture
and industry abroad has enabled them to adopt, and
which my experience of Irish work convinces me our
people would have adopted long ago if they had had
similar educational advantages. And I would further

N

point out that there is no better way of promoting the reform of education in the ordinary, the pedagogic, sense, than by bringing to bear upon the minds of parents those educational influences which are calculated to convince them of the advantage of improved practical education for their children. So to the economist and to the educationist alike I would submit that the new work of economic and social reform should be judged as a whole, and not prejudged by that hypercriticism of details which ignores the fact that the conditions with which it is attempted to deal are wholly unprecedented. I am quite content that the movement which I am about to describe should be ultimately known and judged by its fruits. Meanwhile, I think that to the intelligent critic it will sufficiently justify its existence if it continues to exist.

The story of the new movement, which must now be told, begins in the year 1889, when a few Irishmen, the writer of these pages among them, set themselves the task of bringing home to the rural population of Ireland the fact that their prosperity was in their own hands much more than they were generally led to believe. I have already pointed out that in order to direct the Irish mind towards practical affairs and in order effectively to arouse and apply the latent capacities of the Irish people to their chief industry, agriculture, we must rely upon associative, as distinct from individual effort ; or, in other words, we must get the people to do their business together rather than separately as the English do. Fortunately for us, it happened that this course, which was clearly indicated by the character and temperament of the people, was equally prescribed by economic considerations. The population and wealth of Ireland are, I need hardly say, so predominantly agricultural that the welfare of the country must depend upon the welfare of the farming classes. It is notorious that the industry by which these classes live has for the last quarter of a century become less and less profitable. It is also recognised that the prime cause of agricultural depression, foreign competition, is not likely to be removed, while that from the colonies is likely to increase. The extraordinary development of rapid and cheap transit, together with recently invented processes of preservation, have enabled the more favoured producers in the newly developed countries of both hemispheres successfully to enter into competition in the British markets with the farmers of these islands. The agricultural producers in other European countries, although to some extent protected by tariffs, have had to face similar conditions ; but in most of these countries, though not in the United Kingdom, the farmers have so changed their methods, to meet the altered circumstances, that they seem to have gained by improvement at home as much as they have lost by competition from abroad. Thus our farmers find themselves harassed first by the cheaper production from vast tracts of virgin soil in the uttermost parts of the earth, and secondly by a nearer and keener competition from the better organised and better educated producers of the Continent.

While the opening up of what the economists call the 'world market,' has necessitated, as a condition of successful competition, improved methods of production for, and carriage to, the market, a third and less obvious force has effected an important change in the method of distribution in the market. The swarming populations, which the factory system has brought together in industrial centres, have to be supplied with food by a system of distribution which must above all things be expeditious. This requirement can only be met by the regular consignment of food in large quantities, of such uniform quality that the sample can be relied upon to be truly indicative of the quality of the bulk. Thus the rapid distribution of produce in the markets becomes as important a factor in agricultural economy as improved methods of production or cheap and expeditious carriage.

Now this new market condition is being met in two ways. In the United States, and, in a less marked degree, at home, an army of middlemen between the producer and the consumer attends to this business for a share of the profits accruing from it, whilst in many parts of the Continent the farmers themselves attend, partially at any rate, to the business side of their industry instead of paying others to do it all for them. I say all, for middlemen are necessary at the distributive end: but it is absolutely essential, in a

country like Ireland, that at the producing end the
farmers should be so organised that they themselves
can manage the first stages of distribution, and exercise
some control over the middlemen who do the rest.   The
foreign agricultural producers have long been alive to
this necessity, for their superior education enabled them
to grasp the economic situation and even to realise that
the matter is not one of acute political controversy.

Here, then, was a definite practical problem to the
solution of which the promoters of the new movement
could apply their principle of co-operative effort.   The
more we studied the question the more apparent it
became that the enormous advantage which the Continental farmers had over the Irish farmers, both in
production and in distribution, was due to superior
organisation combined with better education.   State-aid
had no doubt done a great deal abroad, but in every case
it was manifest that it had been preceded, or at least
accompanied, by the organised voluntary effort without
which the interference of the Government with the
business of the people is simply demoralising.

Generally speaking, the task before us in Ireland was
the adaptation to the special circumstances of our country
of methods successfully pursued by communities similarly
situated in foreign countries.   We had to urge upon
farmers that combination was just as necessary to their
economic salvation as it was recognised to be by their
own class, and by those engaged in other industries,
elsewhere.   They must combine, so we urged on them,

for example, to buy their agricultural requirements at the
cheapest rate and of the best quality in order to produce
more efficiently and more economically ; they must combine to avail themselves of improved appliances beyond
the reach of individual producers, whether it be by the
erection of creameries, for which there was urgent need,
or of cheese factories and jam factories which might
come later ; or in ordinary farm operations, to secure the
use of the latest agricultural machinery and the most
suitable pure-bred stock ; they must combine—not to
abolish middle profits in distribution, whether those of
the carrying companies or those of the dealers in agricultural produce—but to keep those profits within reasonable
limits, and to collect in bulk and regularise consignments
so that they could be carried and marketed at a moderate
cost ; they must combine, as we afterwards learned, for the
purpose of creating, by mutual support, the credit required
to bring in the fresh working capital which each new
development of their industry would demand and justify.
In short, whenever and wherever the individuals in a
farming community could be brought to see that they
might advantageously substitute associated for isolated
production or distribution, they must be taught to form
themselves into associations in order to reap the anticipated advantages.

This brief statement of our general aims will furnish a
rough idea of the economic propaganda which we initiated,
and if I give a few illustrations of the practical application of the new principle to the farming industry, I

shall have done all that will be required to leave on the reader's mind a true though perhaps an incomplete impression of the character and scope of the self-help side of the new movement. I shall first give a sketch of the unrecorded struggles of its pioneers, because these struggles prove to those engaged in social and economic work in Ireland that, in the wholly abnormal condition of our national life, no project which is theoretically sound need be rejected because everybody says it is impracticable. The work of the morrow will largely consist of the impossible of to-day. If this adds to the difficulty, it also adds to the fun.

When we arrived at the conclusion that the introduction of the principle of agricultural co-operation was a vital necessity, the first practical question which had to be decided was how the industrial army, which was to do battle for Ireland's position in the world market, should be organised and disciplined for the task. It is evident that before a body of men who have never worked together can form a successful commercial combination, they must be provided with a constitution and set of rules and regulations for the conduct of their business. These must be so skilfully contrived that they will harmonise all the interests involved. And when an arrangement has been come to which is, not only in fact but also obviously, equitable, it remains as part of the process of organisation to teach the participants in the new project the meaning, and to imbue them with the spirit, of the

joint enterprise into which they have been persuaded to
enter with perhaps no very clear understanding of all
that is involved.   There were in Ireland no precedents
to guide us and no examples to follow, but the co-
operative movement in England appeared to furnish most
of the principles involved and a perfect machinery for
their application.*   So Lord Monteagle and Mr. R. A.
Anderson, my first two associates in the New Movement,
joined me as regular attendants at the annual Co-operative
congresses.   We were assiduous seekers after information at the head-quarters of the Co-operative Union in
Manchester.   We had the good fortune to fall in with
Vansittart Neale, and Tom Hughes, both of whom have
passed away, and with Mr. Holyoake, the venerable historian of the co-operative movement, all of whom took
a keen interest in the younger movement of the sister
isle.   Mr. J. C. Gray, who succeeded Mr. Vansittart
Neale as the General Secretary of the Co-operative
Union, gave us invaluable help and continues to do so
to this day.   The leaders of the English movement

* The story of the conversion of some of the tenants on the
Vandeleur estate into a co-operative community in 1831 by Mr. E. T.
Craig, a Scotchman who took up the agency of the property, told in
the *History of Ralahine* (London, Trübner & Co., 1893) is worth
reading.   The experiment, most hopeful as far as it went, was only two
years in existence when the landlord gambled away his property at
cards in a Dublin club and the Utopia was sold up.   But in the
co-operative world Mr. Craig, who died as recently as 1894, is revered
as the author of the most advanced experiment in the realisation of
co-operative ideals.   The economic significance of the narrative is
obviously not important, and I doubt whether joint ownership of land,
except for the purpose of common grazing, is a practical ideal.   The
ready response, however, of the Irish peasants to Mr. Craig's enthusiasm
and the way in which they took up the idea form an interesting study
of the Irish character.

sympathised with our efforts. The Union paid us the compliment of constituting our first converts its Irish Section. Liberal support was given out of the central English funds towards the cost of the missionary work which was to spread co-operative light in the sister isle. We can never forget the generosity of the workingmen in England in giving their aid to the Irish farmers, especially when it is remembered that they had no sanguine anticipations for the success of our efforts and no prospect of advantages to themselves if we did succeed.

It must be admitted that the outlook was not altogether rosy. Agricultural co-operation had never succeeded in England, where it seemed to be accepted as one of the disappointing limitations of the co-operative movement that it did not apply to rural communities in these islands. There were also in Ireland the peculiar difficulties arising from ceaseless political and agrarian agitation. It was naturally asked—did Irish farmers possess the qualities out of which co-operators are made? Had they commercial experience or business education? Had they business capacity? Would they display that confidence in each other which is essential to successful association, or indeed that confidence in themselves without which there can be no business enterprise? Could they ever be induced to form themselves into societies, and to adopt, and loyally adhere to those rules and regulations by which alone equitable distribution of the responsibility and profit among the participants in the joint undertaking can be assured, and harmony and successful working be rendered possible? Then, our best-informed Irish critics assured us that voluntary association for humdrum business purposes, devoid of some religious or political incentive, was alien to the Celtic temperament and that we should wear ourselves out crying in the wilderness. We were told that Irishmen can conspire but cannot combine. Economists assured us that even if we succeeded in getting farmers to embark on the projected enterprises, financial disaster would be the inevitable result of our attempts to substitute in industrial undertakings, ever becoming more technical and requiring more and more commercial knowledge and experience, democratic management for one-man control.

On the other hand there were some favouring conditions, the importance of which our studies of the human problems already discussed will have made my readers realise.   Isolated, the Irish farmer is conservative, sceptical of innovations, a believer in routine and tradition.   In union with his fellows, he is progressive, open to ideas, and wonderfully keen at grasping the essential features of any new proposal for his advancement.   He was, then, himself eminently a subject for co-operative treatment, and his circumstances were equally so.   The smallness of his holding, the lack of capital, and the backwardness of his methods made him helpless in competition with his rivals abroad.   The process f organisation was also, to some extent, facilitated by the insight the people had been given by the Land League into the power of combination, and by the education they had received in the conduct of meetings. It was a great advantage that there was a machinery ready at hand for getting people together, and a procedure fully understood for giving expression to the sense of the meeting. On the other hand, the domination of a powerful central body, which was held to be essential to the success of the political and agrarian movement, had exercised an influence which added enormously to the difficulty of getting the people to act on their own initiative.

Though the economic conditions of the Irish farmer clearly indicated a need for the application of co-operative effort to all branches of his industry, it was necessary at the beginning to embrace a more limited aim. It happened at the time we commenced our Irish work that one branch of farming, the dairying industry, presented features admirably adapted to our methods. This industry was, so to speak, ripe for its industrial development, for its change from a home to a factory industry. New machinery, costly but highly efficient, had enabled the factory product, notably that of Denmark and Sweden, to compete successfully with the home-made article, both in quality and cost of production. Here, it will be observed, was an opportunity for an experiment in co-operative production, under modern industrial conditions, which would put the associative qualities of the Irish farmer to a test which the British artisan had not stood quite as well as the founders of the co-operative movement had anticipated. To add to the interest of the situation, capitalists had seized upon

the material advantages which the abundant supply of
Irish milk afforded, and the green pastures of the
" Golden Vein " were studded with snow white
creameries which proclaimed the transfer of this
great Irish industry from the tiller of the soil to the man
of commerce. The new-comers secured the milk of the
district by giving the farmer much more for his milk than
it was worth to him, so long as he pursued the old
methods of home manufacture. This induced farmers to
go out of the butter-making business. After a while the
price was reduced, and the proprietor, finding it necessary to give the suppliers only what they could make
out of their milk without his modern equipment, realised
profits altogether out of proportion to his share of the
capital embarked or the labour involved in the production
of the butter.

The economic position was ideal for our purpose, and
we had no difficulty in explaining it to the farmers
themselves. The social problem was the real difficulty.
To all suggestions of co-operative action they at first
opposed a hopeless *non possumus*. Their objections
may be summed up thus :—They had never combined for
any business purpose. How could they trust the Committee they were asked to elect from amongst themselves to expend their money and conduct their business ?
It was all very well for the proprietor with his ample
capital, free hand, and business experience, to work
with complicated machinery and to consign his butter
out of the reach of the local butter buyer, and to save

the waste and delay of the local butter market. But
they knew nothing of the business and would only make
fools of themselves. The promoters—they were not
putting anything into the scheme—how much did they
intend to take out?*

There was nothing in this attitude of mind which we
had not fully anticipated. We were confident that, as we
were on sound economic ground, no matter what difficulties might confront us it was only a question of time
for the attainment of our ends. All that was required
was that we should keep pegging away. My own
experience was not encouraging at first. I was, and am,
a poor speaker, and in Ireland a man who cannot express
his thoughts with facility, whether he has got them or
not, accentuates the difficulties under which a prophet
labours in his own country. I made up for my deficiencies in the first essential of Irish public life by
engaging a very eloquent political speaker, the late Mr.
Mulhallen Marum, M.P., to stump the country. He
gave to the propaganda a relish which my prosaic
economics altogether lacked. The nationalist band
sometimes came out to meet him. We all know the
efficiency of the drum in politics and religion, but it
seemed to me a little out of place in economics. However, he created an excellent impression, but unhappily

* The late Canon Bagot had done good service in explaining the
value of the new machinery; but unhappily the vital importance of
co-operative organisation was not then understood. He formed some
joint stock companies with the result that, having no co-operative
spirit to offset their commercial inexperience, they all proved, instead
of co-operative successes, competitive failures. This fact added to our
early difficulties.

he died of heart disease before he had attended more than three or four meetings. This was a severe blow to us, and we toiled away under some temporary discouragement. My own diary records attendance at fifty meetings before a single society had resulted therefrom. It was weary work for a long time. These gatherings were miserable affairs compared with those which greeted our political speakers. On one occasion the agricultural community was represented by the Dispensary Doctor, the Schoolmaster, and the Sergeant of Police. Sometimes, in spite of copious advertising of the meeting, the prosaic nature of the objects had got abroad, and nobody met.

Mr. Anderson, who sometimes accompanied me and sometimes went his rounds alone, had similar experiences. I may quote a passage from some of his reminiscences, recently published in the *Irish Homestead*, the organ of the co-operative movement in Ireland.

It was hard and thankless work. There was the apathy of the people and the active opposition of the Press and the politicians. It would be hard to say now whether the abuse of the Conservative *Cork Constitution* or that of the Nationalist *Eagle*, of Skibbereen, was the louder. We were " killing the calves," we were " forcing the young women to emigrate," we were " destroying the industry." Mr. Plunkett was described as a " monster in human shape," and was adjured to " cease his hellish work." I was described as his " Man Friday " and as " Roughrider Anderson." Once, when I thought I had planted a Creamery within the precincts of the town of Rathkeale, my co-operative apple-cart was upset by a local solicitor who, having elicited the fact that our movement recognised neither political nor religious differences—that the Unionist-Protestant cow was as dear to us as her Nationalist-Catholic sister—gravely informed me that our programme would not suit Rathkeale. "Rathkeale," said he, pompously, "is a Nationalist town—Nationalist to the backbone—and every pound of butter made in this Creamery must be made on Nationalist principles, or it shan't be made at all." This sentiment was applauded loudly, and the proceedings terminated.

On another occasion a similar project was abandoned because the flow of water to the disused mill which it was proposed to convert into a creamery, passed through a conduit lined with cement originally purchased from a man who now occupied a farm from which another had been evicted. To some minds these little complications would have spelled failure. To my associates they but accentuated the need for the movement which they had so laboriously thought out, and the very nature of the difficulties confirmed them in their belief that the economic doctrine they were preaching was adapted to meet the requirements of the case. And so the event proved.

In the year 1894 the movement had gathered volume to such an extent—although the societies then numbered but one for every twenty that are in existence to-day— that it became beyond the power of a few individuals to direct its further progress. In April of that year a meeting was held in Dublin to inaugurate the Irish Agricultural Organisation Society, Ltd. (now commonly known as the I.A.O.S.), which was to be the analogue

of the Co-operative Union in England. In the first
instance it was to consist of philanthropic persons, but
its constitution provided for the inclusion in its membership of the societies which had already been created
and those which it would itself create as time went on.
It had, and has to-day, a thoroughly representative
Committee. I was elected the first President, a position
which I held until I entered official life, when Lord
Monteagle, a practical philanthropist if ever there
was one, became my successor. Father Finlay, who
joined the movement in 1892, and who has devoted
the extraordinary influence which he possesses over the
rural population of Ireland to the dissemination of our
economic principles, became Vice-President. Both he
and Lord Monteagle have been annually re-elected ever
since.

The growth of the movement in the last nine years
under the fostering care of the I.A.O.S. is highly satis-
factory. By the autumn of this year (1903) considerably
over eight hundred societies had been established, and
the number is ever growing; of these 360 were dairy,
and 140 agricultural societies, nearly 200 agricultural
banks, 50 home industries societies, 40 poultry societies,
while there were 40 others with miscellaneous objects.
The membership may be estimated—I am writing towards the end of the Society's statistical year—at about
80,000, representing some 400,000 persons. The combined trade turnover of these societies during the present
year will reach approximately £2,000,000, a figure the

meaning of which can only be appreciated when it is remembered that the great majority of the associated farmers are in so small a way of business that in England they would hardly be classed as farmers at all.

These societies consist, as has been explained, of groups of farmers who have been taught by organisers that certain branches of their business can be more profitably conducted in association than by individuals acting separately. The principle of agricultural co-operation with its economic advantages will, as time goes on, be further extended by the combined action of societies. With this end in view federations are constantly being formed with a constitution similar to that of the societies, the only difference being that the members of the federation are not individuals but societies, the government of the central body being carried on by delegates from its constituent associations. The two largest of these federations, one for the sale of butter, and another for the combined purchase by societies of their agricultural requirements, have been working successfully for several years. Federations, too, are being formed, as societies find that their business can be conducted more economically, for example, in dairying by centralising the manufacture of butter, or in the egg export trade by the alliance of many districts to enable large contracts to be undertaken. In the near future a further development of federation will be required to complete a scheme now under consideration for the mutual insurance of live stock. Such a scheme

o

involves the existence of two prime conditions, a local
organisation for the purpose of effective supervision, and
the spreading of the risk over a large area.

In all such enterprises and economic changes the
Organisation Society is either the initiator, or is called
in for advice, and its continued existence in a purely
advisory capacity as a link between the societies where
concerted action is required, will be necessary even
when the organisation of farmers into societies is
completed. The economic life of rural communities is in
continual need of adjustment. Now it is an invention
like a steam separator which revolutionises an industry.
At another time the crisis created by a change in the
tariff of a foreign country forces the producer either to
find a new outlet for his wares, or to abandon a hitherto
profitable employment. A striking instance of the value
of organisation and connection with a central advisory
body occurred in 1887, when swine fever broke out in
Denmark, and the exports of live swine fell from
230,000 in one year to 16,000 in the next. The organisation of the farmers, however, enabled them easily to con-
sult together how best to meet the emergency, and their
decision to start co-operative bacon-curing factories was
the foundation of their present great export trade in
manufactured bacon.

I must not overburden with details a narrative intended for readers to whom I merely wish to give a
deeper and wider understanding of Irish life than most
of them probably possess. But there is just one form of

agricultural co-operation to which I can usefully devote a few paragraphs, because it throws much light upon the associative qualities of the people and also upon the educational and social value of the movement. I refer to the Agricultural Banks, more properly called Credit Associations, which have been organised upon the Raiffeisen system. Before the Irish Agricultural Organisation Society was formed we had read of these institutions, and of the marvellously beneficial effect they had produced upon the most depressed rural communities abroad. But only in the last few years have we fully realised that they are even more required and are likely to do more good in Ireland than in any other country; for on the psychological side of our work we formerly but dimly saw things which we now see clearly.

The exact purpose of these organisations is to create credit as a means of introducing capital into the agricultural industry. They perform the apparent miracle of giving solvency to a community composed almost entirely of insolvent individuals. The constitution of these bodies, which can, of course, be described only in broad outline here, is somewhat startling. They have no subscribed capital, but every member is liable for the entire debts of the association. Consequently the association takes good care to admit men of approved character and capacity only. It starts by borrowing a sum of money on the joint and several security of its members. A member wishing to borrow from the association is not required to give tangible security, but must bring two sureties. He fills up an application form which states, among other things, what he wants the money for. The rules provide—and this is the salient feature of the system—that a loan shall be made for a productive purpose only, that is, a purpose which, in the judgment of the other members of the association as represented by a committee democratically elected from among themselves, will enable the borrower to repay the loan out of the results of the use made of the money lent.

Raiffeisen held, and our experience in Ireland has fully confirmed his opinion, that in the poorest communities there is a perfectly safe basis of security in the honesty and industry of its members. This security is not valuable to the ordinary commercial lender, such as the local joint stock bank. Even if such lenders had the intimate knowledge possessed by the committee of one of these associations as to the character and capacity of the borrower, they would not be able to satisfy themselves that the loan was required for a really productive purpose, nor would they be able to see that it was properly applied to the stipulated object. One of the rules of the co-operative banks provides for the expulsion of a member who does not apply the money to the agreed productive purpose. But although these " Banks " are almost invariably situated in very poor districts, there has been no necessity to put this rule in force in a single instance. Social influences seem to be quite sufficient to secure obedience to the association's laws.

Another advantage conferred by the association is that the term for which money is advanced is a matter of agreement between the borrower and the bank. The hard and fast term of three months which prevails in Ireland for small loans is unsuited to the requirements of the agricultural industry— as for instance, when a man borrows money to sow a crop, and has to repay it before harvest. The society borrows at four or five per cent. and lends at five or six per cent. In some cases the Congested Districts Board or the Department of Agriculture have made loans to these banks at three per cent. This enables the societies to lend at the popular rate of one penny for the use of one pound for a month. The expenses of administration are very small. As the credit of these associations develops, they will become a depository for the savings of the community, to the great advantage of both lender and borrower. The latter generally makes an enormous profit out of these loans, which have accordingly gained the name of 'the lucky money,' and we find, in practice, that he always repays the association and almost invariably with punctuality.

The sketch I have given of the agricultural banks will, perhaps, be sufficient to show what an immense educational and economic benefit they are likely to confer when they are widely extended throughout Ireland, as I hope they will be in the near future. Under this system, which, to quote the report of the Indian Famine Commission, 1901, 'separates the working bees from the

drones,' the industrious men of the community who had
no clear idea before of the meaning or functions of
capital or credit, and who were generally unable to get
capital into their industry except at exorbitant rates of
interest and upon unsuitable terms, are now able to
get, not always, indeed, all the money they want, but
all the money they can well employ for the improvement
of their industry. There is no fear of rash investment
of capital in enterprises believed to be, but not in reality
productive—the committee take good care of that. The
whole community is taught the difference between borrowing to spend and borrowing to make. You have the
collective wisdom of the best men in the association
helping the borrower to decide whether he ought to
borrow or not, and then assisting him, if only from
motives of self-interest, to make the loan fulfil the
purpose for which it was made. I was delighted to find
when I was making an enquiry into the working of the
system that, whereas the debt-laden peasants had formerly concealed their indebtedness, of which they were
ashamed, those who were in debt to the new banks were
proud of the fact, as it was the best testimonial to their
character for honesty and industry.*

---

* It should be noted that this form of association for credit
purposes, owing to its peculiar constitution, applies only to a grade of
the community whose members all live on about the same scale and
that a fairly low one. It is obvious that unlimited liability would lose
its efficacy in developing the sense of responsibility if some members
of the association were so substantial that its creditors would make them
primarily responsible in the event of failure. The fact, however, that
the scheme has worked with unvarying success among the poorest of
the poor, and the most Irish of the Irish, renders it as good an illustra-

One other sphere of activity worked by the co-operative associations needs a passing notice. The desire that, together with material amelioration, there should be a corresponding intellectual advancement and a greater beauty in life has prompted many of the farmers' societies to use their organisation for higher ends. A considerable number of them have started Village Libraries, and by an admirable selection of books have brought to their members, not only the means of educating themselves in the more difficult technical problems of their industry, but also a means of access to that enchanted world of Irish thought which inspires the Gaelic Revival to which I have already referred. Social gatherings of every kind, dances, lectures, concerts, and such like entertainments, which have the two-fold effect of brightening rural life and increasing the attachment of the members to their society, are becoming a common feature in the movement, and this more human aspect has attracted to it the attention of many who do not understand its economic side. We have gratifying evidence from many of the clergy that the movement thus developed has kept at home young people who would otherwise have fled from the continued hardship and intellectual emptiness of rural life at home.

tion as can be found of what may be done by sympathetic and intelligent treatment of Irish economic problems. Mr. Henry W. Wolff, the foremost authority on People's Banks in these islands, and Mr. R. A. Yerburgh, M.P., a generous subscriber to the Irish Agricultural Organisation Society, have taken great interest in this part of the movement and have rendered much assistance.

These results are in no small measure due to the zeal and devotion of the governing body and staff of the I.A.O.S. The general policy of the society is guided by a committee of twenty-four members, one-half of whom are elected by the individual subscribers and the other half by the affiliated societies. It is representative in the best sense and influential accordingly. The success of the Committee is no doubt mainly due to the wisdom which they have displayed in the selection of the staff. In the most important post, that of Secretary, they have kept on my chief fellow-worker in the early struggle, Mr. R. A. Anderson, who has devoted himself to the cause with all the energy of a nature at once enthusiastic, unselfish, and practical, and who has succeeded in inspiring his staff of organisers and experts with his own spirit. Among these, two deserve special mention, Mr. George W. Russell, one of the Assistant Secretaries, who has, under the *nom de plume* " A. E.," attained fame for a poetry of rare distinction of thought and diction, and Mr. P. J. Hannon, the other Assistant Secretary, who has proved himself a splendid propagandist. Each of these gentlemen has brought to the movement a zeal and ability which could only come of a devotion to high ideals of patriotism, curiously combined with a shrewd practical instinct for carrying on varied and responsible business undertakings.

With the growing work the staff has been repeatedly augmented to enable the central society to keep pace with the demand made by groups of farmers to be

initiated into the principles of co-operative organisation
and the details of its application to the particular
branches of farming carried on in their several districts.
At the same time the societies which have been established need, during their earlier years, and with each extension of their operations, constant advice and supervision. Hence skilled organisers have to be kept to form
co-operative dairy societies, inspect creameries, and give
technical advice upon the manufacture and sale of butter,
the care of machinery, the adequacy of the water supply,
the drainage system, and many similar technical questions. Others are employed to start poultry societies,
which when organised have still to be instructed by a
Danish expert in the proper method of packing, selecting,
and grading the eggs for export. In tillage districts
there is a constant demand for organisers of purely
agricultural societies, which aim at the joint purchase of
seeds and manures, of implements and other farm
requisites, and at the better disposal of produce; while
the growing importance of an improved system of agricultural credit keeps four organisers of agricultural
banks constantly at work. Home industries, bee-keeping,
and horticulture, may be added to the objects for which
societies have been formed and which require separate
expert organisers. And in addition to all this work,
the central association has found it necessary to keep a
staff of accountants, versed in the principles of co-
operative organisation, to instruct these miscellaneous
societies in simple and efficient systems of book-keeping,

and in the general principles of conducting business. To complete the description of the propagandist activities of the central body, there is a ceaseless flow of leaflets and circulars containing advice and direction to bodies of farmers who, for the first time in their lives, have combined for business purposes; while a little weekly paper, the *Irish Homestead*, acts as the organ of the movement, promotes the exchange of ideas between societies scattered throughout the country, furnishes useful information upon all matters connected with their business operations, and keeps constantly before the associated farmers the economic principles which must be observed, and, above all, the spirit in which the work must be approached, if the movement is to fulfil its mission.*

One of the difficulties incidental to a movement of this kind, which, for the reasons already set forth, had to be rapidly and widely extended, was the enormous cost to its supporters. It is needless to say that such a staff as I have described could not be kept continuously travelling by rail and road for so many years without the provision of a large fund. These officers must obviously be men with exceptional qualifications, if they are not only to impress the thought of their agricultural

* Those who wish to go more fully into the details of the co-operative agricultural movement in Ireland should write to the Secretary Irish Agricultural Organisation Society, 22 Lincoln-place, Dublin. The publications of the Society are somewhat voluminous, and the inquirer should intimate any particular branches of the subject in which he is especially interested. Those wishing to keep *au courant* with the further development of the movement would do well to take in the *Irish Homestead*, post free 6s. 6d. per annum.

audiences, but also to move them to action, and to sustain the newly organised societies through the initial difficulties of their unfamiliar enterprise. Such men are not to be found idle, and if they preach this gospel, they are entitled to live by it. They are not by any means overpaid, but their salaries in the aggregate amount to a large annual sum. Before the creation of the Department of Agriculture and Technical Instruction in 1900 large sums were spent by the I.A.O.S. not only in its proper work of organisation, but also in giving technical instruction, which was found to be essential to commercial success. When the Society was relieved of this educational work many of its supporters withdrew their subscriptions under the impression that there was now no longer any need for its continued existence. But so far from the Society's usefulness having ceased, it has now become more important than ever that the doctrine of organised self-help, which must be the foundation of any sound Irish economic policy, should be insisted upon and put into practical operation as widely as possible. All those who are devoting their lives to the firm establishment of this self-help movement among the chief wealth-producers of the country are agreed that no better educational work can be done at the moment than that which is bringing about so salutary a change in the economic attitude of the Irish mind.

It is not to be wondered at that the greater part of the necessary funds should have been drawn from a very limited circle of public-spirited men capable of grasping the significance of a movement the practical effect of which would appear to be permanent only to those who had a deep insight into Irish problems.* The difficulty of a successful appeal to a wider public has been the impossibility of giving in brief form an adequate explanation, such as that which it is hoped these pages will afford, of the part the movement was to play in Irish life. We were asked whether our scheme was business or philanthropy. If philanthropy, it would probably do more harm than good. If business, why was it not self-supporting? I remember hearing the movement ridiculed in the House of Commons by a prominent Irish member on the ground that the accounts of the I.A.O.S. showed that £20,000 (£40,000 would be nearer the mark now) had been put into the 'business,' and that this large capital had been entirely lost! When we proved that agricultural co-operation brought a large profit to the members of the societies we formed, it was suggested that a small part of this profit would give us all we required for our organising work. So it will in time, but if instead of merely refusing financial assistance to our converts, we were, on the other hand, to demand it from them, we certainly should not lessen the difficulty of launching our movement among the farmers of Ireland. Some of our critics denounced the expenditure of so much money for which, in their opinion, there was nothing to

---

* The chief donors belong to the class of philanthropists who do not care to advertise their beneficence. I, therefore, respect their wishes and withhold their names.

show, and said that the time had come to stop this 'spoon-feeding.' When those for whose exclusive benefit the costly work had been undertaken learned that all we had to offer was the cold advice that they should help themselves, they not infrequently raised a wholly different objection to our economic doctrine. Spoonfeeding they might have tolerated, but there was nothing in the spoon!

The movement has survived all these criticisms. The lack of moral and of financial support which retarded its progress in the early years, has been so far surmounted. The movement may now, I think, appeal for further help as one that has justified its existence. The opinion that it has done so is not held only by those who are engaged in promoting it, nor by Irish observers alone. The efforts of the Irish farmers so to reorganise their industry that they may hopefully approach the solution of the problems of rural life are being watched by economists and administrators abroad. Enquirers have come to Ireland during the last two years from Germany, France, Canada, the United States, India, South Africa, Cyprus and the West Indies, having been drawn here by the desire to understand the combination of economic and human reform. It was not alone the economic advantages of the movement which interested them, but the way in which the organisation at the same time acted upon the character and awoke those forces of self-help and comradeship in which lies the surety of any enduring national prosperity. A native governor from a famine district in the Madras Presidency, who, perhaps, better than any one realised the importance of these human factors, because the lethargy of his own people had forced it on his notice, said, when he was referred to the Department of Agriculture and Technical Instruction for information, "Oh, don't speak to me about Government Departments. They are the same all over the world. I come here to learn what the Irish people are doing to help themselves and how you awaken the will and the initiative." I hope to show later that State assistance properly applied is not necessarily demoralising but very much the reverse. It is consoling, too, to our national pride, long wounded by contemptuous references to our industrial incapacity as compared with our neighbours, to find that our latest efforts are regarded by them as worthy of imitation. From the other side of the Channel no less than five County Councils have sent deputations of farmers to Ireland to study the progress of the movement, and already an English Organisation Society, expressly modelled upon its Irish namesake, has been established and is endeavouring to carry out the same work.

It is not surprising that the facts which I have cited should be interesting to the honest inquirer. A summary of actual achievement will show that this movement has spread all over Ireland, that its principle of organised self-help has been universally accepted, and that nothing but time and the necessary funds are required by its promoters to give it, within the range of its applicability, general effect. It is no exaggeration to say that there has been set in motion and carried beyond the experimental stage a revolution in agricultural methods which will enable our farmers to compete with their rivals abroad, both in production and in distribution, under far more favourable conditions than before. Alike in its material and in its moral achievements this movement has provided an effective means whereby the peasant proprietary about to be created will be able to face and solve the vital problems before it, problems for which no improvement in land tenure, no rent reductions actual or prospective, could otherwise provide an adequate solution. Furthermore, nothing could be more evident to any close observer of Irish life than the fact that had it not been for the new spirit which the workers in this movement, mostly humble unknown men, had generated, the attitude of the Irish democracy towards England's latest concession to Ireland would have been very different from what it is. In the last dozen years hundreds and thousands of meetings have been held to discuss matters of business importance to our rural communities. At these meetings landlord and tenant-farmer have often met each other for the first time on a footing of friendly equality, as fellow-members of co-operative societies. It is significant that all through the negotiations which culminated in the Dunraven Treaty, landlords who had come into the life of the people in connection with the co-operative movement took a prominent part in favour of conciliation.

I would further give it as my opinion, whatever it may

be worth, that the movement has exercised a profound influence in those departments of our national life where, as I have shown in previous chapters, new forces must be not only recognised but accepted as essential to national well-being, if we are to cherish what is good and free ourselves from what is bad in the historical evolution of our national life. In the domain of politics it is hard to estimate even the political value of the exclusion of politics from deliberations and activities where they have no proper place. In our religious life, where intolerance has perpetuated anti-industrial tendencies, the new movement is seen to be bringing together for business purposes men who had previously no dealings with each other, but who have now learned that the doctrine of self-help by mutual help involves no danger to faith and no sacrifice of hope, while it engenders a genuinely Christian interpretation of charity.*

I cannot conclude the story of this movement without paying a brief tribute of respect and gratitude to those true patriots who have borne the daily burden of the

---

* I recall an occasion when the Vice-President of the I.A.O.S. (a Nationalist in politics and a Jesuit priest), who has been ever ready to lend a hand as volunteer organiser when the prior claims of his religious and educational duties allowed, found himself before an audience which he was informed, when he came to the meeting, consisted mainly of Orangemen. He began his address by referring to the new and somewhat strange environment into which he had drifted. He did not, however, see why this circumstance should lead to any misunderstanding between himself and his audience. He had never been able to understand what a battle fought upon a famous Irish river two centuries ago had got to do with the practical issues of to-day which he had come to discuss. The dispute in question was, after all, between a Scotchman and a Dutchman, and if it had not yet been decided, they might be left to settle it themselves—that is if too great a gulf did not separate them!

work. I hope the picture I have given of their aims and achievements will lead to a just appreciation of their services to their country. By these men and women applause or even recognition was not expected or desired : they knew that it was to those who had the advantages of leisure, and what the world calls position, that the credit for their work would be given. But it is of national importance that altruistic service should be understood and given freedom of expansion. I have, therefore, presented as faithfully as I could the origin and development of one of the least understood, but in my opinion, most fruitful movements which has ever been undertaken by a body of social and economic reformers. As Irish leaders they have preferred to remain obscure, conscious that the most damaging criticism which could be applied to their work would be that it depended on their own personal qualities or acts for its permanent utility. But most assuredly the real conquerors of the world are those who found upon human character their hopes of human progress.

P

CHAPTER VIII.

THE RECESS COMMITTEE.

The new movement, six years after its initiation, had succeeded beyond the most sanguine expectations of its promoters. All over the country the idea of self-help was taking firm hold of the imagination of the people. Co-operation had got, so to speak, into the air to such an extent that, whereas at the beginning, as I well remember, our chief difficulty had been to popularise a principle to which one section of the community was strongly opposed, and in which no section believed, it was now no longer necessary to explain or support the theory, but only to show how it could be advantageously applied to some branch of the farmer's industry. It was not, strange to say, the economic advantage which had chiefly appealed to the quick intelligence of the Irish farmer, but rather the novel sensation that he was thinking for himself, and that while improving his own condition he was working for others. This attitude was essential to the success of the movement, because had it not been for a vein of altruism, the "strong" farmers would have held aloof, and the small men would have been discouraged by the abstention of the better-off and presumably more enlightened of their class.

Perhaps, too, we owed something to the recognition
on the part of the working farmers of Ireland that they
were showing a capacity to grasp an idea which had so
far failed to penetrate the bucolic intelligence of the
predominant partner. Whatever the causes to which the
success of the movement was attributable, those who
were responsible for its promotion felt in the year 1895
that it had reached a stage in its development when it
was but a question of time to complete the projected
revolution in the farming industry, the substitution of
combined for isolated methods of production and distribution. It was then further brought home to them
that the principle of self-help was destined to obtain
general acceptance in rural Ireland, and that the time
had come when a sound system of State aid to agriculture
might be fruitfully grafted on to this native growth of
local effort and self-reliance.

From time to time our public men had included in the
list of Irish grievances the fact that England enjoyed a
Board of Agriculture while Ireland had no similar institution. As a matter of fact a mere replica of the English
Board would not have fulfilled a tithe of the objects we
had in view. That much at least we knew, but beyond
that our information was vague. What, having regard
to Irish rural conditions, should be the character and
constitution of any Department called into being to
administer the aid required? Here indeed was a vital
and difficult problem. Even those of us who had given
the closest thought to the matter did not know exactly

what was wanted ; nor, if we had known our own minds, could we have formulated our demand in such a way as to have obtained a backing from representative public bodies, associations, and individuals sufficient to secure its concession. Instead, therefore, of agitating in the conventional manner we determined to try to direct the best thought of the country to the problem in hand, with a view to satisfying the Government, and also ourselves, as to what was wanted. We had confidence that a demand presented to Parliament, based upon calm and deliberate debate among the most competent of Irishmen, would be conceded. The story of this agitation, its initiation, its conduct, and its final success will, I am sure, be of interest to all who feel any concern for the welfare of Ireland.

I have accepted the common characterisation of the Irish as a leader-following people. When we come to analyse the human material out of which a strong national life may be constructed, we find that there are in Ireland—in this connection I exclude the influence of the clergy, with which I have dealt specifically in another chapter—two elements of leadership, the political and the industrial. The political leaders are seen to enjoy an influence over the great majority of the people which is probably as powerful as that of any political leaders in ancient or modern times; but as a class they certainly do not take a prominent, or even an active part in business life. This fact is not introduced with any controversial purpose, and I freely acknowledge can be interpreted in a sense altogether creditable to the Nationalist members. The other element of leadership contains all that is prominent in industrial and commercial life, and few countries could produce better types of such leaders than can be found in the northern capital of the country. But, unhappily, these men are debarred from all influence upon the thought and action of the great majority of the people, who are under the domination of the political leaders. This is one of the strange anomalies of Irish life to which I have already referred. Its recognition, and the desire to utilise the knowledge of business men as well as politicians, took practical effect in the formation of the Recess Committee.

The idea underlying this project was the combination of these two forces of leadership—the force with political influence and that of proved industrial and commercial capacity—in order to concentrate public opinion, which was believed to be inclining in this direction, on the material needs of the country. The General Election of 1895 had, by universal admission, postponed, for some years at any rate, any possibility of Home Rule, and the cessation of the bitter feelings aroused when Home Rule seemed imminent provided the opportunity for an appeal to the Irish people in behalf of the views which I have adumbrated. The appeal took the form of a letter, dated August 27th, 1895, by the author to the Irish Press, under the quite sincere, if somewhat grandiloquent, title, "A proposal affecting the general welfare of Ireland."

The letter set out the general scope and purpose of the scheme. After a confession of the writer's continued opposition to Home Rule, the admission was made that if the average Irish elector, who is more intelligent than the average British elector, were also as prosperous, as industrious, and as well educated, his continued demand, in the proper constitutional way, for Home Rule would very likely result in the experiment being one day tried. On the other hand, the opinion was expressed that if the material conditions of the great body of our countrymen were advanced, if they were encouraged in industrial enterprise, and were provided with practical education in proportion to their natural intelligence, they would see that a political development on lines similar to those adopted in England was, considering the necessary relations between the two countries, best for Ireland; and then they would cease to desire what is ordinarily understood as Home Rule. A basis for united action between politicians on both sides of the Irish controversy was then suggested. Finding ourselves still opposed upon the main question, but all anxious to promote the welfare of the country, and confident that, as this was advanced, our respective policies would be confirmed, it would appear, it was suggested, to be alike good patriotism and good policy to work for the material and social advancement of the people. Why then, it was asked, should any Irishman hesitate to enter at once upon that united action between men of both parties which alone, under existing conditions, could enable either party to do any real and lasting good to the country?

The letter proceeded to indicate economic legislation which, though sorely needed by Ireland, was hopelessly unattainable unless it could be removed from the region of controversy. The *modus co-operandi* suggested was as follows:—a committee sitting in the Parliamentary recess, whence it came to be known as the Recess Committee, was to be formed, consisting in the first instance, of Irish Members of Parliament nominated by the leaders of the different sections. These nominees were to invite to join them any Irishmen whose capacity, knowledge, or experience might be of service to the Committee, irrespective of the political party or religious persuasion to which they might belong. The day had come, the letter went on to say, when "we Unionists, without abating one jot of our Unionism, and National-ists, without abating one jot of their Nationalism, can each show our faith in the cause for which we have fought so bitterly and so long, by sinking our party differences for our country's good, and leaving our respective policies for the justification of time."

Needless to say, few were sanguine enough to hope that such a committee would ever be brought together. If that were accomplished some prophesied that its members would but emulate the fame of the Kilkenny cats. A severe blow was dealt to the project at the outset by the refusal of Mr. Justin McCarthy, who then spoke for the largest section of the Nationalist representatives, to have anything to do with it. His reply to the letter must be given in full :—

My dear Mr. Plunkett,

I am sure I need not say that any effort to promote the general welfare of Ireland has my fullest sympathy.   I readily acknowledge and entirely believe in the sincerity and good purpose of your effort, but I cannot see my way to associate myself with it.   Your frank avowal in your letter of August 27th is the expression of a belief that if your policy could be successfully carried out the Irish people " would cease to desire Home Rule."   Now, I do not believe that anything in the way of material improvement conferred by the Parliament at Westminster, or by Dublin Castle, could extinguish the national desire for Home Rule.   Still, I do not feel that I could possibly take part in any organisation which had for its object the seeking of a substitute for that which I believe to be Ireland's greatest need—Home Rule.

Yours very truly,

Justin McCarthy.

73, Eaton-terrace, S.W., October 22nd, 1895.

I had not much hope that I could influence Mr. McCarthy's decision ; but it was so serious an obstacle to further action that I made one more appeal. I wrote to my respected and courteous correspondent, pointing out the misconception of my proposal, which had arisen from the use made of the six words quoted by him, which were hardly intelligible without the context. I asked him to reconsider his refusal to join in the proposal for promoting the material improvement of our country, on account of a contingency which he confidently declared could not arise. But in those days economic seed fell upon stony political ground.

The position was rendered still more difficult by the action of Colonel Saunderson, the leader of the Irish Unionist party, who wrote to the newspapers declaring that he would not sit on a Committee with Mr. John Redmond. On the other hand, Mr. Redmond, speaking then for the " Independent " party, consisting of less than a dozen members, but containing some men who agreed with Mr. Field's admission in the House of Commons that "man cannot live on politics alone," joined the Committee and acted throughout in a manner which was broad, statesmanlike, conciliatory, and as generous as it was courageous. His letter of acceptance ran as follows :—

DEAR MR. PLUNKETT,

I received your letter, in which you ask me to co-operate with you in bringing together a small Committee of Members of Parliament to discuss certain measures to be proposed next Session for the benefit of Ireland. While I cannot take as sanguine a view as you do of the benefits likely to flow from such a proceeding, I am unwilling to take the responsibility of declining to aid in any effort to promote useful legislation for Ireland.

I will, under the circumstances, co-operate with you in bringing such a Committee as you suggest together.

Very truly yours,

J. E. REDMOND.

October 21st, 1895.

Before these decisions were officially announced the idea had " caught on." Public bodies throughout the country endorsed the scheme. The parliamentarians,

who formed the nucleus of the Committee, came together and invited prominent men from all quarters to
join them. A committee which, though informal and
self-appointed, might fairly claim to be representative
in every material respect, was thus constituted on the
lines laid down.

Truly, it was a strange council over which I had
the honour to preside. All shades of politics were there
—Lords Mayo and Monteagle, Mr. Dane and Sir
Thomas Lea (Tories and Liberal Unionist Peers and
Members of Parliament) sitting down beside Mr. John
Redmond and his parliamentary followers. It was found
possible, in framing proposals fraught with moral,
social, and educational results, to secure the cordial
agreement of the late Rev. Dr. Kane, Grand Master of
the Belfast Orangemen, and of the eminent Jesuit
educationist, Father Thomas Finlay, of the Royal
University. The O'Conor Don, the able Chairman of
the Financial Relations Commission, and Mr. John Ross,
M.P., now one of His Majesty's Judges, both Unionists,
were balanced by the Lord Mayor of Dublin, and Mr.
T. C. Harrington, M.P., who now occupies that post,
both Nationalists. The late Sir John Arnott fitly
represented the commercial enterprise of the South,
while such men as Mr. Thomas Sinclair, universally
regarded as one of the wisest of Irish public men,
Sir William Ewart, head of the leading linen concern in
the North, Sir Daniel Dixon, now Lord Mayor of
Belfast, Sir James Musgrave, Chairman of the Belfast

Harbour Board, and Mr. Thomas Andrews, a well-known flax-spinner and Chairman of the Belfast and County Down Railway, would be universally accepted as the highest authorities upon the needs of the business community which has made Ulster famous in the industrial world. Mr. T. P. Gill, besides undertaking investigation of the utmost value into State aid to agriculture in France and Denmark, acted as Hon. Secretary to the Committee, of which he was a member.

The story of our deliberations and ultimate conclusions cannot be set forth here except in the barest outline. We instituted an inquiry into the means by which the Government could best promote the development of our agricultural and industrial resources, and despatched commissioners to countries of Europe whose conditions and progress might afford some lessons for Ireland. Most of this work was done for us by the late eminent statistician, Mr. Michael Mulhall. Our funds did not admit of an inquiry in the United States or the Colonies. However, we obtained invaluable information as to the methods by which countries which were our chief rivals in agricultural and industrial production have been enabled to compete successfully with our producers even in our own markets. Our commissioners were instructed in each case to collect the facts necessary to enable us to differentiate between the parts played respectively by State aid and the efforts of the people themselves in producing these results. With this information before us, after long and earnest deliberation we came to a unanimous agreement upon the main facts of the situation with which we had to deal, and upon the recommendations for remedial legislation which we should make to the Government.

The substance of our recommendations was that a Department of Government should be specially created, with a minister directly responsible to Parliament at its head. The central body was to be assisted by a Consultative Council representative of the interests concerned. The Department was to be adequately endowed from the Imperial Treasury, and was to administer State aid to agriculture and industries in Ireland upon principles which were fully described. The proposal to amalgamate agriculture and industries under one Department was adopted largely on account of the opinion expressed by M. Tisserand, late Director-General of Agriculture in France, one of the highest authorities in Europe upon the administration of State aid to agriculture.* The creation of a new minister directly responsible to Parliament was considered a necessary provision. Ireland is governed by a number of Boards, all, with the exception of the Board of Works (which is really a branch of the Treasury), responsible to the Chief Secretary—practically a whole cabinet under one hat—who is supposed to be responsible for them to Parliament and to the Lord Lieutenant. The bearers of this burden are generally men of great ability. But no Chief Secretary could

* The memorandum which he kindly contributed to the Recess Committee was copied into the Annual Report of the United States Department of Agriculture for 1896.

possibly take under his wing yet another department
with the entirely new and important functions now to be
discharged. What these functions were to be need not
here be described, as the Department thus 'agitated' for
has now been three years at work and will form the
subject of the next two chapters.

On August 1st, 1896, less than a year from the issue
of the invitation to the political leaders, the Report was
forwarded to the Chief Secretary to the Lord Lieutenant for Ireland, with a covering letter, setting out the
considerations upon which the Committee relied for the
justification of its course of action. Attention was drawn
to the terms of the original proposal, its exceptional
nature and essential informality, the political conditions
which appeared to make it opportune, the spirit in which
it was responded to by those who were invited to join,
and the degree of public approval which had been
accorded to our action. We were able to claim for the
Committee that it was thoroughly representative of those
agricultural and industrial interests, North and South,
with which the Report was concerned.

There were two special features in the brief
history of this unique coming together of Irishmen which will strike any man familiar with the conditions of Irish public life. The first was the way in which
the business element, consisting of men already deeply
engaged in their various callings—and, indeed, selected
for that very reason—devoted time and labour to the
service of their country. Still more significant was the

fact that the political element on the Committee should have come to an absolutely unanimous agreement upon a policy which, though not intended to influence the trend of politics, was yet bound to have far-reaching consequences upon the political thought of the country, and upon the positions of parties and leaders. It was thought only fair to the Nationalist members of the Committee that every precaution should be taken to prevent their being placed in a false position. ' To avoid any possible misconception,' the covering letter ran, ' as to the attitude of those members of the Committee who are not supporters of the present Government, it is right here to state that, while under existing political conditions they agreed in recommending a certain course to the Government, they wish it to be understood that their political principles remain unaltered, and that, were it immediately possible, they would prefer that the suggested reforms should be preceded by the constitutional changes of which they are the well-known advocates.'

It is interesting to note that the Committee claimed favourable consideration for their proposals on the ground that they sought to act as ' a channel of communication between the Irish Government and Irish public opinion.'   Little interest, they pointed out, had been hitherto aroused in those economic problems for which the Report suggested some solution.   They expressed the hope that their action would do something to remedy this defect, especially in view of the importance which foreign Governments had found it necessary to attach to public opinion in working out their various systems of State aid to agriculture and industries. At the same time the Committee emphasied, in the covering letter, their reliance on individual and combined effort rather than on State aid. They were able to point out that, in asking for the latter, they had throughout attached the utmost importance to its being granted in such a manner as to evoke and supplement, and in no way be a substitute for self-help. If they appeared to give undue prominence to the capabilities of State initiation, it was to be remembered that they were dealing with economic conditions which had been artificially produced, and which, therefore, might require exceptional treatment of a temporary nature to bring about a permanent remedy.

I fear those most intimately connected with the above occurrences will regard this chapter as a very inadequate description of events so unprecedented and so full of hope for the future. My purpose is, however, to limit myself, in dealing with the past, to such details as are necessary to enable the reader to understand the present facts of Irish life, and to build upon them his own conclusions as to the most hopeful line of future development. I shall, therefore, pass rapidly in review the events which led to the fruition of the labours of the Recess Committee.

Public opinion in favour of the new proposals grew rapidly. Before the end of the year (1896) a deputation, representing all the leading agricultural and industrial interests of the country, waited upon the Irish Government, in order to press upon them the urgent need for the new department. The Lord Lieutenant, after describing the gathering as 'one of the most notable deputations which had ever come to lay its case before the Irish Government,' and noting the 'remarkable growth of public opinion' in favour of the policy they were advocating, expressed his heartfelt sympathy with the case which had been presented, and his earnest desire—which was well known—to proceed with legislation for the agricultural and industrial development of the country at the earliest moment. The demand made upon the Government was, argumentatively, already irresistible. But economic agitation of this kind takes time to acquire dynamic force. Mr. Gerald Balfour introduced a Bill the following year, but it had to be withdrawn to leave the way clear for the other great Irish measure which revolutionised local government. The unconventional agitation went on upon the original lines, appealing to that latent public opinion which we were striving to develop. In 1899 another Bill was introduced, and, owing to its masterly handling by the Chief Secretary in the House of Commons, ably seconded by the strong support given by Lord Cadogan, who was in the Cabinet, it became law.

I cannot conclude this chapter without a word upon the extraordinary misunderstanding of Mr. Gerald Balfour's policy to which the obscuring atmosphere sur-

rounding all Irish questions gave rise. In one respect
that policy was a new departure of the utmost importance. He proved himself ready to take a measure from
Ireland and carry it through, instead of insisting upon
a purely English scheme which he could call his own.
these pre-digested foods had already done much to
destroy our political digestion, and it was time we were
given something to grow, to cook, and to assimilate for
ourselves. It will be seen, too, in the next chapter, that
he had realised the potentiality for good of the new
forces in Irish life to which he gave play in his two great
linked Acts—one of them popularising local government, and the other creating a new Department which
was to bring the government and the people together
in an attempt to develop the resources of the country.
Yet his eminently sane and far-seeing policy was regarded in many quarters as a sacrifice of Unionist interests in Ireland. Its real effect was to endow Unionism
with a positive as well as a negative policy. But all reformers know that the further ahead they look, the
longer they have to wait for their justification. Meanwhile, we may leave out of consideration the division of
honour or of blame for what has been done. The only
matter of historic interest is to arrive at a correct
measure of the progress made.

The new movement had thus completed the first and
second stages of its mission. The idea of self-help had
become a growing reality, and upon this foundation an
edifice of State aid had been erected. When a Nationalist

Q

member met a Tory member of the Recess Committee he laughed over the success with which they had wheedled a measure of industrial Home Rule out of a Unionist Government. None the less they cordially agreed that the people would rise to their economic responsibility. The promoters of the movement had faith that this new departure in English government would be more than justified by the English test, and that in the new sphere of administration the government would be accorded, without prejudice, of course, to the ultimate views either of Unionists or Home Rulers, not only the consent, but the whole-hearted co-operation of the governed.

CHAPTER IX.

A New Departure in Irish Administration.

To the average English Member of Parliament, the passing of an Act "for establishing a Department of Agriculture and other Industries and Technical Instruction in Ireland and for other purposes connected therewith," probably signified little more than the removal of another Irish grievance, which might not be imaginary, by the concession to Ireland of an equivalent to the Board of Agriculture in England. In reality the difference between the two institutions is as wide as the difference between the two islands. The chief interest of the new Department consists in the free play which it gives to the pent-up forces of a re-awakening life. A new institution is at best but a new opportunity, but the Department starts with the unique advantage that, unlike most Irish institutions, it is one which we Irishmen planned ourselves and for which we have worked. For this reason the opportunity is one to which we may hope to rise.

Before I can convey any clear impression of the part which the Department is, I believe, destined to play on the stage of Irish public life, it will be necessary for me to give a somewhat detailed description of its functions and constitution. The subject is perhaps dull

and technical ; but readers cannot understand the Ireland of to-day unless they have in their minds not only
an accurate conception of the new moral forces in Irish
life and of the movements to which these forces have
given rise, but also a knowledge of the administrative
machinery and methods by which the people and the
Government are now, for the first time since the Union,
working together towards the building up of the Ireland
of to-morrow.

The Department consists of the President (who is the
Chief Secretary for the time being) and the Vice-
President. The staff is composed of a Secretary, two
Assistant Secretaries (one in respect of Agriculture and
one in respect of Technical Instruction), as well as
certain heads of Branches and a number of inspectors,
instructors, officers and servants. The Recess Committee, it will be remembered, had laid stress upon the
importance of having at the head of the Department a
new Minister who should be directly responsible to
Parliament ; and, accordingly, it was arranged that
the Vice-President should be its direct Ministerial head.
The Act provided that the Department should be
assisted in its work by a Council of Agriculture and
two Boards, and also by a Consultative Committee
to advise upon educational questions. But before
discussing the constitution of these bodies, it is necessary to explain the nature of the task assigned to
the new Department which began work in April,
1900. It was created to fulfil two main purposes.

In the first place, it was to consolidate in one authority certain inter-related functions of government in connection with the business concerns of the people which, until the creation of the Department, were scattered over some half-dozen Boards, and to place these functions under the direct control and responsibility of the new Minister. The second purpose was to provide means by which the Government and the people might work together in developing the resources of the country so far as State intervention could be legitimately applied to this end.

To accomplish the first object, two distinct Government departments, the Veterinary Department of the Privy Council and the Office of the Inspectors of Irish Fisheries, were merged in the new Department. The importance to the economic life of the country of having the laws for safeguarding our flocks and herds from disease, our crops from insect pests, our farmers from fraud in the supply of fertilisers and feeding stuffs and in the adulteration of foods (which compete with their products), administered by a Department generally concerned for the farming industry need not be laboured. Similarly, it was well that the laws for the protection of both sea and inland fisheries should be administered by the authority whose function it was to develop these industries. There was also transferred from South Kensington the administration of the Science and Arts grants and the grant in aid of technical instruction, together with the control of several national institutions, the most important being the Royal College of Science and the Metropolitan School of Art; for they, in a sense, would stand at the head of much of the new work which would be required for the contemplated agricultural and industrial developments. The Albert Institute at Glasnevin and the Munster Institute in Cork, both institutions for teaching practical agriculture, were, as a matter of course, handed over from the Board of National Education.

The desirability of bringing order and simplicity into these branches of administration, where co-related action was not provided for before, was obvious. A few years ago, to take a somewhat extreme case, when a virulent attack of potato disease broke out which demanded prompt and active Governmental intervention, the task of instructing farmers how to spray their potatoes was shared by no fewer than six official or semi-official bodies. The consolidation of administration effected by the Act, in addition to being a real step towards efficiency and economy, relieved the Chief Secretary of an immense amount of detailed work to which he could not possibly give adequate personal attention, and made it possible for him to devote a greater share of his time to the larger problems of general Irish legislation and finance.

The newly created powers of the Department, which were added to and co-ordinated with the various pre-existing functions of the several departments whose consolidation I have mentioned above, fairly fulfilled the recommendation of the Recess Committee that the Department should have 'a wide reference and a free hand.' These powers include the aiding, improving, and developing of agriculture in all its branches; horticulture, forestry, home and cottage industries; sea and inland fisheries; the aiding and facilitating of the transit of produce; and the organisation of a system of education in science and art, and in technology as applied to these various subjects. The provision of technical instruction suitable to the needs of the few manufacturing centres in Ireland was included, but need not be dealt with in any detail in these pages, since, as I have said before, the questions connected therewith are more or less common to all such centres and have no specially Irish significance.

For all the administrative functions transferred to the new Department moneys are, as before, annually voted by Parliament. Towards the fulfilment of the second purpose mentioned above—the development of the resources of the country upon the principles of the Recess Committee—an annual income of £166,000, which was derived in about equal parts from Irish and imperial sources, and is called the Department's Endowment, together with a capital sum of about £200,000, were provided.

It will be seen that a very wide sphere of usefulness was thus opened out for the new Department in two distinct ways. The consolidation, under one authority, of many scattered but co-related functions was clearly

a move in the right direction.   Upon this part of its recommendations the Recess Committee had no difficulty
in coming to a quick decision.   But the real importance
of their Report lay in the direction of the new work
which was to be assigned to the Department.   Under
the new order of things, if the Department, acting with
as well as for the people, succeeds in doing well what
legitimately may and ought to be done by the Government towards the development of the resources of the
country, and, at the same time, as far as possible confines
its interference to helping the Irish people to help themselves, a wholly new spirit will be imported into the industrial life of the nation.

The very nature of the work which the Department
was called into existence to accomplish made it absolutely essential that it should keep in touch with the
classes whom its work would most immediately affect,
and without whose active co-operation no lasting good
could be achieved.   The machinery for this purpose was
provided by the establishment of a Council of Agriculture
and two Boards, one of the latter being concerned with
agriculture, rural industries, and inland fisheries, the
other with technical instruction.   These representative
bodies, whose constitution is interesting as a new
departure in administration, were adapted from similar
continental councils which have been found by experience, in those foreign countries which are Ireland's
economic rivals, to be the most valuable of all means
whereby the administration keeps in touch with the

agricultural and industrial classes, and becomes truly responsive to their needs and wishes.

The Council of Agriculture consists of two members appointed by each County Council (Cork being regarded as two counties and returning four members), making in all sixty-eight persons. The Department also appoint one half this number of persons, observing in their nomination the same provincial proportions as obtained in the appointments by the popular bodies. This adds thirty-four members, and makes in all one hundred and two Councillors, in addition to the President and Vice-President of the Department, who are *ex-officio* members. Thus, if all the members attended a Council meeting, the Vice-President would find himself presiding over a body as truly representative of the interests concerned as could be brought together, consisting, by a strange coincidence, of exactly the same number as the Irish representatives in Parliament.

The Council, which is appointed for a term of three years, the first term dating from the 1st April, 1900, has a two-fold function. It is, in the first place, a deliberative assembly which must be convened by the Department at least once a year. The domain over which its deliberations may travel is certainly not restricted, as the Act defines its function as that of "discussing matters of public interest in connection with any of the purposes of this Act." The view Mr. Gerald Balfour took was that nothing but the new spirit he laboured to evoke would make his machine work. Although he

gave the Vice-President statutory powers to make
rules for the proper ordering of the Council debates,
I have been well content to rely upon the usual
privileges of a chairman. I have estimated beforehand
the time required for the discussion of matters of inquiry :
the speakers have condensed their speeches accordingly,
the business has been expeditiously transacted, and in the
mere exchange of ideas invaluable assistance has been
given to the Department.

The second function of the Council is exercised only
at its first meeting, and consequently but once in three
years. At this first triennial meeting it becomes an
Electoral College. It divides itself into four Provincial
Committees, each of which elects two members to represent its province on the Agricultural Board and one
member to represent it on the Board of Technical Instruction. The Agricultural Board, which controls a sum
of over £100,000 a year, consists of twelve members,
and as eight out of the twelve are elected by the four
Provincial Committees—the remaining four being appointed by the Department, one from each province—
it will be seen that the Council of Agriculture exercises
an influence upon the administration commensurate
with its own representative character. The Board of
Technical Instruction, consisting of twenty-one members,
together with the President and Vice-President of the
Department, has a less simple constitution, owing to the
fact that it is concerned with the more complex life of
the urban districts of the country. As I have said, the

Council of Agriculture elects only four members—one for each province. The Department appoints four others; each of the County Boroughs of Dublin and Belfast appoints three members; the remaining four County Boroughs appoint one member each; a joint Committee of the Councils of the large urban districts surrounding Dublin appoint one member; one member is appointed by the Commissioners of National Education, and one member by the Intermediate Board of Education.

The two Boards have to advise upon all matters submitted to them by the Department in connection, in the one case, with agriculture and other rural industries and inland fisheries, and, in the other case, in connection with Technical Instruction. The advisory powers of the Boards are very real, for the expenditure of all moneys out of the Endowment funds is subject to their concurrence. Hence, while they have not specific administrative powers and apparently have only the right of veto, it is obvious that, if they wished, they might largely force their own views upon the Department by refusing to sanction the expenditure of money upon any of the Department's proposals, until these were so modified as practically to be their own proposals. It is, therefore, clear that the machinery can only work harmoniously and efficiently so long as it is moved by a right spirit. Above all it is necessary that the central administrative body should gain such a measure of popular confidence as to enable it, without loss of influence, to resist proposals for expenditure upon schemes which might ensure great popularity at the moment, but would do permanent harm to the industrial character we are all trying to build up. I need not fear contradiction at the hands of a single member of either Board when I say that up to the present perfect harmony has reigned throughout. The utmost consideration has been shown by the Boards for the difficulties which the Department have to overcome ; and I think I may add that due regard has been paid by the administrative authority to the representative character and the legitimate wishes of the bodies which advise and largely control it.

The other statutory body attached to the Department has a significance and potential importance in strange contrast to the humble place it occupies in the statute book.   The   Agriculture   and   Technical   Instruction (Ireland) Act, 1899, has, like many other Acts, a part entitled ‘ Miscellaneous,’ in which the draughtsman's skill has attended to multifarious practical details, and made provision for all manner of contingencies, many of which the layman might never have thought of or foreseen.   Travelling expenses for Council, Boards, and Committees, casual vacancies thereon, a short title for the Act, and a seal for the Department, definitions, which show how little we know of our own language, and a host of kindred matters are included.   In this miscellany appears the following little clause :—

For the purpose of co-ordinating educational administration

there shall be established a Consultative Committee consisting of the following members :—

(*a.*) The Vice-President of the Department, who shall be
chairman thereof ;

(*b.*) One person to be appointed by the Commissioners
of National Education ;

(*c.*) One person to be appointed by the Intermediate
Education Board ;

(*d.*) One person to be appointed by the Agricultural
Board ; and

(*e.*) One person to be appointed by the Board of Technical Instruction.

Now the real value of this clause, and in this I think it
shows a consummate statesmanship, lies not in what it
says, but in what it suggests.   The Committee, it will be
observed, has an immensely important function, but no
power beyond such authority as its representative character may afford.   Any attempt to deal with a large
educational problem by a clause in a measure of this kind
would have alarmed the whole force of unco-ordinated
pedagogy, and perhaps have wrecked the Bill.   The
clause as it stands is in harmony with the whole spirit of
the new movement and of the legislation provided for its
advancement.   The Committee may be very useful in
suggesting improvements in educational administration
which will prevent unnecessary overlapping and lead to
co-operation between the systems concerned. Indeed it
has already made suggestions of far-reaching importance,
which have been acted upon by the educational authorities represented upon it.   As I have said in an earlier

chapter when discussing Irish education from the practical point of view, I have great faith in the efficacy of the economic factor in educational controversy, and this Committee is certainly in a position to watch and pronounce on any defects in our educational system which the new efforts to deal practically with our industrial and commercial problems may disclose.

There remains to be explained only one feature of the new administrative machinery, and it is a very important one. The Recess Committee had recommended the adaptation to Ireland of a type of central institution which it had found in successful operation on the Continent wherever it had pursued its investigations. So far as schemes applicable to the whole country were concerned, the central Department, assuming that it gained the confidence of the Council and Boards, might easily justify its existence. But the greater part of its work, the Recess Committee saw, would relate to special localities, and could not succeed without the cordial co-operation of the people immediately concerned. This fact brought Mr. Gerald Balfour face to face with a problem which the Recess Committee could not solve in its day, because, when it sat, there still existed the old grand jury system, though its early abolition had been promised. It was extremely fortunate that to the same minister fell the task of framing both the Act of 1898, which revolutionised local government, and the Act of 1899, now under review. The success with which these two Acts were linked together by the provisions of the latter forms an interesting lesson in constructive statesmanship. Time will, I believe, thoroughly discredit the hostile criticism which withheld its due meed of praise from the most fruitful policy which any administration had up to that time ever devised for the better government of Ireland.

The local authorities created by the Act of 1898 provided the machinery for enabling the representatives of the people to decide themselves, to a large extent, upon the nature of the particular measures to be adopted in each locality and to carry out the schemes when formulated.   The Act creating the new Department empowered the council of any county or of any urban district, or any two or more public bodies jointly, to appoint committees, composed partly of members of the local bodies and partly of co-opted persons, for the purpose of carrying out such of the Department's schemes as are of local, and not of general importance.   True to the underlying principle of the new movement—the principle of self-reliance and local effort—the Act lays it down that ' the Department shall not, in the absence of any special considerations, apply or approve of the application of money . . . to schemes in respect of which aid is not given out of money provided by local authorities or from other local sources.'   To meet this requirement the local authorities are given the power of raising a limited rate for the purposes of the Act. By these two simple provisions for local administration and local combination, the people of each district were made voluntarily contributory both in effort and in money, towards the new practical developments, and given an interest in, and responsibility for their success. It was of the utmost importance that these new local authorities should be practically interested in the business concerns of the country which the Department was to serve. Mr. Gerald Balfour himself, in introducing the Local Government Bill, had shown that he was under no illusion as to the possible disappointment to which his great democratic experiment might at first give rise. He anticipated that it would "work through failure to success." To put it plainly, the new bodies might devote a great deal of attention to politics and very little to business. I am told by those best qualified to form an opinion (some of my informants having been, to say the least, sceptical as to the wisdom of the experiment), that notwithstanding some extravagances in particular instances, it can already be stated positively that local government in Ireland, taken as a whole, has not suffered in efficiency by the revolution which it has undergone. This is the opinion of officials of the Local Government Board,* and refers mainly to the transaction of the fiscal business of the new local authorities. From a different point of observation I shall presently bear witness to a display of administrative capacity on the part of the many statutory committees, appointed by County, Borough, and District Councils to co-operate with the Department, which is most creditable to the thought and feeling of the people.

It would be quite unfair to a large body of farmers in

* See Report of the Local Government Board, 1901-2,

Ireland if, in describing the administrative machinery for carrying out an economic policy based upon self-help and dependent for its success upon the conciliatory spirit abroad in the country, I were to ignore the part played by the large number of co-operative associati ns, the organisation, work and multiplication of which have been described in a former chapter. The Recess Committee, in their enquiries, found that, in the countries whose competition Ireland feels most keenly, Departments of Agriculture had come to recognise it as an axiom of their policy that without organisation for economic purposes amongst the agricultural classes, State aid to agriculture must be largely ineffectual, and even mischievous. Such Departments devote a considerable part of their efforts to promoting agricultural organisation. Short a time as this Department has been in existence it has had some striking evidence of the justice of these views. As will be seen from the First Annual Report of the Department, it was only where the farmers were organised in properly representative societies that many of the lessons the Department had to teach could effectually reach the farming classes, or that many of the agricultural experiments intended for their guidance could be profitably carried out. Although these experiment schemes were issued to the County Councils and the agricultural public generally, it was only the farmers organised in societies who were really in a position to take part in them. Some of these experiments, indeed, could not be carried out at all except through such societies.

R

Both for the sake of efficiency in its educational work, and of economy in administration, the Department would be obliged to lay stress on the value of organisation.* But there are other reasons for its doing so: industrial, moral, and social. In an able critique upon Bodley's *France* Madame Darmesteter, writing in the *Contemporary Review*, July, 1898, points out that even so well informed an observer of French life as the author of that remarkable book failed to appreciate the steadying influence exercised upon the French body politic by the network of voluntary associations, the *syndicats agricoles*, which are the analogues and, to some extent, the prototypes, in France of our agricultural societies in Ireland. The late Mr. Hanbury, during his too brief career as President of the Board of Agriculture, frequently dwelt upon the importance of organising similar associations in England as a necessary step in the development of the new agricultural policy which he foreshadowed. His successor. Lord Onslow, has fully endorsed his views, and in his speeches is to be found the same appreciation of the exemplary self-reliance of the Irish farmers. I have already referred to the keen interest which both agricultural reformers and English and Welsh County Councils have been taking in the unexpectedly progressive efforts of the Irish farmers to reorganise their industry and place themselves in a position to take advantage of State assistance. I believe that our farmers are going to the

* See Annual General Report of the Department 1900-1901, pp. 25-27.

root of things, and that due weight should be given to the silent force of organised self-help by those who would estimate the degree in which the aims and sanguine anticipations of the new movement in Ireland are likely to be realised.

And it is not only for its foundation upon self-reliance that the latest development of Irish Government will have a living interest for economists and students of political philosophy. They will see in the facts under review a rapid and altogether healthy evolution of the Irish policy so honourably associated with the name of Mr. Arthur Balfour. His Chief Secretaryship, when all its storm and stress have been forgotten, will be remembered for the opening up of the desolate, poverty-stricken western seaboard by light railways, and for the creation of the Congested Districts Board. The latter institution has gained so wide and, as I think, well merited popularity, that many thought its extension to other parts of Ireland would have been a simpler and safer method of procedure than that actually recommended by the Recess Committee, and adopted by Mr. Gerald Balfour. The Land Act of 1891 applied a treatment to the problem of the congested districts—a problem of economic depression and industrial backwardness, differing rather in degree than in kind from the economic problem of the greater part of rural Ireland—as simple as it was new. A large capital sum of Irish moneys was handed over to an unpaid commission consisting of Irishmen who were acquainted with the local circumstances, and who were in a position to give their services to a public philanthropic purpose. They were given the widest discretion in the expenditure of the interest of this capital sum, and from time to time their income has been augmented from annually voted moneys. They were restricted only to measures calculated permanently to improve the condition of the people, as distinct from measures affording temporary relief.

I agree with those who hold that Mr. Arthur Balfour's plan was the best that could be adopted at the moment. But events have marched rapidly since 1891, and wholly new possibilities in the sphere of Irish economic legislation and administration have been revealed. A new Irish mind has now to be taken into account, and to be made part of any ameliorative Irish policy. Hence it was not only possible, but desirable, to administer State help more democratically in 1899 than in 1891. The policy of the Congested Districts Board was a notable advance upon the inaction of the State in the pre-famine times, and upon the system of doles and somewhat objectless relief works of the latter half of the nineteenth century ; but the policy of the new departure now under review was no less notable a departure from the paternalism of the Congested Districts Board. When that body was called into existence it was thought necessary to rely on persons nominated by the Government. When the Department was created eight years later it was found possible, owing to the broadening of the basis of local

government and to the moral and social effect of the
new movement, to rely largely on the advice and assistance of persons selected by the people themselves.

The two departments are in constant consultation as
to the co-ordination of their work, so as to avoid conflict
of administrative system and sociological principle in
adjoining districts; and much has already been done
in this direction.   My own experience has not only made
me a firm believer in the principle of self-help, but I
carry my belief to the extreme length of holding that
the poorer a community is the more essential is it to
throw it as much as possible on its own resources, in order
to develop self-reliance.   I recognise, however, the unde-
sirability of too sudden changes of system in these
matters.   Meanwhile, I may add in this connection that
the Wyndham Land Act enormously increases the importance of the Congested Districts Board in regard to its
main function—that of dealing directly with congestion,
by the purchase and resettlement of estates, the migration of families, and the enlargement of holdings.*

I have now said enough about the aims and objects,
the constitution and powers, and the relations with other
Governmental institutions, of the new Department, to
enable the reader to form a fairly accurate estimate of
its general character, scope and purpose.   From what it
is I shall pass in the next chapter to what it does, and
there I must describe its everyday work in some detail.
But I wish I could also give the reader an adequate

* *Cf. ante*, pp 46-49.

picture of the surge of activities raised by the first
plunge of the Department into Irish life and thought.
After a time the torrent of business made channels
for itself and went on in a more orderly fashion ; practical ideas and promising openings were sifted out
at an early stage of their approach to the Department
from those which were neither one nor the other ; time
was economised, work distributed, and the functions of
demand and supply in relation to the Department's work
throughout Ireland were brought into proper adjustment
with each other.   Yet, even at first, to a sympathetic and
understanding view, the waste of time and thought
involved in dealing with impossible projects and dispel-
ling false hopes was compensated for by the evidence
forced upon us that the Irish people had no notion of
regarding the Department as an alien institution with
which they need concern themselves but little, however
much it might concern itself with them.   They were
never for a moment in doubt as to its real meaning and
purpose.   They meant to make it their own and to utilise
it in the uplifting of their country.   No description of
the machinery of the institution could explain the real
place which it took in the life of the country from the
very beginning.   But perhaps it may give the reader a
more living interest in this part of the story, and a more
living picture of the situation, if I try to convey to his
mind some of the impressions left on my own, by my experiences during the period immediately following the pro-
jection of this new phenomenon into Irish consciousness.

When in Upper Merrion-street, Dublin, opposite to the Land Commission, big brass plates appeared upon the doors of a row of houses announcing that there was domiciled the Department of Agriculture and Technical Instruction, the average man in the street might have been expected to murmur, 'Another Castle Board,' and pass on. It was not long, however, before our visiting list became somewhat embarrassing. We have since got down, as I have said, to a more humdrum, though no less interesting, official life inside the Department. But let the reader imagine himself to have been concealed behind a screen in my office on a day when some event, like the Dublin Horse Show, brought crowds in from the country to the Irish capital. Such an experience would certainly have given him a new understanding of some then neglected men and things. While I was opening the morning's letters and dealing with " Files " marked " urgent," he would see nothing to distinguish my day's work from that of other ministers, who act as a link between the permanent officials of a spending Department and the Government of the day. But presently a stream of callers would set in, and he would begin to realise that the minister is, in this case, a human link of another kind—a link between the people and the Government. A courteous and discreet Private Secretary, having attended to those who have come to the wrong department, and to those who are satisfied with an interview with him or with the officer who would have to attend to their particular business,

brings into my not august presence a procession of
all sorts and conditions of men. Some know me
personally, some bring letters of introduction or want
to see me on questions of policy. Others—for
these the human link is most needed—must see the
ultimate source of responsibility, which, in Ireland,
whether it be head of a family or of a Department, is
reduced from the abstract to the concrete by the preg-
nant pronoun 'himself.' I cannot reveal confidences, but
I may give a few typical instances of, let us say, callers
who might have called.

First comes a visitor, who turns out to be a 'man
with an idea,' just home from an unpronounce-
able address in Scandinavia. He has come to tell me
that we have in Ireland a perfect gold mine, if we
only knew it—in extent never was there such a gold field
—no illusory pockets—good payable stuff in sight for
centuries to come—and so on for five precious minutes,
which seem like half a day, during which I have realised
that he is an inventor, and that it is no good asking him
to come to the point. But I keep my eye riveted on his
leather bag which is filled to bursting point, and manifest
an intelligent interest and burning curiosity. The suggestion works, and out of the bag come black bars and balls,
samples of fabrics ranging from sack-cloth to fine linen,
buttons, combs, papers for packing and for polite correspondence, bottles of queer black fluid, and a host of
other miscellaneous wares. I realise that the particular
solution of the Irish Question which is about to be un-

folded is the utilisation of our bogs. Well, this *is* one of
the problems with which we have to deal. It is physically possible to make almost anything out of this Irish
asset, from moss litter to billiard balls, and though one
would not think it, aeons of energy have been stored
in these inert looking wastes by the apparently unsympathetic sun, energy which some think may, before
long, be converted into electricity to work all the smoke-
less factories which the rising generation are to see.
Indeed, the vista of possibilities is endless, the only
serious problem that remains to be solved being ' how to
make it pay,' and upon that aspect of the question, unhappily, my visitor had no light to throw.

The next visitor, who brings with him a son and a
daughter, is himself the product of an Irish bog in the
wildest of the wilds. His Parish Priest had sent him
to me. A little awkwardness, which is soon dispelled,
and the point is reached. This fine specimen of
the ' bone and sinew ' has had a hard struggle to
bring up his ' long family '; but, with a capable wife,
who makes the most of the *res angusta domi*—of the pig,
the poultry, and even of the butter from the little black
cows on the mountain—he has risen to the extent of his
opportunities. The children are all doing something.
Lace and crochet come out of the cabin, the yarn from
the wool of the ' mountainy ' sheep, carded and spun at
home, is feeding the latest type of hosiery knitting
machine and the hereditary handloom. The story of this
man's life which was written to me by the priest cannot

find space here. The immediate object of his visit is to get his eldest daughter trained as a poultry instructress to take part in some of the ' County Schemes ' under the Department, and to obtain for his eldest son, who has distinguished himself under the tuition of the Christian Brothers, a travelling scholarship. For this he has been recommended by his teachers. They had marked this bright boy out as an ideal agricultural instructor, and if I could give the reader all the particulars of the case it would be a rare illustration of the latent human resouices we mean to develop in the Ireland that is to be.   I explain that the young man must pass a qualifying examination, but am glad to be able to admit that the circumstances of his life, which would have to be taken into account in deciding between the qualified, are in his case of a kind likely to secure favourable con- sideration.

And now enters a sporting friend of mine, a ' practical angler,' who comes with a very familiar tale of woe. The state of the salmon fisheries is deplorable : if the Department does not fulfil its obvious duties there will not be a salmon in Ireland outside a museum in ten years more. He has lived for forty-five years on the banks of a salmon river, and he knows that I don't fish. But this much the conversation reveals : his own knowledge of the sub- ject is confined to the piece of river he happens to own, the gossip he hears at his club, and the ideas of the particular poacher he employs as his gillie. His sug- gested remedy is the abolition of all netting. But I have

to tell him that only the day before I had a deputation
from the net fishermen in the estuary of this very river,
whose bitter complaint was that this 'poor man's industry' was being destroyed by the mackerel and herring
nets round the coast, and—I thought my friend would
have a fit—by the way in which the gentlemen on the
upper waters neglect their duty of protecting the spawn-
ing fish! Some belonging to the lower water interest
carried their scepticism as to the efficacy of artificial pro-
pagation to the length of believing that hatcheries are
partially responsible for the decrease. As so often happens, the opposing interests, disagreeing on all else, find
that best of peacemakers, a common enemy, in the Government. The Department is responsible—for two opposite
reasons, it is true, but somehow they seem to confirm
each other. We must labour to find some other common
ground, starting from the recognition that the salmon
fisheries are a national asset which must be made to
subserve the general public interest. I assure my friend
that when all parties make their proper contribution in
effort and in cash, the Department will not be backward
in doing their part.

At the end of this interview a messenger brings a
telegram for 'himself' from a stockowner in a remote
district.* 'My pigs,' runs one of the most business-like

---

* No fiction about this, nor about the following letter to the
Secretary :—

        ' The Scratatory, Vitny Dept.
  ' Honord Sir,
     'I want to let ye know the terible state we're in now. Al
the pigs about here is dyin in showers. Send down a Vit at
oncet.'

communications I ever received, 'are all spotted. What shall I do?' I send it to the Veterinary Branch, which, with the Board of Agriculture in England, is engaged in a scheme for staying the ravages of swine fever, a scheme into which the late Mr. Hanbury threw himself with his characteristic energy. The problem is of immense importance, and the difficulty is not mainly quadrupedal. Unless the police 'spot' the spotted pigs, we too often hear nothing about them. I am sure it must be daily brought home to the English Board, as it is to the Irish Department, that an enormous addition might be made to the wealth of the country if our veterinary officers were intelligently and actively aided, in their difficult duties for the protection of our flocks and herds, by those most immediately concerned.

So far it has been an interesting morning bright with the activities out of which the future is to be made. The element of hope has predominated, but now comes a visitor who wishes to see me upon the one part of my duties and responsibilities which is distasteful to me— the exercise of patronage. He has been unloaded upon me by an influential person, upon whom he has more legitimate claims than upon the Department. He has prepared the way for a favourable reception by getting his friends to write to my friends, many of whom have already fulfilled a promise to interview me in his behalf. His mother and two maiden aunts have written letters which have drawn from my poor Private Secretary, who has to read them all, the dry quotation, 'there's such

a thing as being so good as to be good for nothing.'
The young hopeful quickly puts an end to my specula-
tions as to the exact capacity in which he means to serve
the Department by applying for an inspectorship. I ask
him what he proposes to inspect, and the sum and substance of his reply is that he is not particular, but would
not mind beginning at a moderate salary, say £200 a year.
As for his qualifications, they are a sadly minus quantity,
his blighted career having included failure for the army,
and a clerkship in a bank, which only lasted a week when
he proved to be deficient in the second and dangerous in
the third of the three R's. His case reminds me of a
story of my ranching days, which the exercise of patronage has so often recalled to my mind that I must out
with it. Riding into camp one evening, I turned my
horse loose and got some supper, which was a vilely
cooked meal even for a cow camp. Recognising in the
cook a cowboy I had formerly employed, I said to him,
'You were a way up cow hand, but as cook you are no
account. Why did you give up riding and take to cook-
ing? What are your qualifications as a cook any way?'
'Qualifications!' he replied, 'why, don't you know I've
got varicose veins?' My caller's qualifications are of an
equally negative description, though not of a physical
kind. He is one of the young Micawbers, to whom the
Department from its first inception has been the something which was to turn up. He had, of course, testimonials which in any other country would have com-
manded success by their terms and the position of the

signatories, but which in Ireland only illustrate the charity with which we condone our moral cowardice under the name of good nature. I am glad when this interview closes.

One more type—a Nationalist Member of Parliament! He does not often darken the door of a Government office—they all have the same structural defect, no front stairs—he never has asked and never thought he would ask anything from the Government.   But he is interested in some poor fishermen of County Clare who pursue their calling under cruel disadvantages for want of the protection from the Atlantic rollers which a small breakwater would afford. It is true that they were the worst constituents he had—went against him in ' The Split,'— but if I saw how they lived, and so on. I knew all about the case. A breakwater to be of any use would cost a very large sum, and the local authority, though sympathetic, did not see their way to contribute their proportion, and without a local contribution, I explained, the Department could not, consistently with its principles, unless in most exceptional—— Here he breaks in : ' Oh ! that red tape. You're as bad as the rest—exceptional, indeed!   Why, everything is exceptional in my constituency. I am a bit that way myself. But, seriously, the condition of these poor people would move even a Government official. Besides, you remember the night I made thirteen speeches on the Naval Estimates—the Government wanted a little matter of twenty millions—and you met me in the Lobby and told me you wished to go to bed,

and asked me what I really wanted, and—I am always
reasonable—I said I would pass the whole Naval Programme if I got the Government to give them a boat-
slip at Ballyduck.—" Done !" you said, and we both went
home.—I believe you knew that I had got constituency
matters mixed up, that Ballyduck was inland, and that it
was Ballycrow that I meant to say.—But you won't deny
that you are under a moral obligation.'

Well, I would go into the matter again very carefully
—for I thought we might help these fishermen in some
other way—and write to him. He leaves me ; and, while
outside the door he travels over the main points with my
Private Secretary, the lights and shades in the picture
which this strange personality has left on my mind
throw me back behind the practical things of to-day.
In Parliament facing the Sassanach, in Ireland facing
their police, he has for years—the best years of his life—
displayed the same love of fighting for fighting's sake.
In the riots he has provoked, and they are not a few, he
is ever regardless of his own skin, and would be truly
miserable if he inflicted any serious bodily harm on a
human being—even a landlord. It is impossible not to
like this very human anachronism, who, within the limitations imposed by the convenience of a citizenship to
which he unwillingly belongs, does battle

> For Faith, and Fame, and Honour, and the ruined hearths
> of Clare.

The reader may take all this as fiction. I am sure no
one will annoy me by trying on any of the caps I have

displayed on the counter of my shop. What I do fear is
that the picture of some of my duties which I have
given may have made a wrong impression of the
Department's work upon the reader's mind. He may
have come to the conclusion that, contrary to all
the principles laid down, an attempt was being made to
do for the people things which the new movement was
to induce the people to do for themselves. The Department may appear to be using its official position and
Government funds to constitute itself a sort of Universal
Providence, exercising an authority and a discretion over
matters upon which in any progressive community the
people must decide for themselves. However near to the
appearances such an impression might be, nothing could
be further from the facts. If I have helped the reader to
unravel the tangled skein of our national life, if I have
sufficiently revealed the mind of the new movement to
show that there is in it 'a scheme of things entire
it should be quite clear that the deliberate intention
both of Mr. Gerald Balfour and of those Irishmen
whom he took into his confidence are being fulfilled
in letter and in spirit. It only remains for me to attempt
an adequate description of the work of the Department
created by that Chief Secretary, and, above all, of the
way in which the people themselves are playing the part
which his statesmanship assigned to them.

CHAPTER X.

GOVERNMENT WITH THE CONSENT OF THE GOVERNED.

In the preceding chapter I attempted to give to the reader a rough impression of the general purpose and miscellaneous functions of the new Department. I described in some detail the constitution and powers of the Council of Agriculture—a sort of Business Parliament—which criticises our doings and elects representatives on our Boards; and of the two Boards which, in addition to their advisory functions, possess the power of the purse. I laid special stress upon the important part these instruments of the popular will were intended to play as a link between the people and the Department. I gave a similar description and explanation of the Committees of Agriculture and Technical Instruction, appointed by local representative bodies, by means of which the people were brought into touch with the local as distinct from the central work, and made responsible for its success. The details were necessarily dull; and so also must be those which will now be required in order to indicate the general nature and scope of the work for the accomplishment of which all this machinery was designed. Yet I am not without

S

hope that even the general reader may find a deep
human interest in the practical endeavour of the humbler
classes of my fellow-countrymen to reconstruct their
national life upon the solid foundation of honest work.

The Department has at the time of writing been in
existence for three years, the term of office, it will be
remembered, of the Council of Agriculture and of the
two Boards. It would be unreasonable to expect in so
short a time any great achievement; but the understanding critic will attach importance rather to the spirit
in which the work was approached than to the actual
amount of work which was accomplished. He may say
that no true estimate of its value can be formed until the
enthusiasm aroused by its novelty has had time to wear
off. Those of us who know the real character of
the work are quite satisfied that the interest which it
aroused during the period in which the people had
yet to grasp its meaning and utility is not likely to become less real as the blossom fades and the fruit begins
to swell. The attitude of the Irish people towards the
Department and its work has not been that of a child
towards a new toy, but of a full-grown man towards a
piece of his life's work, upon which he feels that he
entered all too late. Indeed, so quickly have the people
grasped the significance of the new opportunities for
material advancement now placed within their reach, that
the Department has had to carry out, and to assist the
statutory local committees in carrying out, a number
and variety of schemes which, at any rate, proved that

public opinion did not regard it as a transitory experiment, but as a much-needed institution which, if properly utilised, might do much to make up for lost time, and which, in any case, had come to stay. The amount of the work which we were thus constrained to undertake was somewhat embarrassing; but so general and so genuine was the desire to make a start that we have done our best to keep pace with the local demands for immediate action. The staff of the Department caught the spirit in which the task had been set by the country, and showed a keen anxiety to get to work; and I am glad to have an opportunity of acknowledging that both the indoor and outdoor support it has received leaves the Department without excuse if it has not already justified its existence.

I shall deal as mercifully as I can with my readers in helping them towards an understanding of what has been actually done in the three years under review. I am aware that if I were to attempt a description of all the schemes which the variety of local needs suggested, and in the execution of which the assistance of the many-sided Department was sought and obtained, I should lose the patient readers, who have not already fainted by the way, in a jungle where they could not see the wood for the trees. These things can be studied by those interested,—and they I hope, in Ireland at any rate, are not few—in the Annual Reports and other official publications of the Department. For the general reader I must try to indicate in broad outline the nature and scope of that side of the new movement which seeks to supplement organised self-help and open the way for individual enterprise by a well considered measure of State assistance. I shall be more than satisfied if I succeed in giving him a clear insight into the manner in which the delicate task of making State interference with the business of the people not only harmless but beneficial has been set about. It is obvious that the fulfilment of this object must depend upon the soundness of the economic policy pursued, and upon the establishment and maintenance of mutual confidence between the central authority and the popular representative bodies through which the people utilise the new facilities afforded by the State.

I think the best way of giving the information which is required for an understanding of our somewhat complicated scheme for agricultural and industrial development under democratic control is first to explain the line of demarcation which we have drawn between the respective functions of the Department and the people's committees throughout the country; and then I must give a rapid description of some of the most important features of the Department's policy and programme. I shall add a sufficiency of detail from the actual work accomplished in these organising and experimental years, to illustrate both the difficulties which are incidental to such a policy, and the manner in which these difficulties may be surmounted.

When it became manifest that both the country

and the Department were anxious to drive ahead, the first thing to do was to lay down a *modus operandi* which would assign to the local and central bodies their proper shares in the work and responsibilities and secure some degree of order and uniformity in administration. This was quickly done, and the plan adopted works smoothly. The Department gives the local committee general information as to the kind of purpose to which it can legally and properly apply the funds jointly contributed from the rates and the central exchequer. The committee, after full consideration of the conditions, needs and industrial environment of the community for which it acts, selects certain definite projects which it considers most applicable to its district, allocates the amount required to each project, and sends the scheme to the Department for its approval. When the scheme is formally approved, it becomes the official scheme in the locality for the current year; and the local committee has to carry it out.

Although harmony now usually exists between the local and central authorities to the advantage and comfort of both, a considerable amount of friction was inevitable until they got to understand each other. The occasional over-riding of local desires by the 'autocratic' Department, which in the first rush of its work had to act in a somewhat peremptory fashion, was, no doubt, irritating. Now, however, it is generally recognised that the central body, having not only the advice of its experts and access to information from similar Departments in other countries to guide it, but also being in a position to profit by the exchange of ideas which is constantly going on between it and all the local committees in Ireland, is in a position of special advantage for deciding as to the bearing of local schemes upon national interests, and sometimes even as to their soundness from a purely local point of view.

Passing now from the conditions under which the Department's work is done, we come to review some typical portions of the work itself so far as it has proceeded. This falls naturally, both as regards that which is done by the central authority for the country at large and that which is locally administered, into two divisions. The first consists of direct aid to agriculture and other rural industries, and to sea and inland fisheries. The second consists of indirect aid given to these objects, and also to town manufactures and commerce, through education—a term which must be interpreted in its widest sense. Needless to say, direct aids, being tangible and immediately beneficial, are the more popular : a bull, a boat, or a hand-loom is more readily appreciated than a lecture, a leaflet, or an idea. Yet in the Department we all realise —and, what is more important, the people are coming to realise—that by far the most important work we have to do is that which belongs to the sphere of education, especially education which has a distinctly practical aim. To this branch of the subject I shall, therefore, first direct the reader's attention.

It must be remembered that, for reasons fully set out in the earlier portions of the book, I am treating the Irish Question as being, in its most important economic and social aspects, the problem of rural life. The Department's scheme of technical instruction, therefore, need not here be detailed in its application to the needs of our few manufacturing towns, but only in its application to agriculture and the subsidiary industries. I do not suggest that the questions relating to the revival of industry in our large manufacturing centres and provincial towns are not of the first importance. The local authorities in these places have eagerly come into the movement, and the Department has already taken part in founding, in our cities and larger towns, comprehensive schemes of technical education, as to the outcome of which we have every reason to be hopeful. Not only that, but it is highly necessary for the Department to consider these schemes in close relation to its work upon the more specially rural problems, for, as I have said elsewhere,* the interdependence of town and country, and the establishment of proper relations between their systems of industry and education, is a prime factor in Irish prosperity. But the rural problem, as I have so often reiterated, is the core of the Irish Question ; and to deal at all adequately with technical education, so far as we carry it on upon lines common both to Great Britain and Ireland, would lead us too far afield on the present occasion. I must, therefore, con-

* Pages 38, 39.

tent myself with indicating my reasons for leaving it rather on one side, and pass on to a brief description of the Department's educational work in respect of its twofold aim of developing agriculture and the subsidiary industries.

In the case of agriculture our task is perfectly plain. We know pretty well what we want to do, for we are dealing with an existing industry, and with known conditions. The productivity of the soil, the demand of the market, the means of transport from the one to the other, are all easily ascertainable. What most needs to be provided in Ireland is a much higher technical skill, a more advanced scientific and commercial knowledge, as applied to agricultural production and distribution.* This, in our belief, depends, more than upon any other agency, upon the soundness of the education which is provided to develop the capacities of those in charge of these operations. Our chief difficulty is that of co-ordinating our teaching of technical agriculture with the general educational systems of the country—a difficulty which the other educational authorities are all united with us in seeking to remove.

When, on the other hand, education—again, I believe, the chief agency for the purpose—is considered as a means for the creation of new industries, we come face to face with a wholly different problem. We have no

* It must be borne in mind that the Department is not officially concerned with the question of the economic distribution of land referred to on pp. 46-49.

longer an industry which we are seeking to foster and develop going on under our eyes, steadying us in our theorising, and in our experimenting upon the mind of the worker, by bringing us into close touch with the actual conditions of his work.   Our chief aim must be to develop his adaptability for the ever-changing and, we hope, improving economic industrial conditions amidst which he will have to work.   But unless we can satisfy parents that the schemes of development in which their children are being educated to take their place have an assured prospect of practical realisation, they will naturally prefer an inferior teaching which seems to them to offer a better prospect of an immediate wage or salary.   The teachers in the secondary schools of the country, who, so far, have shown a desire to assist us in giving an industrial and commercial direction to our educational policy, would also in that event have to meet the wishes of the parents; and thus education would fall back into the old rut with its cramming, its examinations and result fees—all leading to the multiplication of clerks and professional men, and preventing us from turning the thoughts and energies of the people towards productive occupations.

The natural trend of our educational policy will now be clear.   Leaving out of account large towns, where our problem is, as I have said, the same as that which confronts the industrial classes in the manufacturing centres of Great Britain, we are chiefly concerned with the application of science to the cultivation of the soil and

the improvement of live stock, and of business principles to the commercial side of farming; with the
teaching of dairying, horticulture, apiculture, and what
has been called farm-yard lore, outside the rural home,
and with domestic economy inside. On the industrial
as distinct from the agricultural side of the work in rural
localities, technical instruction must be directed towards
the development of subsidiary rural industries.

We early came to the conclusion that we could not
expect to find a system which we could simply transplant
from some other country. The system adopted in Great
Britain, where each county or group of counties maintains
an agricultural college and an experimental farm, and
many more elaborate systems on the continent, were all
found on examination to be inapplicable to our own
rural conditions, unsuitable to the national character,
and unrelated to the history of our agriculture. Many
of these schemes might have turned out a few highly
qualified authorities on the theory of agriculture, and
even good practical directors for those who farm on a
large scale. But we are dealing with a country with
great possibilities from an agricultural point of view, but
where, nevertheless, agriculture in many parts is in a very
backward condition, and where it is probably safe
to say that three-fifths of the farms are crowded on
one-fourth of the land. We are dealing with a
community with whom the systems of elementary,
secondary and higher education have not tended to
prepare the student for agricultural pursuits. A system

of agricultural and domestic education suited to the wants of those who are to farm the land must recognise and foster the new spirit of self-help and hope which is springing up in the country, and must be made so interesting as to become a serious rival to the race meeting and the public-house. The daily drudgery of farm work must be counteracted by the ambition to possess the best stock, the neatest homestead and fences, the cleanest and the best tilled fields. The unsolved problem of agricultural education is to devise a system which will reach down to the small working farmers who form the great bulk of the wealth producers of Ireland, to give them new hope, a new interest, new knowledge and, I might add, a new industrial character.

We were met at the outset by the difficulty which would apply to any system—that of finding trained teachers. This deficiency was felt in two directions—first, in the secondary school, in which the preliminary scientific studies should be undertaken, which are necessary to enable a lad to profit by more advanced instruction later on; and, secondly, in the special training of technical agriculture. It would not have been desirable to overcome these difficulties by any very extensive importation of teachers from without. I certainly hold the occasional importation of teachers with outside experience to be most desirable, but these should not form more than a leaven of the pedagogic lump; for it is a serious hindrance when to the task of familiarising students with a new system of education there is added that of familiarising a large body of teachers with the intellectual, social and economic conditions of the people among whom they are to work.

The manner in which the teacher difficulty was surmounted may be briefly stated, first, as regards the school, and, secondly, as regards the teaching of agriculture. Those already engaged in the teaching profession could not be relegated again to the *status pupillaris*. There was only one way in which they could assist us to overcome the difficulty, and that involved a great sacrifice on their part, the sacrifice of their well-earned vacation, but a sacrifice which they willingly made. The teachers most urgently needed were those of practical science, with knowledge of experimental work ; and about five hundred teachers from secondary schools, in order to qualify themselves, have attended summer courses specially organised by the Department at several centres in Ireland, while about four hundred have availed themselves of special summer courses in such subjects as drawing, manual instruction, domestic economy, building construction, wood-carving and modelling.

For the provision of a future supply of thoroughly trained teachers of science and of technology, including agriculture, the Royal College of Science has been reorganised. Although this institution was brought under the new conditions little more than three years ago, it will be seen that no time has been lost when I state that the first batch of men who have received a three years' course of training under the new programme are already at work under County Committees. For the training of these teachers, scholarships had to be provided, and new professors and teachers, particularly in agriculture, had to be appointed.

In regard to agricultural instruction we had to begin by carefully considering what, among many alternative plans, should be our immediate as well as our more remote aims. The Department's officers had studied Continental systems, and some of them had taken part in establishing systems of agricultural education in Great Britain. But it was not until the summer of 1901 that we had sufficiently studied the question in Ireland itself, with direct reference to the history, the environment, and the ideals of the people, to justify us in initiating a policy or formulating a definite programme for its execution.* The main object was to secure for the youth of the present generation who will later be concerned with agriculture, sound and thorough instruction in its principles and practice. Everyone who has given any thought to the subject knows how difficult it is to teach technical agriculture unless provision has been made in the general education of the country for instruction in those fundamental principles of science which, recognised or unrecognised, lie at the root of, and profoundly influence agricultural practice. This foundation, as I have shown, is now being

---

* For a full description of the Department's scheme of agricultural education I may refer to a *Memorandum on Agricultural Education in Ireland*, written by the author and published by the Department, July, 1901.

laid in Ireland. In our scheme the boy who has managed to avail himself of a two or three years' course of practical science in one of the secondary schools is then prepared to take full advantage of courses of technology, and will have to make up his mind as to the career he is to follow. We are now considering the case of a boy who is going to become a farmer, the class to which we chiefly look for the future well-being of Ireland. It is necessary that he should be taught the practical as well as the technical side of agriculture. The practical work he can learn upon his father's farm during spring and summer, and the technical by continuing his studies during the winter months in a school of agriculture. The establishment of such winter schools is in contemplation. But, in the meanwhile, to bring home to farmers the advantages of a first-class agricultural education for their sons, and at the same time to teach these farmers the more practical application of science to agriculture, the Department decided on a preliminary period of Itinerant Instruction.

The teacher difficulty, experienced on all sides of our work, was probably felt more acutely in regard to the specialised teachers of agriculture than in any other connection. Here it was necessary to take the young men brought up upon farms and possessed of the normal qualifications of the Irish practical farmer. We then had to make them into teachers by adding to their inherited and home-manufactured capacities a scientific training. In the training of agricultural teachers the Albert

Institute, Glasnevin, has been utilised by the Department. This school has also been re-organised to meet the new programme, and it will probably form in future a link between the winter schools of agriculture and the Royal College of Science in the training of our agricultural teachers.

Partly by these methods, partly by the temporary engagement of lecturers on special subjects, and partly by the appointment of trained teachers from England or Scotland, the system of itinerant instruction has been brought into operation as fully as could be expected in the time. Already half the County Committees have been provided with County instructors, while the remainder have nearly all drafted schemes and allocated funds for a similar purpose, ready to go to work as soon as more teachers have been trained.

The Itinerant Instruction scheme, it may be pointed out, besides one obvious, has another less immediately recognisable purpose. The direct business of the itinerant instructor is, by the aid of experimental plots, simple lectures, and demonstrations, to teach the farmers of his district as much as they can take in without the scientific preparation in which, as adults who have grown up under the old system of education, they are still lacking. But he does more than that. He not only conducts a school for adults, but in the very process of instruction he necessarily makes them aware of the vital necessity of a school for the young; and they begin, as parents, to understand and to desire the kind of instruction in the

schools of the country which will prepare their children
to take more advantage of the advanced teaching in agriculture than they themselves can ever hope to do.

This preparation is provided for as follows. To the
Department, as has already been explained, was handed
over the administration of the Science and Art Grants
formerly administered by South Kensington. The Department accordingly drew up a programme of experimental science and drawing, carrying capitation grants,
for day secondary schools. The Intermediate Education
Board, acting on the suggestion of the Consultative
Committee for Co-ordinating Education,* adopted this
programme and at the same time undertook to accept
the reports of the Department's inspectors as the basis
of their awards in the new "subject." These steps
insured the rapid and general introduction of this practical teaching in secondary schools, and, owing particularly
to the spirit in which their authorities and teaching staffs
accepted the innovation, the work has been carried out
with the happiest results.

I now come to the subjects grouped together under the
classification of 'domestic economy.' These differ only
in detail in their application to town and country. To
these subjects the Department attaches great importance. In the industrial life of manufacturing
towns I am persuaded that far too little thought
has been given to this element of industrial efficiency. From a purely economic point of view a

* See *ante*, pp. 236-238.

saving in the worker's income due to superior house-
wifery is equivalent to an increase in his earnings; but,
morally, the superior thrift is, of course, immensely
more important. " Without economy," says Dr. Johnson,
" none can be rich, and with it few can be poor," and the
education which only increases the productiveness of
labour and neglects the principles of wise spending will
place us at a disadvantage in the great industrial struggle.
When we come to consider domestic economy as an
agency for improving the conditions of the peasant
home, not only by thrift, but by increasing the general
attractiveness of home life, the introduction of a sound
system of domestic economy teaching becomes not only
important, but vital.

The establishment of such a system and the task of
making it operative and effective in the country is beset
with difficulties. The teacher difficulty confronts us
again, and also that of making pupils and their parents
understand that there are other objects in domestic
training than that of qualifying for domestic service.
A corps of instructresses in domestic economy is, however, already abroad throughout the country, nearly
all the County Councils having already appointed
them. Some of these teachers, who have made the
best contributions towards the as yet only partially
determined question of the ultimate aim and present
possibilities of a course of instruction in hygiene,
laundry work, cookery, the management of children,
sewing, and so forth, have told me that the demand

T

in rural districts seems to be chiefly for the class
of instruction which may lead to success in town life.
I have heard of a class of girls in a Connaught village
who would not be content with knowing the accomplish-
ments of a farmer's wife until they had learned how to
make asparagus soup and cook sweetbreads. No doubt
they had read of the way things are done in the kitchens
of the great. This tendency should never be encouraged,
but neither can it always be inflexibly repressed without
endangering the main objects of the class.

Women teachers of poultry-keeping, dairying, domestic
science and kindred subjects are trained at the Munster
Institute, Cork, and the School of Domestic Economy,
Kildare Street, Dublin, both of which have been equipped
to meet the needs of the new programme. The want of
teachers, and not any lack of interest on the part of the
country, has alone prevented all the counties from adopting schemes for encouraging improvement in all these
branches of work. I may add that more than one
hundred and fifty of these qualified teachers are now
at work under County Committees.

I have already, in this chapter, indicated that outside
large industrial centres, our educational policy is, broadly
speaking, twofold. We seek, in the first place, through
our programme in Experimental Science and its allied
subjects, now so generally adopted by secondary schools
in Ireland, to give that fundamental training in science
and scientific method which, most thinkers are agreed,
constitutes a condition precedent to sound specialised

teaching of agriculture as well as other forms of industry. We seek further, by methods less academic in character—for example, by itinerant instruction which is of value chiefly to those with whom 'school' is a thing of the past—to teach not only improved agricultural methods but also simple industries, and to promote the cultivation of industrial habits which are as essential to the success of farming as to that of every other occupation. Classes in manual work of various kinds—woodwork, carpentry, applied drawing and building construction, lace and crochet making, needlework, dressmaking and embroidery, sprigging, hosiery and other such subjects, have been numerously and steadily attended.

I do not ignore the argument that such home industries must in time give way before the competition of highly-organised factory industries. The simple answer is that it is desirable, and indeed necessary, to employ the energy now running to waste in our rural districts— energy which cannot in the nature of things be employed in highly-organised industries. To the small farmer and his family, time is a realisable, though too often unrealised, asset, and it is part of our aim to aid the family income by employing their waste time. Even if we can only cause them to do at home what they now pay someone else to do, we shall not only have improved their budget but shall have contributed to the elevation of the standard of home life, and thus, in no small measure, to the solution of the difficult problem of rural life in Ireland.

I think the reader will now understand the general character of the problem with which we were confronted and the means by which its solution is being sought. Our policy was not one which was likely to commend itself to the " man in the street." Indeed, to be quite candid, it was a little disappointing even to myself that I could not immortalise my appointment by erecting monuments both to my constructive ability and to my educational zeal in the shape of stately edifices at convenient railway centres, preferably along the tourist routes. We have had to stand the fire of the critic fresh from his holiday on the Continent where he had seen agricultural and technological institutions, magnificently housed and lavishly equipped, fitting generations of young men and young women for competition with our less fortunate countrymen. It is hard to prevail in argument against the man who has gone and seen for himself. It is useless to point out to the man with a kodak that the Corinthian façade and the marble columns of the *aula maxima* which aroused his patriotic envy are but a small part of the educational structure which he saw and thought he understood. If he would read the history of the systems and trace the successive stages by which the need for these great institutions was established, he would have a little more sympathy with the difficulties of the Department, a little more patience with its Fabian policy.

I must not, however, utter a word which suggests that the Department has any ground of complaint against the

country for the spirit in which it has been met ; especially as there was one factor to be taken into account
which made it difficult for public opinion to approve of
our policy. As I have already explained, a large capital
sum of a little over £200,000 was handed over to the
Department at its creation. During the first year, what
with the organisation of the staff, the thinking out of a
policy on every side of the Department's work, the constitution of the statutory committees to administer its
local schemes in town and country, the agreement, after
long discussion, between the central body and these
committees upon the local schemes, and all the other
preparatory steps which had to be taken before money
could wisely be applied, it is obvious that the Department could not have spent its income. In the second
year, and even the third year, savings were effected, and
the original capital sum has been largely increased. What
more natural than that in a poor country a spending
Department which was backward in spending should
appear to be lacking in enterprise, if not in administrative
capacity? But whether the policy was right or wrong it
has unquestionably been approved by the best thought in
the country, a fact which throws a very interesting light
upon the constitutional aspects of the Department. At
each successive stage the policy was discussed at the Council of Agriculture and its practical operation was dependent upon the consent of the Boards which have the power
of the purse. A Vice-President who had not these bodies
at his back would be powerless, in fact would have to

resign.   Thoughtless criticism has now and again condemned not only the parsimonious action of the Department, but the invertebrate conduct of the Council of·
Agriculture and the Boards in tolerating it.   The time
will soon come when the service rendered to their country
by the members of the first Council and Boards, who gave
their representative backing to a slow but sure educational policy, and scorned to seek popularity in showy
projects and local doles, will be gratefully remembered
to them.

Already we have had some gratifying evidences that
the country is with us in the paramount importance we
attach to education as the real need of the hour.   Most
readers will be surprised to hear that in the short time
the Department has been at work it has aided in the
equipment of nearly two hundred science laboratories
and of about fifty manual instruction workshops, while
the many-sided programme involved in the movement as
a whole is in operation in some four hundred schools
attended by thirty-six thousand pupils.

Nothing can be more gratifying than the unanimous
testimony of the officers of the Department to the
increasing practical intelligence and reasonableness
of the numerous Committees responsible for the
local administration of the schemes which the Department has to approve of and supervise.   The demand
for visible money's worth has largely given place
to a genuine desire for schemes having a practical
educational value for the industry of the district.   County

Clare is not generally considered the most advanced part of Ireland, nor can Kilrush be very far distant from 'the back of Godspeed'; yet even from that storm-battered outpost of Irish ideas I was memorialised a year ago to induce the County Council to pay less attention to the improvement of cattle and more to the technical education of the peasantry.

Under the heading of direct aids to agriculture, rural industries, and sea and inland fisheries, there is much important and useful work which the Department has set in motion, partly by the use of its funds and partly by suggestion and the organisation of local effort. The most obvious, popular and easily understood schemes were those directed to the improvement of live stock. The Department exercised its supervision and control with the help of advisory committees composed of the best experts it could get to volunteer advice upon the various classes of live stock. It is unnecessary to give any details of these schemes. The Department profited by the experience of, and received considerable assistance from the Royal Dublin Society, which had for many years administered a Government grant for the improvement of horses and cattle. The broad principle adopted by the Department was that its efforts and its available resources should be devoted rather to improving the quality, than to increasing the quantity, of the stock in the country, the latter function being regarded as belonging to the region of private enterprise.

It is impossible to over-estimate the importance to the country of having a widespread interest aroused and discussion stimulated on problems of breeding which affect a trade of vast importance to the economic standing of the country—a trade which now reaches in horned cattle alone an annual export of nearly three quarters of a million animals. All manner of practical discussions were set on foot, ranging from the production of the ideal, the general purposes cow, to that controversy which competes, in the virulence with which it is waged, with the political, the educational, and the fiscal questions—the question whether the hackney strain will bring a new era of prosperity to Ireland, or whether it will irretrievably destroy the reputation of the Irish hunter. The discussion of these problems has been accompanied by much practical work which, in due time, cannot fail to produce a considerable improvement upon the breed of different classes of live stock. In one year over one thousand sires have been selected by the experts of the Department for admission to the stock improvement schemes. Probably an equal number of breeding animals offered for inspection have been rejected. Many a *cause célèbre* has not unnaturally arisen over the decisions of the equestrian tribunal, and there have not been wanting threats that the attention of Parliament should be called to the gross partiality of the Department which has cast a reflection upon the form of stallion A or upon the constitutional soundness of stallion B. On the whole, as far as I can gather, the best authorities in the country are agreed that since the Department has been at work there has been established a higher standard of excellence in the bucolic mind as regards that vastly important national asset, our flocks and herds

Again for details I must refer the reader to official documents. There he will find as much information as he can digest about the vast variety of agricultural activities which originate sometimes with the Department's officers or with its *Journal* and leaflets, the circulation of which has no longer to be stimulated from our Statistics and Intelligence bureau, and sometimes emanate from the local committees, whose growing interest in the work naturally leads to the discovery of fresh needs and hitherto unthought of possibilities of agricultural and industrial improvement. I may, however, indicate a few of the subjects which have been gone into even in these years while the new Department has been trying so far as it might, without sacrifice of efficiency and sound economic principle, to keep pace with the feverish anxiety of a genuinely interested people to get to work upon schemes which they believe to be practical, sound, and of permanent utility.

A question which has troubled administrators of State aid to every progressive agricultural community, and which each country must settle for itself, is by what form of object lesson in ordinary agriculture intelligent local interest can best be aroused. We have advocated widely diffused small experimental plots, and they have done much good. Probably the most useful

of our crop improvement schemes have been those
which have demonstrated the profitableness of artificial
manures, the use of which has been enormously increased.
The profits derivable in many parts of Ireland from the
cultivation of early potatoes has been demonstrated in
the most convincing manner. To what may be called
the industrial crops, notably flax and barley, a great deal
of time and thought has been applied and much information disseminated and illustrated by practical experiments. In many quarters interest has been aroused in
the possibilities of profitable tobacco culture.   Many
negative and some positive results have been attained by
the Department in the as yet incomplete experiments
upon this crop. Much has been learned about the functions of central and local agricultural and small industry
shows, those occasional aids to the year's work which
disseminate knowledge and stimulate interest and friendly
rivalry among the different producers.   The reduction in
the death-rate among young stock, due to preventible
causes such as white scour and blackleg, is well worthy
of the attention of those who wish to study the more
practical work of the Department.

The branch of the Department's work which deals
with the Sea-fisheries can only be very briefly touched
on.   It falls into two main heads which may roughly be
termed the administrative and the scientific ; the latter, of
course, having economic developments as its ultimate
object.   The issue of loans to fishermen for the purchase
of boats and gear, contributing to the cost of fishery

slips and piers, circulating telegraphic intelligence, the making of by-laws for the regulation of the fisheries, the patrolling of the Irish fishing grounds to prevent illegalities, and the attempts which are being made to develop the valuable Irish oyster fishery by the introduction, with modifications suited to our own seaboard, of a system of culture comparable to those which are pursued with success in France and Norway, may be mentioned as falling under the more directly economic branch of our activities. Irish oysters are already attaining considerable celebrity, owing to the distance of our oyster beds from contaminating influences; and it is hoped that when the Department's experiments are complete the Irish oyster will be made subject to direct control for all its life, until it is despatched to market. Attention is also being given to the relative value of seed oysters, other than native, for relaying on Irish beds.

On the more directly scientific side, the Department has undertaken the survey of the trawling grounds around the coast to obtain an exact knowledge of the movements of the marketable fish at different times of their life, so that we may be guided in making by-laws and regulations by a full knowledge of the times and places at which protection is necessary. The biological and physical conditions of the western seas are also being studied in special reference to the mackerel fishery, with the object of correlating certain readily observable phenomena with the movements of the fish, and so of predicting the probable success of a fishery in a particular season. The routine observations of the Department's fishery cruiser have been so arranged as to synchronise with those of other nations, in order to assist the international scheme of investigation now in progress, wherever its objects and those of the Department are the same.

While these various practical projects have been in operation, we have done our best to keep abreast of the times by sending missions to other countries, consisting of an expert accompanied by practical Irishmen who would bring home information which was applicable to the conditions of our own country. The first batch of itinerant instructors in agriculture, whose training for the important work of laying the foundations for our whole scheme of agricultural instruction I have referred to, were taken on a continental tour by the Professor of Agriculture at the Royal College of Science, in order to give special advantages to a portion of our outdoor staff upon the success of whose work the rate of our progress in agricultural development might largely depend. And not only have we in our first three years gleaned as much information as possible by sending qualified Irishmen to study abroad the industries in which we were particularly interested, but we also took steps to give the mass of our people at home an opportunity of studying these industries for themselves. With the somewhat unique experiment carried out for this object, I will conclude the story of the new Department's activities in its early years.

The part we took at the Cork Exhibition of 1902 was well understood in Ireland, but not perhaps elsewhere. We secured a large space both in the main Industrial Hall and in the grounds, and gave an illustration not of what Ireland had done, but of what, in our opinion, the country might achieve in the way of agricultural and industrial development in the near future. Exhibiting on the one hand our available resources in the way of raw material, we gave, on the other hand, demonstrations of a large number of industries in actual operation. These exhibits, imported with their workers, machinery and tools, from several European countries and from Great Britain, all belonged to some class of industry which, in our belief, was capable of successful development in Ireland. In the indoor part of the exhibit there was nothing very original, except perhaps in its close relation to the work of a government department. But what attracted by far the greatest interest and attention was a series of object lessons in many phases of farm activities, where, in our opinion, great and immediate improvements might be made. Here were to be seen varieties of crops under various systems of treatment, demonstrations of sheep-dipping, calf-rearing on different foods, illustrations of the different breeds of fowl and systems of poultry management, model buildings and gardens for farmer and labourer; while in separate buildings the drying and pressing of fruit and vegetables, the manufacture of butter and cheese, and a very comprehensive forestry exhibit enabled our visitors to combine profitable suggestion with, if I may judge from my frequent opportunities of observing the sightseers in whom I was particularly interested, the keenest enjoyment.

We kept at the Exhibition, for six months, a staff of competent experts, whose instructions were to give to all-comers this simple lesson. They were to bring home to our people that, here in Ireland before their very eyes, there were industries being carried on by foreigners, by Englishmen, by Scotchmen, and in some instances by Irishmen, but in all cases by men and women who had no advantage over our workers except that they had the technical training which it was the desire of the Department to give to the workers of Ireland. The officials of the Department entered into the spirit of this scheme enthusiastically and cheerfully, some of them, in addition to their ordinary work, turning the office into a tourist agency for these busy months. With the generous help of the railway companies they organised parties of farmers, artisans, school teachers, members of the statutory committees, and, in fact, of all to whom it was of importance to give this object lesson upon the relations between practical education and the promotion of industry. Nearly 100,000 persons were thus moved to Cork and back before the Exhibition closed—an achievement largely due to the assistance given by the Irish Agricultural Organisation Society and the clergy throughout the country.

This experiment, both in its conception and in its

results, was perhaps unique. There were not wanting
critics of the new Department who stood aghast at so
large an expenditure upon temporary edifices and a
passing show; but those who are in touch with its
educational work know that this novel application of
State assistance fulfilled its purpose. It helped substantially to generate a belief in, and stimulate a demand for,
technical instruction which it will take us many years
adequately to supply.

An American visitor who, as I afterwards learned,
takes an active part in the discussion of the rural problems of his own country, disembarked at Queenstown
in order to 'take in' the Cork Exhibition. In his rush
through Dublin he 'took in' the Department and the
writer. 'Mr. Vice-President,' he said, before the hand-
shaking was completed, 'I have visited all the great
Expositions held in my time. I have been to the Cork
Exposition. I often saw more things, but never more
idees.'

With this characteristically rapid appreciation of a
movement which seeks to turn Irish thought to action,
my strange visitor vanished as suddenly as he came.

———

Those whose sympathy with Ireland has induced them
to persevere through the mass of details with which this
story of small beginnings is pieced together may wonder
why the bearing of hopeful efforts for bringing prosperity
and contentment to Ireland upon the mental attitude of
millions of Irishmen scattered throughout the British

Empire and the United States, and so upon the lives
of the countries in which they have made their homes,
is apparently ignored. I fully recognise the vast
importance of the subject. A book dealing com-
prehensively with the actual and potential influence
of Irish intellect upon English politics at home, and
upon the politics of the United States, a carefully
reasoned estimate of the part which Irish intellect is
qualified, and which I firmly believe it is destined, to
play wherever the civilisation of the world is to be under
the control of the English-speaking peoples—more especially where these peoples govern races which speak
other tongues and see through other eyes—a clear and
striking exposition of the true relation between the
small affairs of the small island and that greater Ireland
which takes its inspiration from the sorrows, the passions,
the endeavours, and the hopes of those who cling to the
old home—such a book would possess a deep human
interest, and would make a high and wide appeal.
Nevertheless, I feel that at the present time the most
urgent need, from every point of view on which I have
touched, is to focus the thought available for the Irish
Question upon the definite work of a reconstruction of
Irish life.

Such is the purpose of this book. I do not wish to
attach any exaggerated importance to the scheme of
social and economic reform of which I have attempted
to give a faithful account ; nor is it in their practical
achievement be it great or small, that the initiators

and organisers of the new movement take most pride.
What these Irishmen are proud of is the manner in
which the people have responded to their efforts to bring
Irish sentiment into an intimate and helpful relation
with Irish economic problems. They had to reckon with
that greatest of hindrances to the spirit of enterprise, a
rooted belief in the potentiality of government to bring
material prosperity to our doors. As I have pointed
out, the practical demonstration which Ireland had
received of the power of government to inflict lasting economic injury gave rise to this belief; and I
have noted the present influences to which it seems to
owe its continuance until to-day. I believe that, if any
enduring interest attaches to the story which I have
told, it will consist in the successive steps by which this
initial difficulty has been overcome.

Let me summarise in a few words what has been, so
far, actually accomplished. Those who did the work or
which I have written first launched upon Irish life a
scheme of organised self-help which, perhaps more by
good luck than design, proved to be in accordance with
the inherited instincts of the people, and, therefore, moved
them to action. Next they called for, and in due season
obtained, a department of government with adequate
powers and means to aid in developing the resources of
the country, so far as this end could be attained without
transgressing the limits of beneficial State interference
with the business of the people. In its constitution this
department was so linked with the representative insti-

U

tutions of the country that the people soon began to feel that they largely controlled its policy and were responsible for its success.   Meanwhile, the progress of economic thought in the country had made such rapid strides that, in the administration of State assistance, the principle of self-help could be rigidly insisted upon and was willingly submitted to.   The result is that a situation has been created which is as gratifying as it may appear to be paradoxical.   Within the scope and sphere of the movement the Irish people are now, without any sacrifice of industrial character, combining reliance upon government with reliance upon themselves.

That a movement thus conceived should so rapidly have overcome its initial difficulties and should, I might almost add, have passed beyond the experimental stage, will suggest to any thoughtful reader that above and beyond the removal by legislation of obstacles to progress —and much has been accomplished in this way of recent years—there must have been new, positive influences at work upon the national mind.   These will be found in the growing recognition of the fact that the path of progress lies along distinctively Irish lines, and that otherwise it will not be trodden by the Irish people. Much good in the same direction has been done, too, by the generous and authoritative admission by England that the future development of Ireland should be assisted and promoted 'with a full and constant regard to the special traditions of the country.' *   But

* Speech of the Lord Lieutenant to the Incorporated Law Society, November 20th, 1902.   See also p. 170.

after all, while these concessions to Irish sentiment, vitally important though they be, may speed us on our road to national regeneration, they will not take us far. It remains for us Irishmen to realise—and the chief value of all the work I have described consists in the degree in which it forces us to realise—the responsibility which now rests with ourselves. We have been too long a prey to that deep delusion, which, because the ills of the country we love were in past days largely caused from without, bids us look to the same source for their cure. The true remedies are to be sought elsewhere ; for, however disastrous may have been the past, the injury was moral rather than material, and the opportunity has now arrived for the patient building up again of Irish character in those qualities which win in the modern struggle for existence. The field for that great work is clear of at least the worst of its many historic encumbrances. Ireland must be re-created from within. The main work must be done in Ireland, and the centre of interest must be Ireland. When Irishmen realise this truth, the splendid human power of their country, so much of which now runs idly or disastrously to waste, will be utilised ; and we may then look with confidence for the foundation of a fabric of Irish prosperity, framed in constructive thought, and laid enduringly in human character.

EPILOGUE

After a Year of Criticism

"Give me liberty to know, to utter, and to argue freely according to my conscience, above all liberties."—*Milton.*

EPILOGUE

IN this book I have placed my countrymen neither in the dock, on a pedestal, nor on the stage. My offence is more grave—I have criticised them. The reviler, the panegyrist, and the caricaturist of the Irish have each a recognised position, but not the critic. So when a member of the class held chiefly responsible for past mis-government, occupying an official position in the Govern-ment of the day, ventured to place upon Irishmen them-selves a large measure of responsibility for the removal of their present ills, the first effect was bound to be a considerable disturbance, if not a storm. The chances of such a book as this doing good might seem to be, to say the least, problematical. What induced me to publish it when I did was the urgency of the crisis caused by the emigration drain, and by the social and economic revolu-tion now about to be consummated by the transfer of the land from the owner to the occupier. I felt that, with these two dominant and present facts of Irish life upper-most in their minds, men of practical patriotism, to what-ever party they belonged, would understand the meaning of what I said and the necessity for saying it.

This expectation has been largely fulfilled. In addi-tion to all the public criticism which the book has re-ceived, it has brought me a voluminous correspondence from my own countrymen at home and abroad—most of them Nationalists and Roman Catholics—who have welcomed the frank expression of my opinions, and have, with equal frankness, given me their own in return. It is to these last, who share the feelings of the great majority of the people, that this afterword is gratefully addressed. For where they have failed to grasp my meaning they seek for explanations, which they have every right to ask, and which I am the more anxious to give, because I see clearly that the misunderstanding is, in most cases, due to a failure to appreciate the exact purpose I had in my mind when I decided to write this book.

That purpose was to concentrate thought upon certain social and economic problems hitherto neglected in Ireland, and to expound a practical programme of national development. Thought and work on these lines is to my mind the condition precedent to the solution of the Irish Question. But our people have been taught by history, and under present influences are held to the belief, that all such efforts are doomed to failure until that Question has been solved. The foregoing pages may be regarded as one man's endeavour to break this vicious circle in which poor Ireland revolves.

The difficulties of such a task are obvious. Those who are familiar with the story of Ireland know how it came about that between the two sections of the Irish people there stands a great dividing wall, the foundations of which are racial, the stones political, and the cement religious. Historical causes have left us with a

public opinion* thus trebly partisan, which has little
tolerance for the man who in the search for truth does
not seek for it on one side only. And as I took some
national shortcomings for my theme, it was inevitable
that the greater the truth of what I wrote the more
bitterly should I be condemned by those who mould
popular opinion in Ireland. Obviously the best defence
against my most hostile critics would be to quote some
of their pronouncements, as a proof that I had not misrepresented the tone or temper of Irish controversy.
But I prefer to be patient, as I dare say their most
vehement denunciations are more often prompted by a
sense of patriotic duty than indulged in as a congenial
pastime. I will content myself with citing a single
sentence, which has served as a text for many lay
and some clerical sermons, and which will illustrate only too well the general character of a
vast amount of the hostile comment which these
pages have provoked. In the course of one of its almost
daily attacks upon the Department for the administration of which I have been chiefly responsible, the
most widely circulated Nationalist organ in Ireland
solemnly declared that the writer of this book "has
demonstrated his unfitness for his position by wantonly
and deliberately insulting the character and religion of

* By the term ' public opinion ' I mean that part of a people's
thoughts and feelings the free expression of which is tolerated
by the forces which rule in the matter. I must not be understood
as implying that, in the strife and clamour of our public life, the
spoken, or even the written word is always an accurate reflection
of our thoughts and emotions.

the great majority of the Irish people, to whom he appeals for co-operation."*

No man fitted for public life in Ireland would feel even a passing soreness at judgments thus conceived.   Nor will any one who has read the book ask me to defend it or myself against any of the charges in this comprehensive indictment.   It is only in a country where newspapers are much read and books very little, and where people morbidly dread any public association with unpopular men or movements, that attacks like this do harm.   But there is another line of criticism which, much as I regret its personal bearings, I am forced on public grounds to meet.

Some who are in general agreement with my views, but who are anxious for the success of the practical programme I have described, say that I ought not to have given any opportunity to those who feel bound to renounce me and all my works, to attack the Department and the movement with which I was connected.   Even when they have grasped the moral situation in its economic bearings, they think the moral revolution involved in the remedy to be visionary and Utopian.   Such critics ask what useful purpose could, in the circumstances, be served by honest criticism, however constructive, and however moderately expressed.   The answer to this question may be as complex as are the conditions out of which it arises, but I will try to make it direct and clear.

I found in the state of public opinion in Ireland a fatal

* *Freeman's Journal*, 27th June, 1904.

hindrance to the work of national development—a hindrance which, if my diagnosis of its nature be right, would be equally disastrous under any system of government, however ideal. We cherish the belief that we are a liberty-loving people groaning under the tyranny of alien rule. The contrary would be nearer to the truth. Seldom a Sunday passes but we indulge the luxury of denouncing the Government with oratory which, if published in the columns of the Continental press, would fill rulers with amazement, peoples with envy, and, possibly, some prisons with editors! So far, at any rate, in our struggle for freedom we are free; but on the ruins of the old ascendancy there has been built up by censors, who combine a total disregard for the feelings of others with a morbid sensitiveness for their own, a moral domination more grievous than any repression sustained by physical force. This tyranny, the work of moral cowards—for it is they, and not physical cowards, who are the proverbial bullies—is upheld as a discipline essential to the attainment of national autonomy. Meanwhile, many of us, Nationalist and Unionist alike, are sighing for just a little Home Rule in the region of thought.

This narrow compass of our liberties escapes the ordinary observer of Irish life who has not grasped the wide difference between its surface and its depths. At first sight we appear to be the people of all others who have the courage of our convictions. But alas! it is generally the courage of somebody else's convictions and not our own. Still more misleading is the buoyancy of our temperament, which

seems incompatible with the existence of the moral ser-
vitude I have sketched. But that is our historical attitude of mind—we had more gaiety in the darkest of the
Penal days. Miss Lawless, the best exponent of this
aspect of the Irish temperament, in one of her too few
Irish poems, admirably hits the impression made upon
the foreigner by the Irish soldiers who took service in
continental armies nearly two centuries ago. One of
their comrades asks whether these 'exiles merry of
heart' can really be 'the men of a thousand wrongs,' of
whose woes so much had been heard. Their apologist
replies :—

> 'Fool, did you never hear
> Of sunshine which broke through rain,
> Sunshine which came with storm,
> Laughter that rang with pain ?
> Boastings begotten of grief,
> Vauntings to hide a smart,
> Braggings with trembling lip,
> Tricks of a broken heart ? '*

It is no longer the 'tricks of a broken heart,' but rather
the response of a subdued spirit to the only freedom that
it knows, which deceives the observer of to-day. We are
more serious in these happier times, but we are still content (if I may use an Irish phrase eloquent of long suffering and inextinguishable hope) to 'enjoy bad health.'

The consideration of these national peculiarities is
very pertinent to an explanation why this book was
written. Their historical origin is easily traceable, their
historical excuse is more than plausible ; but none the

* 'Clare Coast (*circa* 1720)' in *With the Wild Geese.*

less a defect in character is clearly indicated. This
'lack of moral fibre'—whether the cause or the effect of
the moral tyranny, or both, it matters not—I gradually
came to regard, and in this book treated, as the chief
present evil of Irish life. It was and is my
confident belief that, if once the disastrous effects
of the evil were more generally recognised by
those who possess political and religious influence, or
who wield the power of the press, the remedy would
begin to be radically applied.* It was this conviction
which led to the publication of my book, having as its
main proposition that the Irish Question is, above all
and before all, a problem of character.

Yet I sometimes find that readers who would
willingly admit the truth of this as an academic

---

* A recent utterance of one of the most powerful living Irish
political leaders gives reason to hope that this recognition will come.
" A mere physical row," said Mr. William O'Brien, "is the last
thing which would daunt an Irishman. I only wish we had as
plentiful a supply of moral courage."—(*Freeman's Journal*, November 7th, 1904.) So do I ; and I hope that Mr. O'Brien will go on
helping to teach us our needs in this respect. Few men could do
more in that direction than one who has so unmistakably shown his
possession of both kinds of courage.
In this connection the following extract from a letter I have
received from a correspondent in high position in the Roman Catholic
Church in Ireland will be of interest. Alluding to my references to
moral fibre and civic virtue, he writes : " I quite understand that
it is not precisely in the balance of the Commandments you weigh our
people and find them wanting. You are speaking of character with
its strength, independence, stability and fidelity ; and none can gain-
say the supreme importance of the foundation. Well, to be sure, the
rust of slavery has widely eaten its way. But I altogether disagree
with the opinion that the desirable ' character ' is limited to individuals. I know whole glens in this county filled with people
who would shame your Cabinet for character." I gladly endorse
the high appreciation of the communities my correspondent has
in his mind, but, of course, to the comparison which he draws I
must officially demur !

proposition, are as far as ever from grasping its
vital practical importance, or from understanding why
I was ready to provoke so much hostility in order to
drive it home. But surely a little consideration ought to
show that, if the proposition be true, it ought to be
acted upon by those who are desirous of promoting the
real progress of our country. And it is just at this
point, where an attempt is made to translate theory
into practice, that one begins to tread on dangerous ground. I might have reiterated my cardinal doctrine again and again without offence—
and without effect. But when I endeavoured to
examine the main influences operating on national
character, when I introduced such subjects as politics
and religious systems into a book, one of the chief
objects of which was to explain, and gain support for, a
programme of social and economic reform, I no doubt
caused grave misgivings in the minds of many who were
in intellectual sympathy with my point of view.   They
fear that I shall retard my work without effecting any
change in the body of opinion opposed to my own. But
they fail to observe that I do not want to change either
political or religious convictions. I want merely to draw
attention to the harmful and unnecessary way in which
these convictions are made to affect interests which
are neither political nor religious.

So much then for the reasons which led to the publication of the book. I shall now try to clear up the existing, and avert further, misunderstanding of both its aim

and argument. This I can best do by offering to my readers, (1) a brief restatement of the argument as to character; (2) an explanation of the reasons which made it necessary to dwell on the effects produced upon character, and consequently upon industry, by political agitation; and (3) a clearer exposition of what I hold to be the relation between religious systems and economic progress.

(1) THE NATIONAL CHARACTER.

As an Irishman I take pride in the high qualities of heart and mind which the race, through much tribulation, has preserved. I am a firm believer in the latent capacities of the Irish people, but feel that the time has come when we should search our consciences and ask ourselves why these capacities have remained latent so long; whether we can honestly say that all the causes of our present shortcomings are still external to ourselves— that the Irish light is really concealed under the English bushel.

To these questionings I gave an answer which angered many who deny, and more who feel its truth. I urged that our national character has some defects which, if Ireland is to realise the hopes of her children, call for a great national effort of reform. Unhappily, large numbers of my readers have completely misunderstood both the meaning and the purpose of my reflections upon the national character. Some seem to have been misled by my use of such terms as ‘moral fibre,’ and in some cases

appear to have confused *morale* with *morals*. I thought
I had protected myself from a misconception so hurtful to
the usefulness of the book when at the outset I affirmed
my belief that " our failure to rise to our opportunities
and to give practical evidence of the intellectual qualities
with which the race is admittedly gifted, was due to
certain defects of character, not ethically grave, but
economically paralysing."

I have repeated these words because they were written
in the preface, which, I am now told, only reviewers read.
They were intended to make it clear that my purpose
was purely practical, my criticism constructive. So far
from having any desire to be censorious, I have
always felt and contended that the moral evolution, even
in the economic sphere, which has taken place in Ireland,
was largely what might have been expected in view of
the past government of the country. If in practical life
what is Celtic in us ' reacts against the despotism of
fact,' that is the natural outcome of six long centuries
of revolt against the fact of despotism. I agree with
those who hold that the strongest indictment which can
be made against past misgovernment is the demoralising
influence it exerted upon the character of the governed,
and who explain our failures by insisting that the
industrial character and vitality of the people still suffers
from the effect of former commercial restrictions, of
the Penal Laws, and of the land system before 1881.
But I strongly disagree with those who, while cherish-
ing the remembrance of these wrongs, denounce those

who call attention to their inevitable effects. I hold that it is mere demagogy to pander to popular sentiment by proclaiming to the world that we have been morally plundered, and yet are morally whole. The triumph of the race is that on one side of its character—and that, happily, the higher side—it came out of the ordeal even purified by its trials. But it is the folly of follies to say that on its other side the national character has preserved that strength, self-reliance, and sense of responsibility, or that appreciation of true liberty, which a modern people must possess if it is to succeed, or even to survive, in the industrial fight.

The importance of this point lies in the fact that the success of a people depends upon those qualities wherein we Irish are, from whatever cause, deficient. To the best of my judgment—and I speak now from official experience—our people are endowed in a high degree with administrative capacity. Compared with the English, who, no doubt, are steadier, they show a remarkable appreciation of the needs, and regard for the susceptibilities, of those within the sphere of their administration. And yet the mere presence of a reporter or of a noisy gallery will be often enough to reveal a sense of irresponsibility, and a lack of moral courage, grievously at odds with the good feeling and good judgment which would otherwise almost certainly prevail. Thus it is that resolutions are passed which are obviously carried by their sound rather than by their significance, and questions of practical importance,

X

with which the meeting is fully competent to deal wisely, are not discussed on their merits. Thus it is that administrative officers are too often appointed, not with regard to their fitness for the work to be done, but under the pressure of influences brought to bear on behalf of the applicants. Indeed, I think it is not irrelevant to add that but too many of the patrons, often in the highest social and official positions, who supply applicants with testimonials, do not seem to be more richly endowed with moral courage than some of the bodies to whom these reckless panegyrics are addressed.* I gladly acknowledge, however, that in the period which has elapsed since new duties in connection with agricultural an industrial development devolved upon them, our local authorities have shown a growing appreciation of the fact that their success depends upon getting the best men to carry out their work. It is only fair to add that the Local Government Board, in their annual reports, bear testimony to the increasing efficiency of the County

---

* Recently a friend of mine was asked to sign a memorial, which was being promoted by the clergymen of the district, both Catholic and Protestant, magistrates, &c., in favour of a prisoner who was described as having been " previously of unblemished character." He afterwards learned that there were sixty-four previous convictions recorded against this man ! Personally, I prefer the practice of telling the brutal truth in testimonials, which prevailed where I got my business education—a method well illustrated by the following incident which recurs to my memory. An Indian called at the ranch where I was living at the time and handed me a letter from the Agent of his Reservation. This characteristic and, as I afterwards learned, just testimonial ran :— " Tinbelly is a worthless Indian. Anyone who gives him anything will be that much out." Do any of us know of a country where the: estimonial would be phrased :—" Mr. P. J. Tinbelly is qualified to discharge efficiently and faithfully any duties which may be entrusted to him " ?

and District Councils in the discharge of their local government work. Indeed I would not have hinted at the deficiencies I have mentioned, were I not impressed with the supreme importance of turning all the administrative capacity the Irish democracy possesses to the task of applying State assistance to the development of our industrial resources, on the lines successfully followed in almost every competing continental country.

In the sphere of private citizenship the dependence of a country's industrial life upon its moral atmosphere is quite as real as in the case of public administration. Any commercial traveller of wide experience, any one who has conducted industrial undertakings among different peoples, will confirm this truth. History and reason alike approve the judgment that what counts industrially in the long run is character. Both the capitalist, seeking an investment for his capital, and the captain of industry, seeking an opening, make an estimate of the moral qualities of a community in order to determine whether they will find the business efficiency, the persistence, the sobriety and punctuality—qualities which are far more conducive to success than mere mechanical skill. In measuring the capacity of a country for industrial and commercial development, every man of the world gives to these qualities a high place among the deciding factors.

I am here considering not the views of moral philosophers or other theorists, but the principles which guide the action of practical business men, to whom we must look for help in our efforts towards industrial development. I know the minds of such men, because I have of late years approached many capitalists and captains of industry with a view to getting them to give a lead to Irish capital, which is, at present, significantly shy. The plain truth is that the moral atmosphere in Ireland is not yet considered, either at home or abroad, favourable for industrial enterprise. My own opinions on this vitally important question were formed in the course of active business in Great Britain and the United States, which gave me my standards of comparison. As a result of a fairly wide and varied business experience I state positively that the laws under which we live are now at least as favourable to industrial enterprise as those of any State in the Union ; and, this being so, I am driven to the conclusion that our comparatively backward industrial state is due to the moral conditions which, however caused, it is the first duty of Irishmen to improve. Fortunately, the adaptability of our people is unimpaired; and this gives us reason to believe that the remedy can be rapidly and effectively applied.

Believing, therefore, in the existence of the evil, and in the feasibility of its effectual cure if once it were generally recognised, how could I remain silent and preserve my self-respect? It is true that I occupy a responsible official position which I should have to vacate the moment public confidence in my character or capacity were withdrawn; but I cannot enjoy that confidence if

it is to be retained by concealing thoughts which must
affect the discharge of my duties as a public servant.
And as for the timeliness or expediency of my candour,
I could not persuade myself that, in the admittedly
backward state of the country, in face of the continuing
outflow of so much that is strong, consideration of this
all-essential matter ought to have been shelved or
postponed.

(2) POLITICS *versus* INDUSTRY.

In the above survey of certain moral conditions unfavourable to industry, I purposely did not include what
one of the unknown correspondents this book has
brought me declares to be the principal deterrent to the
investment of capital in Ireland—'the intricate inter-
weaving of politics with business.' This condition, incidental to the Land War, is gradually ceasing with the
cessation of the strife, and will, we may hope, ultimately
disappear as the agrarian settlement proceeds. We shall
then be able to make much more rapid progress with
the industrial movement, whose hopeful beginnings I
have described in the last four chapters. It will be
remembered that I treated this movement as being
especially valuable on account of its influence upon the
adverse moral conditions I have just discussed; and my
chapter on politics was introduced solely because many
influential politicians appeared to regard organised

efforts towards economic improvement with feelings
ranging from suspicion to active hostility.

Whatever doubt may have previously existed as to
the necessity for frankly discussing the attitude of politicians towards our industrial progress, was removed by
the publication of the following letter from the leader of
the Irish Nationalist Party to the editor of the *Irish
World* of New York.   The letter is in effect a denial to
the entire industrial movement of the right to exist, on
the ground that its ostensible are not its real objects.
Even those who think I provoked such an attack will
agree that I am in duty bound to make some defence—
not of myself but of the movement. Here is the letter:—

NEW YORK, *October 4th*, 1904.

MY DEAR MR. FORD—I am anxious before leaving for
home to say a word of warning with reference to an
insidious attempt which I find is being made in America
by officials and agents of the British Government to divert
the minds of the friends of Ireland from the National
movement under the pretence of promoting an industrial
revival in Ireland.

The promotion of Irish industries is so praiseworthy an
object that I am not surprised some of our people in
America have been deceived in this matter.   I myself,
indeed, at one time entertained some belief in the good
intentions of Sir Horace Plunkett and his friends, but
recent events have entirely undeceived me ; and Sir
Horace Plunkett's recent book, full as it is of undisguised
contempt for the Irish race, makes it plain to me that
the real object of the movement in question is to under-
mine the National Party and divert the minds of our

people from Home Rule, which is the only thing which can ever lead to a real revival of Irish industries.

The men who are conducting this movement are for the most part avowed anti-Home Rulers, and many of them salaried officials of the British Government. I am informed that an agent of theirs is about to visit America for the purpose of still further pushing this movement, and I feel it my duty to issue this word of warning to prevent our friends here from being deceived as to the real meaning of this movement.—Believe me, very truly yours,

JOHN E. REDMOND.

It would be hard to find a more perfect illustration of the disastrous conflict between politics and industry than this letter reveals. It is difficult to understand how it could have been thought necessary to give such a warning to the shrewdest and most progressive section of Irish Nationalists, and I have reason to believe that in the United States it was not taken seriously. But the letter was widely published in Ireland, and there did harm. The definite assertion by the Chairman of the Parliamentary Party that the industrial movement is really a political conspiracy has been used, by those who prefer politics to industry, to discredit the work of economic development described in this book, a work in the initiation of which, it will be remembered, Mr. Redmond himself, in the days of the Recess Committee, bore a prominent part.* With accidental irony this letter appeared in the Irish Press on the same day as the first

* See Chapter VIII.

news of the Russian admiral's attack on the British trawlers in the North Sea, which he mistook for Japanese torpedo boats. I have been too long in Irish public life to be easily surprised ; but I did feel that, even on the stormy seas of Irish politics, and in the prevailing mists, the Irish leader should not have mistaken our little industrial craft for a British political destroyer.

Mr. Redmond does as little justice to his own sagacity as to my sincerity when he says that I deceived him so long and so successfully. But, leaving aside accusations of personal bad faith, against which I have no desire to defend myself, let us see where the real difference lies between the political leaders and those of the industrial movement. To be quite fair to the former, let me admit that they appeal to a broad well-known principle of political philosophy, as well as to expediency. The principle is that the sense of responsibility, needful for industrial as well as every other kind of progress, cannot be developed in a people so long as they are denied the essentials of responsible government. Admitting, for the sake of argument, that responsible government does not exist in Ireland, I reply that, in any country where individual freedom exists, a sense of responsibility can be developed in the process of striving for constitutional betterment no less than in the enjoyment of the attained result. Every worker in the new intellectual and industrial movements acts upon this theory. On the question of principle there are, then, two distinct courses which present themselves as practical politics—constitutional change as a means to national advancement, and national development as a means towards the attainment of whatever may prove to be constitutionally best. Whichever course may be theoretically right, I claim for my plan that it at least furnishes the better working hypothesis.

On the question of expediency, many Nationalists hold that my plan is opposed to what experience has shown to be the only effective tactics for the Irish Parliamentary Party to adopt. They point to the fact that much of the legislation which has apparently come from British statesmen, was advocated by Irish representatives long before it found its way into the programme of English parties; and that, until Parnell developed the present system of Parliamentary tactics, Irish demands did not receive even bare attention in the Imperial Parliament. While this is largely true as regards the past, and while it would be hard to exaggerate the debt the farmers of Ireland owe to the Parnellite movement, I might remind thoughtful Nationalists that the wise use of the land is quite as important now as was formerly its acquisition. What, however, I am really concerned to urge with regard to the methods introduced by Parnell is that, whatever their tactical justification at the time, they inevitably retarded the development of a political character equal to the needs of these democratic days. Being convinced of the interdependence of political character and economic character, I wrote the chapter upon the influence of politics with the aim of showing that, both from the tactical and the moral points of view, our methods of political agitation ought now to be modified. I there submitted, for the consideration of Irish political leaders, that the particular constitutional changes which they hold to be good for us would not only be more likely to be obtained, but would also be better calculated to fulfil their purpose when obtained, if we learned to cultivate independence of thought and action in ourselves, and to respect it in others. Ireland cannot be prosperous until the political leader makes this, not large but vitally important, concession to the political economist.

(3) RELIGION AND ECONOMICS.

Some critics who agree that I could not have ignored the effect of politics upon industry hold that I should not have touched upon the other great power which dominates Irish life. On reflection they will, I hope, see that the available means of improving the material condition of a people peculiarly devoted to their religion, could not have been adequately discussed without reference to the influence upon secular life of the clergy to whom the majority of the people look for guidance in questions of faith and morals, and in many other things besides. Where a plea is being put forward for the recognition and treatment of defective economic qualities, and for the formation of a public opinion which would tolerate that freedom of thought and action which is an essential condition of economic progress, a moral question arises upon which the clergyman and the economist must take counsel together.

My correspondence furnishes gratifying proof that many Irish Catholics, both lay and clerical, have read my remarks upon the influence of our religious systems in the spirit in which they were offered. Others appear to take up the position, which I cannot but conceive to be a weak one, that their church is above criticism, not only as to its doctrinal teaching, but also as to the influence which its ministers exercise upon the society around them. I fully recognise that unless avowedly entering the arena of religious controversy, I am not entitled to discuss doctrinal issues. All that I claim is the right of a citizen in a free state to say openly what I believe to be the effect which any ecclesiastical body produces upon the economic and social life of my country. Some, I know, honestly think that I have transgressed the limits I have here defined. I suspect I have suffered largely for the sins of others, for I frequently find myself in the embarrassing position of being denounced for having taken my opinions from books I had not read, by critics who obviously had not read mine. The following passage in a pastoral letter from the Cardinal Primate to the clergy of the Archdiocese of Armagh, which seriously prejudiced Irish Catholics against this book, furnishes a case in point.

" While these theories," wrote his Eminence, " found expression only among a few sore-heads who, for reasons best known to themselves, seek every pretext to assail religion and her ministers, we could afford to despise them. But when a gentleman whose abilities should have saved him from following the senseless drivel of irresponsible writers, and whose high position should have admonished him to weigh his words, has seriously taken up these theories—*as I infer from a letter in yesterday's paper he has*—it is time to look about for an antidote to the poison."*

I cannot, of course, reply to all my clerical critics in detail. But I feel it incumbent upon me to meet the chief objections, emanating from authoritative sources, which have been taken to my treatment of the real and important issues I felt compelled to raise. Fortunately my chapter on the influence of religious systems in Ireland was criticised in a review which may be taken as at least representative, if not authoritative; happily, too, it is in a form admitting of a succinct reply. This review is from the pen of the Rev. J. F. Hogan, D.D., of Maynooth, and it appeared in the *Irish Ecclesiastical Record*, a publication described in a sub-

---

* The italics are mine. The Pastoral Letter was dated March 2, 1904, and the letter referred to in it appeared on March 1, in the *Freeman's Journal.*

A week after the appearance of this condemnation, the Mullingar Rural District Council held a meeting, and, in the course of business, this book came up for discussion. One councillor, who could claim the distinction of having read the book, assured his colleagues that it was "merely a reproduction of Mr. McCarthy's book, *Priests and People in Ireland.*" The following resolution was thereupon proposed and adopted unanimously:—"That we, the Mullingar Rural District Council, condemn Sir Horace Plunkett's book as an insult to Catholic Ireland, and that a copy of this resolution be forwarded to each District Council in Ireland."—*Westmeath Examiner*, March 12th, 1904.

title as *A Monthly Journal under Episcopal Sanction.**
The article is, of course, written with courtesy, although
evidently under feelings of strong resentment. " For
our part," he writes, " we much mistake the character of the Irish people if they have not intelligence
enough to see through all this mechanism of statecraft,
and ' moral fibre ' enough to say what they think of it."
This passage shows that when Dr. Hogan and I
discuss character from our different points of view, we
are talking of two different things. Otherwise he
would know that it would require far more moral
courage to say a word in defence of this book or its
author than to join the crowd in denouncing both. But
these are side issues. The real issue is clearly presented by Dr. Hogan in a striking passage where he
defends the Roman Catholic position, and at the same
time shows a misconception of my meaning, which is
quite sufficient to account for his impression that I am
attacking his church and faith. The entire review
should, of course, be read, but I may quote the following
passage without the context, as it is complete in itself.

" It is true, of course, that Catholics do not look on
wealth as the highest good either of individuals or of

* See issue for April, 1904. In thus singling out Dr. Hogan's
review I ought also to mention one by another theologian, which
appeared weekly, for almost a year, in the *Leader* (of Dublin), signed
'M. O'R.' I have not a word to say against its tone, but the writer
frequently reads into my words propositions which I certainly never
intended to advance. Moreover, a review is usually a chapter about
a book, but when, as in this case, it assumes the proportions of a book
about a chapter, such space as I could afford to devote to a rejoinder
would appear disrespectfully small.

nations. It is true that they make the value of this life to
depend chiefly on its relation to the life to come. Protestantism is, on the other hand, utilitarian and worldly. It
goes on the principle that as this world is the best we have
any experience of we should make the most of it.
Catholics even go so far as to think that the highest and
most perfect form of life is to leave all this world can offer
and take up the cross and follow the footsteps of their
Master in detachment and poverty. To Protestants all
this is extravagance and folly. But whilst Catholics maintain that their conception of life is founded clearly on the
Gospel, and that the Gospel is neither 'uneconomic or anti-
economic,' they also believe that it is better suited than
any other to raise up and to maintain a strong, pure, and
energetic race. They believe, moreover, that their view of
things is justified by history and by the actual condition of
the world. ' One ounce of fact is worth a ton of theory,'
says Russell Lowell, and when we find such countries as
Belgium, Westphalia, and Lombardy putting British
manufactures out of their market, we are not particularly
alarmed as to how our religion looks from the economic
point of view to an outsider like Sir Horace Plunkett." *

I assume that Dr. Hogan is anxious to promote
mutual tolerance between Catholics and Protestants in
Ireland. I ask him, then, to consider the full meaning
of his words. He defines Protestantism in terms which
apply only to materialism pure and simple, and then
proceeds to argue from this definition. He resents even
the suggestion, beyond which I did not intend to go,
that, in the affairs of this life, the faith and practice of
his church, in Ireland at any rate, do not always appear

* *Irish Ecclesiastical Record*, April, 1904, p. 300.

to make for material progress. What, then, must be the feelings of Protestants when their religion—if such a term be appropriate to the commercial asset they are supposed to enjoy in their conception of Christianity—is represented as being diametrically opposed to the very essence of the teaching of Christ?

But we may eliminate from this discussion, as not being relevant, the alleged anti-Christian tenets of Protestants, and I hope Dr. Hogan will be able to dismiss them from his mind, as they obviously prejudice his view of my opinions on the issue we are discussing. 'To raise up and to maintain a strong, pure and energetic race,' is an admirably expressed ideal towards which the minister of any Christian religion and the economist can work together. In seeking to promote such co-operation, I was, of course, concerned with actual life, as I had observed its conditions, and not with conceptions of life, ideal or otherwise. The Roman Catholic and Protestant Churches alike set the final goal of human effort in another world. But they seem to differ, in practice, at all events, as to the due proportions of economic and religious activities as parts of a Christian life. I was dealing simply with the necessary economic conditions of success in modern times, and nowhere have I contended that Roman Catholicism, as a system, is essentially inimical to such success. A few isolated sentences, sometimes a single word, torn from the context, have sufficed with those who have not read the book to substantiate this complete misinterpretation of my argument as a whole.* 'Roman Catholicism,' I wrote, 'strikes an outsider as being, in some of its tendencies, non-economic, if not actually anti-economic.'† This sentence has been largely quoted, but almost invariably without the qualifying words. Indeed, all that survives of the text, in most of the criticisms that I have seen, is the epithet 'non-economic,' or 'anti-economic,' my critics applying to Roman Catholicism as a system what I applied to "some of its tendencies." Developing my meaning, I proceeded to say that certain characteristics of Roman Catholicism "appear to me calculated, unless supplemented by other influences, to check the growth of the qualities of initiative and self-reliance."

I can account for the heated comments to which this expression of opinion has given rise, only by supposing my critics to have altogether overlooked the important qualifying words in the context. I have been charged with materialism merely because I pointed out that "it behoves a Church to see that its members, while fully acknowledging the claims of another life, should develop the qualities which make for well-being in this life."‡ Is it irreligious to con-

---

* Some readers will recall the somewhat similar experience of Mr. Arthur Balfour. In the stormy days of his Irish administration his enemies discovered that he had written a book. It happened to be a brilliant defence of revealed religion against the Positivist attack; but it bore the suspicious title, "A Defence of Philosophic Doubt." Thenceforth the term 'atheist' was added to the otherwise alliterative epithets which usually adorned his name.

† Page 101.
‡ Page 104

tend that the command not to be over-solicitous for the morrow does not lessen our obligation to provide for to-day, to practise the virtue of thrift, or to make thoughtful provision for the temporal future of ourselves and our families? Surely it is obvious that these issues cannot be neglected if Christian principles are to retain their hold on a civilisation which Christianity has been the chief agency in creating.

My own opinions on this subject are quite definite, but I find it extremely hard to say exactly where they differ from Dr. Hogan's. To my moderate criticism of what appeared to me to be uneconomic in certain tendencies of Roman Catholicism, he retorts, in effect, that such criticism is beside the point, because the ideal of his church is detachment and poverty. But when I suggest that in Ireland the tendencies referred to are exceptionally pronounced, he develops another line of argument, and proceeds to confute my contention by citing the more than British success of certain other Roman Catholic countries in manufacturing enterprise. I may mention incidentally that, in the chapter he was reviewing, I had myself referred to these industrial achievements.

Dr. Hogan apparently fails to observe that I was not dealing with conceptions of Christian perfection, but with the principles of a national economy. So far from setting up two spheres of duty in antagonism to each other, I was seeking to show that no necessary antagonism exists. 'To leave all,' in Dr. Hogan's sense, can be the perfect life only for the few, whose

Y

example may serve to influence the many in
not so greedily following the economic as to stifle
the spiritual life. Must those Catholics who believe that
'the highest and most perfect form of life is to leave all
this world can offer,' hold that this is the ideal of life
for all as well as for some—for the nation as for the
individual? If this were so, Catholicism would not
merely be non-economic or anti-economic; it would be
incompatible with a nation's existence. In nothing that
I have said is there anything which detracts from the
spiritual claims of the Catholic Church; nor, if my qualifying words are taken into account, is there anything
which implies a necessary conflict between her ministry
and the material progress of nations.

The wrong impression as to my opinions upon the relations between Roman Catholicism and economic life
has led to my being charged with a desire to prove that
in Ireland, at any rate, Roman Catholicism is incompatible with material progress. What I sought to prove,
what I have laboured to demonstrate in practical
life, is the exact contrary of that proposition.
Whether Protestantism or Roman Catholicism better
harmonizes with an advanced economic ideal is a merely
academic question. I can, however, well imagine that in
the circumstances of rural Ireland an economy which
does not promise the largest acquisition of wealth may
last the longer. Knowing as I do the part which religion
plays in the life of Irish Roman Catholics, I rely upon
their church to foster contentment under the compara-

tively low standard of physical comfort, and the limited range of industrial opportunity, which must prevail in Ireland while the new peasant proprietary is being constituted and organised. I agree with Dr. Hogan that some of his continental brethren have rendered notable service towards the solution of the problem of rural life ; and, what is more encouraging, the working out of the economic salvation of our own peasantry has been begun by a few priests whom I would not exchange even for those whose flocks have thriven so well in Belgium, Lombardy, and Westphalia.

The exact nature of that work has been sufficiently indicated in the second part of this book. Its most important branches are the reorganisation of agriculture on its commercial and technical sides, certain much-needed improvements in the domestic economy of the rural poor, the training of the people for the gradual development of subsidiary industries, and the furthering of intellectual and social movements. These are all integral and necessary parts of the general scheme for building up a decent and comfortable rural life which will keep our people contentedly at home. It is not, I know, the function of the clergy to do the work of such bodies as the new Department, the Agricultural Organisation Society, or the Gaelic League. But they can help them all by influencing a public opinion which is favourable in the abstract to these agencies of constructive endeavour, but is taught to suspect of ulterior motives every man who devotes himself to their promotion. None

can better help us to realise that it is a sign of strength
to be calm, of dignity to weigh our words, and of
courage to be moderate.   An Irish priest, who is also a
practical economist, with whom I discussed this subject,
said, in words which his brethren will appreciate, ' You
are merely asking us to furnish the supplementary teaching, which must be added to the Rule of Life, for those
whose labour supports the nation.'

No man, with the opinions I have expressed in this
book upon the power of the Roman Catholic clergy
in Ireland, could desire to see their moral influence
impaired.   Taking the view that I do of Irish character,
and in the light of certain political events which all can
remember, I hold that a conflict between clerical influence and modern life, such as other countries have
witnessed, would probably involve in Ireland a moral
débâcle such as any Christian would deplore.   Indeed,
my chief feeling on reading the intemperate denunciations coming from certain of my clerical critics, was the
fear that they might some day come to realise that, in
concerning themselves too much about the straw, they
had ignored the wind.

I must now revert for a moment to those particular
operations of the Roman Catholic Church in Ireland,
my treatment of which has drawn a more angry fire than
have certain anti-clerical diatribes I am supposed to have
endorsed.   I introduced these subjects—the monopoly of
education by the secular clergy and the religious orders,
the alleged excessive church-building, and the contrast

between the failure of the clergy to make their flocks temperate and their success in making and keeping them chaste—in order to furnish concrete illustrations in support of the views I had expressed regarding clerical influence upon secular life in Ireland.

During five years of active administrative work I have given much attention to the provision of means whereby teachers whose calling is primarily spiritual might increase their efficiency for the work of technical education. I have been accused of squandering public money on monastic and conventual institutions by some of my fellow-Protestants, who are, perhaps, ignorant of the total lack of other educational machinery in the greater part of Ireland. From the opposite quarter, my expressed opinion that the almost total exclusion of lay teachers from secondary schools had some educational disadvantages, has been added to the list of my offences. All I would ask of these critics is that they should read the chapters on religion and on education together, when they will, I think, better understand the relevance and force of what I wrote.*

My remarks as to the alleged excessive church-building were, I regret to say, made in a form which laid me open to misconception. Some readers feel that I did not make sufficient allowance for the fact that much church-building was absolutely required for the mere physical accommodation of a people among whom regular church

* See Chapters IV. and V., more especially pp. 108-9, and 135-6.

attendance is practically universal, and who had been deprived of all the ancient churches in the country. It is also urged that the extravagance complained of is the exception and not the rule. All this I gladly admit. Still, what strikes many observers is the undisputed fact that while the number of Catholic churches and religious houses is rapidly rising, the Catholic population itself is rapidly falling. Had the reverse been true, my strictures would have been more open to objection. I trust, however, that I shall give no fresh offence if I express the hope that the zeal now put forth in church-building may find a counterpoise in a vigorous effort to improve the economic condition of a people who must be preserved to the country if the churches are not to be emptied of their worshippers.

My references to the attitude of the clergy towards the subjects of temperance and of chastity have been the cause (or the occasion) of a great deal of vehement denunciation. With regard to temperance, I find no serious attempt to dispute the substantial accuracy of the facts as I have presented them. I submitted the suggestion that the ill-success of the clergy in their efforts to deal with this evil was due to a failure 'to recognise the chief defect in the character of the people, and a misunderstanding of the means by which that character can be strengthened.'* This discussion was not only relevant, but essential, to an argument dealing

* See page 114.

with economic conditions and industrial possibilities. I
think my contention was worthy of a more serious reply
than that 'of all the social evils imported from England
for the ruin of this country, perhaps the greatest was the
public-house.'* In this extraordinary passage Dr.
Hogan seems to attribute the drink evil to some external
power over which Irishmen can exercise no control. Is
the influence of the publicans in so many Irish municipal
bodies to be ascribed to the English connection or to
Irish apathy? I am convinced that the clergy, to whose
zeal in the matter I have paid my humble tribute, could
effect a wonderful reformation if they were to realise
that nowadays this evil must be combated by work done
upon character, and not only upon emotions.†

It was to further illustrate this opinion that I introduced the more delicate subject of chastity; and here
my point has been missed in a way which, after reading

---

* *Irish Ecclesiastical Record*, April, 1904, p. 309.

† A Roman Catholic correspondent, in a letter expressing his agreement with my views as to the cause and source of Irish intemperance,
writes :—" As for the temperance question, I not only agree with
your views (pp. 112-113), but would wish to emphasise the need of
the Catholic clergy doing their utmost towards completely rebuilding the tissues of the national character. Were this done, the
outlook of Irishmen on many things would instinctively readjust
itself, and most of our anti-industrial faults—the drink-habit
amongst them—would soon die a desirable death. Our priests, I
fear, will always be on the wrong tack while their efforts result
in fostering that type of disposition which seeks to make up in fitful
piety what it lacks in abiding self-control." He adds the following
interesting calculation :—" The drink bill of Ireland is now estimated at
£14,311,000. In proportion to that of the whole United Kingdom it is
as 1 to 11·8. In population Ireland stands to the United Kingdom as
1 to 9·2. Therefore, according to the population basis, Ireland drinks
less than her share. Judged, however, according to relative wealth,
the proportions are different. It is hard to estimate the relative wealth
of the Three Kingdoms precisely, but we can consider it on the basis of

and re-reading my references to the subject, I am wholly unable to understand.* Because, when discussing the standard of chastity attained in Ireland under the stringent discipline enforced by the pastors of the people, I ventured to question the methods by which the result was attained, I have been widely censured for showing indifference to the result itself. It does not require great erudition, but simply a little knowledge of the world, to be aware of the greater moral efficacy of fixed habits of character than of discipline, the effects of which too often last only as long as it is watchfully applied. In this, as in my other references to religious influences, it was not my purpose to discuss the higher ideals of moral and religious life. I ventured no further than to examine the methods by which it is attempted to realise these ideals in Ireland, in so far as those methods seemed to me to have a bearing upon the material well-being of the country. The sole purpose of such an examination was to lead ministers of religion to consider whether the means they employ might not be so modified as to meet vital tem-

reputed fiscal resource. When the Home Rule Bill of 1886 was discussed, such a financier as Mr. Gladstone computed Ireland's fair contribution to Imperial revenue at 1-14th or 1-15th part. If Ireland only drank in these proportions, her drink bill would fall to £12,071,000, or (for 1-15th) £11,267,000. Mr. Parnell, however, traversed the British Cabinet's estimate, contending that 1-20th or 1-21st part was the just contribution of Ireland to the Imperial revenue. On this basis, then, Ireland's drink bill should be only £8,450,000, or (for a 21st part) £8,047,000—either of which latter figures contrasts violently with £14,311,000."

* See pp. 115-117.

poral needs without losing their efficiency for higher purposes.*

I hope that both my Roman Catholic and my Protestant readers will now see why I was moved to impress upon the Roman Catholic clergy the urgent necessity for building up an industrial character in a people whom historical causes have economically depressed. I would remind those who regard such action on the part of a Protestant as being either impertinent or futile, of a notable precedent. In his memorable letter entitled *A Word to the Wise* Bishop Berkeley appealed, from the standpoint of a Protestant economist, to the Roman Catholic clergy for help in the improvement of the material condition of their flocks. ' Give me leave to tell you,' he wrote, ' that no set of men upon earth have it in their power to do good on easier terms, with more advantage to others, and less pain or loss to themselves. Your

---

* The correspondent whose views on the temperance question I have quoted in a previous note, contributes in the same letter the following observations on my reference to chastity. " I more than agree with you as regards the chastity question. Give the people *morale* and their morals will take care of themselves. Some will tell you that the industrial character has not proved itself consistent with the nicest morals, and they contrast the statistics of illegitimacy in Ireland with those of Scotland and other places. But there is another side to the picture. The known facts regarding the moral shipwreck of so many Irish girls in New York and other large cities, cruelly dissipate the notions we hold of our superiority on this head. Our poor girls have no greater natural tendency towards moral laxity than others : it is not moral sense they want, but moral fibre—character and grit.   The lack of industrial training, too, sends them down in the struggle,—many even to the streets, a result hastened, I fear, rather than hindered by a tutelage which represses the emotions rather than disciplines the will. Both our lads and girls need industrial training to give them that economic self-dependence without which there is no abiding self-respect, and consequently no enduring virtue at all."

flocks are, of all others, most disposed to follow directions, and of all others want them most.'* In reply to
this appeal the Catholic clergy of the Diocese of Dublin
assured Bishop Berkeley that they were 'determined to
comply with every particular recommended in it to the
utmost of their power '—a reply which must have heaped
coals of fire upon the heads of those responsible for the
penal laws. I have, in this work, ventured to renew this
appeal with, it is true, no claim comparable to that of the
distinguished philosopher, but in times when I should
have thought it could be made with less danger of giving
offence.

The present-day opportunities of the Irish Roman
Catholic clergy in the economic field are surely far
beyond any which were open to them a century and a
half ago. It may be that, in the larger liberty they now
enjoy, they have lost something of that influence which
they exercised when they shared with their flocks a persecution mainly directed against their religion. Still
they enjoy a prestige and occupy a position among the
majority of the people, which finds no exact parallel in
any other section of the Christian clergy in the world.
Coming from the people, chosen by the discerning eye
of the Church from the most promising of the youth
under her tuition, their influence upon secular life is of
the most far-reaching character, and all the more so
because of the emigration which has so largely drained

---

* *A Word to the Wise : or an Exhortation to The Roman Catholic
Clergy of Ireland.* By George Berkeley, D.D. Bishop of Cloyne.
Dublin: Faulkner, 1752.

the lay portion of the community of every element of leadership other than the political.

I think it opportune to point out here that amongst the causes from which the Irish Roman Catholic clergy derive their unique power must be reckoned the later policy of England, in giving them, by the founding of Maynooth College, facilities for higher education, and at the same time withholding the obviously essential counterpoise of a completed system of education for lay Catholics. A consequence of this policy has been to place under the control of the clergy such education as the majority of the people receive. Curiously enough this inevitable result is often most angrily resented by those who have caused it. 'Clerical domination' is frequently denounced by the very politicians to whom is due that difference of educational opportunities upon which the subordination of the Catholic laity to their clergy so largely rests.

Such being the educational situation, I turned to the Roman Catholic clergy, with the conviction, based upon study and observation, that they have here and now a unique opportunity of harmonising the furtherance of religious interests with the promotion of economic progress. They may also by this means avert in Ireland those conflicts between religious systems and the feverish aspirations of modern life which are raging elsewhere. If they desire to render this double service to their country and their church, they must not neglect the lower but yet essential conditions of such a consummation, even though the case is presented to them by a lay Protestant student of Irish problems.   Despite the angry rejoinders of my less considerate critics, I still indulge the hope that, with men who seriously study the signs of the times, my suggestions will not have been wholly in vain.

THE END.

INDEX

Z

PRINTED BY BROWNE AND NOLAN, LTD., DUBLIN.